Praise for John Glatt and his true crime books

"John Glatt is one of the finest true crime craftsmen writing today."   —Howard Goldberg, VH1.com

"[Glatt] certainly comes through with the goods."
                                        —*Library Journal*

"[A] true crime page turner."
                    —*East Bay Express* on *The Doctor's Wife*

"Author John Glatt goes behind the headlines and into the heart of this fascinating case."
                    —Bookcrossing.com on *Cradle of Death*

"This is a great true crime book."
                    —Bookreporter.com on *Deadly American Beauty*

"Definitive tales of a dozen sets of twins gone bad."
                                        —Twinstuff.com

"A blockbuster."   —*The Globe* on *Depraved*

"An exhaustive account . . . A creepy but mesmerizing read."   —*Woman's Own* on *Depraved*

"A shocking expose of clergymen who kill."
                    —*National Examiner* on *For I Have Sinned*

"Fascinating reading."   —*Arizona Republic* on *Evil Twins*

"Glatt . . . create[s] a mood of relentless darkness."
                                        —*Crime Magazine*

ALSO BY JOHN GLATT

The Perfect Father
The Family Next Door
My Sweet Angel
The Lost Girls
The Prince of Paradise
Love Her to Death
Lost and Found
Playing with Fire
Secrets in the Cellar
To Have and to Kill
Forgive Me, Father
The Doctor's Wife
One Deadly Night
Depraved
Cries in the Desert
For I Have Sinned
Evil Twins
Cradle of Death
Blind Passion
Deadly American Beauty
Never Leave Me
Twisted

THE
LOST
GIRLS

◆━◆━◆

The True Story of the Cleveland Abductions
and the Incredible Rescue of Michelle Knight,
Amanda Berry, and Gina DeJesus

John Glatt

St. Martin's Paperbacks

For Emily and Jerry Freund

CONTENTS

THREE
FREEDOM

ACKNOWLEDGMENTS

At Ariel Castro's sentencing, forensic psychiatrist Dr. Gregory Saathoff described his crimes as "unprecedented," squarely placing him in an evil class of his own. For more than a decade Castro terrorized Cleveland, abducting girls off the same street and then imprisoning them in his house without arousing any suspicion whatsoever.

The well-respected bass guitarist and mainstay of Cleveland's Latin music scene cruelly tricked his own daughters' friends into 2207 Seymour Avenue, brandishing a Luger handgun and threatening to kill them if they ever tried to escape.

Over the long years of Michelle Knight, Amanda Berry, and Gina DeJesus's captivity, there were many missed opportunities to catch him. Indeed, after his arrest Castro expressed surprise that he had not been caught years earlier, mocking the FBI for not doing its job properly.

In 2008, I wrote about the Austrian monster Josef Fritzl in *Secrets of the Cellar*, who imprisoned his own daughter, Elizabeth, for more than twenty years, fathering her seven children. Two years later, my book *Lost and Found* chronicled how Phillip and Nancy Garrido had abducted eleven-year-old Jaycee Lee Dugard in 1991, imprisoning her in their Antioch, California, house for eighteen years, with Phillip siring her two daughters.

But the Ariel Castro case is perhaps the most cunning and evil of all.

"There are cases where there have been longer term abductions in length," said Dr. Saathoff, "but the specific nature of this—to abduct and keep this number of unrelated victims for this length of time within a neighborhood setting is completely unprecedented."

The Lost Girls is the result of more than eighteen months of research and scores of interviews, both on and off the record. In September 2013, I spent almost two weeks in Cleveland, speaking to Ariel Castro's friends and family to get an accurate picture of this evil enigma. I also visited his birthplace of Duey, Puerto Rico, where Castro spent the first six years of his life, which many believe could have shaped his future behavior.

First and foremost, I would like to thank Lillian Roldan for her exclusive interview about her three-and-a-half-year affair with Ariel Castro. Over an emotional lunch in Cleveland, Lillian broke down in tears as she spoke about her feelings for Castro, who she had once hoped to marry. Even now she cannot believe he could be capable of such crimes.

I am also thankful to: Tito DeJesus, Bill Perez, Councilman Brian Cummins, Cesi Castro, Chris Giannini, Craig Weintraub, Scott Taylor, Fernando Colon, Altagracia Tejeda, Angel and Rafael Diaz, Aurora, Daniel, Javier, and Jovita Marti, Angel Cordero, Joe Frolik, and Sgt. Sammy Morris.

Thanks are also due to: Yauco Police Officer Richard Gonzalez for all his help and acting as my translator,

Monserrate Baez, Uriel Reyes, Edwin Torres, and Cuyahoga County Court reporter Nancy Nunes.

As always, I would like to thank my editors at St. Martin's Press, Charles Spicer and April Osborn, for their continuing encouragement and support. *The Lost Girls* is my twentieth true crime book for them.

Much gratitude also to Jane Dystel and Miriam Goderich of Dystel & Goderich Literary Management, who are always there for me.

I also want to thank my wife, Gail, Debbie, Douglas and Taylor Baldwin, G.K. Freund, Danny, Cari and Allie Tractenberg, Annette Witheridge, Dan Callister, Virginia Randall, Allen Alter, Roger Hitts, and Ena Bissell.

PROLOGUE

Around five-fifteen on a sunny spring evening, Aurora Marti dragged her green plastic chair onto her neighbor Altagracia Tejeda's stone porch for a chat. There was a smell of barbecue in the warm spring air, and it felt good to be out after the long cold winter.

The oldest resident on Seymour Avenue on Cleveland's tough West Side, Aurora arrived almost half a century earlier. The seventy-six-year-old grandmother was among the first wave of Puerto Rican immigrants who settled in the booming steel town after World War II.

At that time it had been a respectable street, but everything changed in the late seventies when I-90 was built, plowing through the neighborhood to connect Cleveland and Pennsylvania. Within a few years, Seymour Avenue had declined into a dangerous drug-infested no-man's-land, full of boarded-up clapboard houses and vacant lots.

Predominantly Latino, the impoverished neighborhood's median annual income is under $15,000 a year, with

70 percent of children failing to graduate high school. At night, drugs and prostitution run rampant, as drivers exit off I-90 to get whatever they need. While some West Side residents describe their under-policed streets as "close-knit," others complain of heavy drug use and violence.

But crime was the last thing on Aurora's mind that balmy evening in early May 2013, as she chided Altagracia for not taking her allergy medicine and chatted with their friend Angel Cordero.

Suddenly a frantic scream pierced the evening calm. It came from the white house across the street, flying a Puerto Rican flag. Aurora looked up to see a woman's hand frantically waving through a narrow gap in the front screen door.

"Help me! Help me!" the woman yelled. "My name is Amanda Berry and I've been captured for ten years!"

Like everyone in Cleveland, Aurora knew about Amanda Berry and her mysterious disappearance a decade earlier, on the day before her seventeenth birthday. Then, a year later, fourteen-year-old Gina DeJesus had also gone missing a couple of blocks away from where Amanda was last seen. Detectives believed the two girls' disappearances were connected, and over the years they had become one of the city's biggest mysteries.

Everybody had a theory of what had happened to Amanda and Gina, with most assuming the worst. Indeed, Aurora had often discussed it with her neighbor Ariel Castro, the owner of 2207 Seymour Avenue opposite, where the woman's screams were now coming from.

"Amanda Berry's dead," Aurora shouted across the street. "Everybody knows that."

"No," the woman shouted, "I've been kidnapped in this house for ten years by Ariel Castro."

Aurora had known Castro for more than twenty-five

years and liked him. The gregarious school bus driver was popular in the neighborhood, as well as being one of Cleveland's top salsa musicians. But Aurora also knew he had a terrible temper and could be violent. More than once, he had beaten his former wife and mother of his four children, Nilda Figueroa, so badly that she had run over to Aurora's house, begging for sanctuary. Then, after one particularly brutal attack during Christmas 1993, Nilda had taken the children and left the house forever.

Since then things had quieted down at 2207 Seymour Avenue. Ariel Castro now lived alone, and had become increasingly reclusive over the years.

Now, as they crossed the street toward the Castro house, Angel Cordero said they should not get involved in his business. But Aurora insisted on helping the woman, telling Altagracia to stand lookout in the middle of the road and warn them if Castro returned.

Aurora and Cordero then came up on the porch and tried to wrench the glass storm door open, with Amanda pushing as hard as she could from the inside.

"Kick it! Kick it!" Cordero told her, but the storm door was chained shut and wouldn't budge.

Two doors away, Charles Ramsey was eating a burger on his porch, when he heard the commotion. At first he thought someone had been hit by a car, but after seeing Aurora and Cordero rush across the street, he came over to help the screaming woman.

He and Cordero began kicking the bottom panel of the screen door together, until it finally broke. Then Amanda Berry crawled out into the bright sunlight, wearing a dirty white tank top and blue slacks. A few moments later, a little girl crawled out behind her, in a black wig and pink tights.

"Let's get out of here," Cordero told them, "because if Ariel comes back he's going to kill us all."

* * *

After picking up the little girl, Amanda Berry ran across the street to Altagracia's porch, yelling for a phone to call 911. The child was hysterical, screaming, "Daddy! Daddy! Daddy!" At one point she tried to run back across the street, and as Cordero restrained her, her dirty wig fell off.

Altagracia then handed Amanda her cordless telephone.

"Help me, I'm Amanda Berry," she yelled into the phone.

"Do you need police, fire, or ambulance?" replied the 911 operator.

"I need police."

"What's going on there?" asked the operator.

"I've been kidnapped. I've been missing ten years. I'm here. I'm free now."

Cleveland police officers Anthony Espada and Michael Tracy were in their squad car on Lorain and Twenty-fifth Street, when a Code One alert came in at 5:52 P.M. The dispatcher told them she had just received a call from a hysterical woman claiming to be Amanda Berry.

"So my partner and I looked at each other in amazement," said Officer Tracy, "and said it could be her."

Officer Tracy then turned on the overhead siren and flashing lights, and hit the accelerator, racing toward 2207 Seymour Avenue.

"Before I could even stop the car she was right there at the window," said Tracy. "I recognized her as Amanda Berry and I look at my partner . . . in disbelief."

Officer Tracy's first question was if there was anyone else still in the house.

"Yes," replied Amanda, "Gina DeJesus and Michelle Knight."

ONE

ARIEL CASTRO

1
ROOTS

Ariel Castro was born on July 10, 1960, in Duey, Puerto Rico, the third child of Pedro "Nona" Castro and Lillian Rodriguez. He had two elder siblings, Marisol Alicea and Pedro Jr., and his younger brother, Onil, was the baby of the family.

Duey is a tiny village on the outskirts of Yauco, the coffee capital of Puerto Rico. Over many generations, the Castro family had become *the* preeminent family in the isolated mountainous barrio, owning most of the land in a section called La Parra.

Despite the family's preeminence, however, their living conditions were primitive. Ariel was born in his father's little wooden shack at the very top of La Parra. At that time there was no running water or electricity, and all the cooking was done over coal on the dirt floor. Every morning, Pedro would drive his jeep several miles down the steep mud track to a well to fill up large plastic water buckets. He would then haul them back up the hill so that his family could wash and have fresh drinking water.

When Ariel was a young child, his father started an affair with a young girl named Gladys Torres, who lived one house away down the mountain. Over the next few years Pedro lived a double life, dividing his time between his wife, Lillian, and his girlfriend, who bore him four children.

"Lillian never suspected anything was wrong," said Ariel Castro's aunt, Monserrate Baez, who was married to Lillian's brother Milfon Rodriguez. "Nona had another family, unknown to us, just a few yards down the mountain."

In 1962, Lillian finally discovered Pedro's secret family.

"Lillian was pregnant with her last child when she found out he had another woman and children," said Monserrate. "She was furious."

When Lilllian confronted him, Pedro announced he was leaving her and the children forever. He then packed his bags, moving in next door with Gladys and their children. They married soon afterward.

In despair, Lillian then relocated to Reading, Pennsylvania, with her father, Americano Rodriguez. She left her four young children behind to be brought up by their grandmother, Hercilia Carabello, rarely returning to see them.

"I was abandoned by my father and later by my mother," Ariel would write. "My grandma raised me."

The Castro children had little parental supervision as they grew up. Ariel would later claim to have been sexually abused at the age of five, by a nine-year-old male friend of the family.

Years afterward, Ariel would be asked by a psychiatrist why he hadn't reported the abuse, which lasted more than a year.

"People who are abused keep quiet," he said, "so I did."

He also said he had begun masturbating as a child, starting a lifelong obsession with sex.

In 1966, Lillian Rodriguez sent for her children, who joined her in Reading, where they lived at 435 North Second Street and Ariel was enrolled at Lauer's Park Elementary School.

He would later claim that his mother physically abused him every day, using "belts, sticks and an open hand." He also accused her of verbal harassment, "yelling negative things and cursing at us."

"I would ask God for her to die," he told the psychiatrist.

One Christmas, Ariel's uncle Julio Castro, better known as "Cesi," arrived from Cleveland, bearing presents for his nephews and niece.

"He took Ariel a little guitar," said Cesi's daughter, Maria Montes, "and [we] saw music bud in him."

Little Ariel loved the guitar and soon started entertaining at Castro family gatherings. Cesi Castro took a special interest in Ariel, telling him he was his "special nephew" and a natural musician.

"[He had] the smarts," said Cesi. "There are very few people who can teach themselves how to play bass."

In 1968, Pedro Castro left Puerto Rico with Gladys and their children to settle down in Cleveland, Ohio, where he already had family.

Pedro had a good head for business and opened a used-car lot on Twenty-fifth Street and Sacket Avenue, which was soon thriving. In 1969, his brother Cesi joined him in Cleveland, opening the Caribe grocery store on Twenty-fifth Street and Seymour Avenue. They were followed by their brother Edwin, who opened Cleveland's first Latino record store on Twenty-fifth Street near Clark Avenue.

In 1970, Lillian Rodriguez moved her family to

Cleveland, as well, settling down at 2346 Scranton Road. By now her ex-husband and his brothers had established themselves as successful businessmen, becoming one of the leading Puerto Rican families in the city as they had been in La Parra. And they kept Yaucano traditions alive, later financing a social club and an annual coffee festival to commemorate their hometown.

"The Castro clan is a big clan," explained Adrian Maldonaldo, who grew up on the lower West Side, where the Castros flourished. "They are very industrial- and business-minded."

But in 1971, the Cleveland *Plain Dealer* reported that FBI agents had raided Cesi Castro's Caribe bodega in a Bolita numbers' racket sting. According to the article, agents seized cash, guns and numbers' records from eleven family members, including Pedro and Cesi.

In September 1973, thirteen-year-old Ariel Castro started at Scranton Elementary, before joining Lincoln Road West Junior High School a year later. He was a below-average student, with poor test results for cognitive ability, but he did make the wrestling team, played softball and was in the school band.

While in junior high, Ariel was suspended for "touching a girl's breast," and punished for fighting classmates.

In September 1976, Ariel moved to Lincoln West High School, where his elder brother, Pedro, Jr., had just graduated as a straight-A student.

"Ariel was just a regular kid," recalled Daniel Marti, who was a year below him. "He was smart and already into bikes and classic sports cars."

At Lincoln, Ariel joined his first Latin band, Los Steinos, playing bass with them in local churches. He was also drinking beer and smoking marijuana.

"He was popular, outgoing and smart," said Marti. "He

played the bass real good and had girlfriends. Everybody knew him."

Daniel's brother Javier Marti was in the same class as Castro at Lincoln West High School.

"The guy was just a regular Joe," Daniel recalled. "He's got a great family and always had nice cars and bikes."

On June 30, 1979, Ariel Castro graduated from Lincoln West High School, near the bottom of his class, with a C average and a low grade-point average of 2.15. Over the next several years he worked a variety of menial jobs, including bagger and cleaner for the Pick-N-Pay supermarket on West Sixty-fifth Street. He also began establishing himself as one of Cleveland's most promising Latin musicians, playing weddings, bar mitzvahs and anything else he could get.

"It was mostly like every weekend," he would later tell a judge, "but there were times we did perform two or three times a week."

Still living at home with his mother and two brothers, Ariel now had money to indulge his passions for expensive clothes, sports cars, motorbikes and musical instruments.

In early 1980, Lillian Rodriguez moved the family to a new house at 1649 Buhrer Avenue, just a mile down the road from where they had been living. Ariel soon noticed a shy seventeen-year-old Puerto Rican girl named Nilda Figueroa, who lived opposite with her parents and five siblings. Whenever they passed each other on the street, he would compliment Nilda on her looks, and the insecure girl was flattered by his attention.

One day he invited her to hear him play with his band and she eagerly accepted. Within a week they were a couple.

2

NILDA

Grimilda Figueroa was born on July 30, 1963, in a small village in Puerto Rico, just a few miles from Yauco. When she was sixteen, her father, Ismail, moved the family to New York, where they spent a few months before settling down in Cleveland.

Nilda, as everyone called her, started classes at the Max S. Hayes High School, but struggled with English and soon dropped out. She found a job in a factory and dreamed of settling down and raising a family. Nilda was a plain girl with low self-esteem and had few boyfriends. Her one promising relationship with a young man she had hoped to marry ended shortly before Ariel Castro asked her out.

Over the next few weeks, Nilda saw Ariel Castro play several times, and after the shows he would take her for expensive meals. Nilda's mother, who was close friends with Lillian Rodriguez, approved of the relationship and hoped it might go further.

"We were seeing each other," Ariel Castro testified in September 2005. "[I] was not in love."

But Nilda was enamored with the well-dressed salsa musician, losing her virginity to him one night by the banks of Lake Erie. When he drove her home afterward, Nilda's mother confronted him.

"We were making out," Castro said, "and when I brought her back home, her mother was waiting on the porch. She says, 'Where were you?' And I told her and she had a talk with me. She says now you have to take her."

That night Nilda moved across the street into Ariel Castro's room, and would remain with him for the next fourteen years.

Around Christmas 1980, Nilda Figueroa became pregnant and Ariel Castro found them a two-bedroom apartment, a few blocks from his home. He was now working as a drill press operator for Lesner Products, and making a name for himself in the Cleveland Latino music scene.

The Figueroa family liked Ariel Castro and were delighted Nilda had found somebody.

"He was a nice guy," said her sister Elida Caraballo. "He was real good to my sister at the beginning."

Ariel Anthony Castro, Jr., was born on September 27, 1981, and his twenty-one-year-old father was delighted. He would have Nilda bring their new baby to gigs, so he could show him off to everyone.

But soon after becoming a father, Castro's behavior toward Nilda began changing.

"He just started being too controlling, too possessive," said Elida. "And he would abuse her. I think having the child . . . made him feel she was his property."

In 1985, Nilda, who was just five feet tall and weighed 135 pounds, would testify how Ariel Castro had started attacking her, soon after Ariel, Jr., was born.

"It was over a small argument," she said. "He just punched me in the face and grabbed me by the head and threw me back against the concrete floor. The second time, he punched me so hard that he broke my nose."

Too scared to tell anyone about the abuse, Nilda began wearing a headscarf and heavy makeup to hide the severe bruising from his constant beatings.

Ariel Castro had also instituted a strict set of rules for Nilda to follow. She was never to leave the apartment without his permission, and when she did, she had to wear long dowdy dresses so other men wouldn't look at her. Castro even stipulated where she could do her grocery shopping and what items to buy, right down to breakfast cereals and milk brands.

He would constantly try to catch her out by pretending to have left the apartment, and then lying in wait downstairs. If he ever caught her disobeying him, there would be a savage beating.

"He isolated her," said Elida, "she never had any friends anymore [and] saw us less and less."

Castro even told her what television programs to watch, banning *The Cosby Show*, as he did not like black people. Every night he would come home and run his hand over the back of the television, to see if it had been turned on. Then if it was still warm he would check the *TV Guide* to see what shows had been on, and beat her if she had watched something he disapproved of.

When Nilda became pregnant again in March 1982, the beatings became worse.

"I was pregnant," she recalled, "and he wanted me to get up and do the dishes."

When Nilda said she had morning sickness and would clean up later, Castro viciously attacked her.

"He just punched me in the mouth and knocked two of my teeth out," she said. "I had told him I was too tired to get up."

*   *   *

Ariel Castro was now working for the Cosmo Plastics factory, and with a second child on the way, the family moved into a small apartment in Nilda's father Ismail Figueroa's house to save money. But even living under her father's roof did not temper his violent behavior.

"He regularly locked her in there," Ismail told journalist Allan Hall, "and I know he beat my daughter, [who] told us not to get involved."

On January 13, 1983, Nilda gave birth to a baby girl whom they named Angie. But when Elida and her brother Frank arrived to see the newborn baby, Castro refused to allow them.

"He was so strict," Frank recalled. "Angie was a little baby, and he wouldn't let us touch her. He didn't want anyone near his daughter."

After Angie was born, Ariel Castro's behavior became even more extreme. During one argument he shoved Nilda into a large cardboard box and closed the flaps.

"He told her, 'You stay there until I tell you to get out!'" said Elida. "That's when I got scared and ran downstairs to get my parents."

A few months later, Ariel Castro was fired from the Cosmo Plastics factory and went on welfare. He was now at home most of the time, using Nilda's food stamps to buy cocaine. His toddler son kept out of his father's way as much as possible, especially when he was in a bad temper.

Outside his immediate family, no one suspected what was going on in Ariel Castro's house, as he was so good at hiding it. He had no real friends other than his brothers Pedro and Onil, who both drank heavily and still lived with their mother. On weekends, he would arrive at gigs in his blue Mustang with his bass guitar and amplifier. He could be charming and charismatic, although some thought him weird and eccentric.

"I've known Ariel since he was a kid," said Bill Perez,

who owns Belinda's Nightclub, where Castro often played. "He was a musician at a young age and was always different."

Castro would dress up for a show, wearing a black silk shirt, a panama hat and sporting a flashy diamond earring. Even if the band who had hired him for the night had a uniform, he refused to conform.

"Ariel was weird and used to stand out," said Perez. "He could be demanding and cocky at times, and always wanted to be king of the group."

In 1985, Ariel Castro found a driving job for Cumba Motors, and moved Nilda and their two young children into a new apartment at 9719 Denison Avenue. There his violence escalated even further. During one argument, he punched Nilda in the nose and broke it again. He made her swear not to report him to the police, before allowing her to go to Grace Hospital to have it set.

A few weeks later, Nilda was back in the hospital, after Castro repeatedly kicked her in the ribs when she said something he didn't like.

"They took an X-ray," Nilda later said, "and they found that I had my rib shattered."

On another occasion, Castro dislocated her shoulders by twisting her arm behind her back and throwing her around the bedroom.

"He felt that it was some kind of punishment that I needed," she would explain.

Once he hit her over the head with a metal bar, putting her in the hospital for three days. She suffered a serious concussion and it took more than forty stitches to close up the wound. As before, Castro first made her promise not to call the police before allowing her to get treatment.

"That's the only way he would let me into the hospital," Nilda later explained, "because he wanted me to die that day. He wanted me to bleed to death."

Although the doctors at Grace Hospital were aware of the abuse she suffered, they were powerless to call in the police without her permission.

"They weren't too happy about me going home," she said.

During one attack in 1987, Castro punched her in the eye, causing permanent damage.

"He came at me full force with his fist," she later testified. "He punched me in the eye. There's a lot of nerve damage."

Then in January 1988, when Nilda was pregnant again, he hit her over the head with a barbell.

"I was nine months pregnant," she said. "He hit me over the head with a hand weight. Beat me."

Amazingly, just a few days later, Nilda gave birth to a healthy baby girl they named Emily Lisette.

Over the next two years the savage beatings continued, but on September 30, 1989, it became a police matter. At six that night, Onil Castro arrived at their apartment, wanting to go out for a drink. When Nilda asked where he was going, Ariel started slapping her in the face. When Nilda tried to run away, he grabbed her, slamming her hard against the wall repeatedly. Finally, she managed to escape and ran up the stairs to her neighbors, who called the police.

Ariel Castro was then arrested and taken into custody on suspicion of assault. Nilda and two of her small children were taken by ambulance to St. John's Hospital, where she was treated for a bruised right shoulder and interviewed by police.

A Cleveland Police Department report of the incident

states that she told officers she had been Ariel Castro's common-law wife for nine years.

"Victim states she was assaulted by the suspect on several other occasions," it read, "but made no official complaint."

As Nilda was still too scared to swear out a criminal complaint against Ariel Castro, police had to let him go without charging him.

"Life with my father growing up was abusive and painful," said Ariel, Jr., who was just eight years old when he witnessed this attack. "He was a violent, controlling man and my mother was the one who bore the brunt of his attacks, although I wasn't spared either."

Many times the brave little boy attempted to protect his mother, only to receive a beating himself.

"I remember crying myself to sleep," said Ariel, Jr., "because my legs were covered in welts from belts and seeing my mom getting beat up in our home. No one should ever have to see their mom crumpled up in a corner on the floor the way I did so many times."

A few months later, a young salsa piano player named Tito DeJesus was at a rehearsal with his fiancée, when he met Ariel Castro for the first time. The bassist immediately made a lewd comment to her.

"He came off to me a little weird," recalled DeJesus. "My fiancée had jeans on and was sitting on a table with her legs open. Ariel said, 'Hey, do you want me to take a picture, since you're smiling already?' And he didn't mean it facially. I just looked at him . . . who is this guy? Later my fiancée explained that Ariel had always been trying to get in her pants."

Nevertheless, Tito became close friends with Castro, as they often played in the same bands together.

"He was one of the best bass players in Cleveland," said

Tito. "He didn't read music all that well, but he would sit down and listen to a tape or CD and practice hard and play it almost [perfectly]."

As a freelance musician, Castro performed with many of the top Cleveland Latino bands, including the Roberto Ocasio Latin Jazz Project, Sin Ti, Groupo Fuego, Groupo Kanon and Los Boyz Del Merengue.

But he was often argumentative and difficult at rehearsals, making himself unpopular with many bandleaders, who did not want to work with him.

"At rehearsals," said DeJesus, "Ariel would ask the bandleader, in front of everyone, why he was doing these songs. He'd say, 'This song is too tough. We don't have to be doing this stuff.' And the bandleader didn't want to hear it: 'Listen, just do your job.'"

Then Castro would argue and argue and deliberately play it his way at the show.

"That was his nature," said DeJesus. "If you tell him the sky is blue, he would try and find reasoning to tell you the sky was red. He was a controlling person."

At the beginning of 1990, Nilda became pregnant again, giving birth on September 6 to Ariel Castro's third daughter, Arlene. She would be their last child together.

They were now living in an apartment on West Ninety-eighth Street and Western Avenue, and soon after Arlene was born, Castro was fired by Cumba Motors for laziness.

On December 11, 1990, he filled out an application to become a school bus driver for the Cleveland Board of Education. It asked what qualified him for the job and what his future goals were.

"I enjoy working with children," he wrote. "I have a good driving record. I speak English and Spanish. I plan to drive a bus and working [sic] with young people."

Listing his clerical skills, he wrote he could use a

calculator and adding machine, and gave the names of three friends as character references. He also filled out an affidavit, stating that he had not been convicted of any crime involving "moral turpitude."

On February 19, 1991, Ariel Castro was officially hired by the Cleveland School District to drive a school bus at ten dollars an hour. After taking a road test and passing a physical examination, he reported for training at the Ridge Road Bus Depot.

3
2207 SEYMOUR AVENUE

On April 29, 1992, Ariel Castro, now thirty-two, bought 2207 Seymour Drive from his uncle Edwin Castro for $12,000. It was just a couple of blocks away from his uncle Cesi's thriving Caribe bodega.

The two-story white clapboard house was on the south side of Seymour Avenue. It had five bedrooms and a bathroom, as well as a small front lawn, a backyard and a 760-square-foot basement. Nestled between the busy I-90 freeway and Scranton Cemetery, Seymour Avenue had been scarred by race riots in the 1960s, when many middle-class whites had fled. They had been replaced by immigrants, including many from Puerto Rico, looking for cheap accommodation. When Castro moved in, it was ground zero of a crack epidemic, making it one of the most dangerous places in Cleveland.

Perhaps its one symbol of stability was the redbrick Immanuel Evangelical Lutheran Church, at the end of the block. It had been built in 1880, and every Sunday Pastor

Horst Hoyer would ring the bells to call his parishioners to worship.

After all the years of living in confined apartments, Nilda and her four children might have hoped for more space. But that was not to be. Immediately after moving in, Ariel Castro started installing padlocks everywhere. He turned the basement into a dungeon with a heavy trapdoor, adding a layer of bricks and curtains to soundproof it.

"Growing up in Seymour Avenue . . . my father was always very secretive," said Ariel, Jr., who was eleven at the time. "He kept a lock on the attic and on the basement door. He nailed the windows shut. There were places we could never go."

After finishing his training, Ariel Castro became a professional driver, earning $14.66 an hour. Early every morning he'd leave the house to pick up the children on his route and drive them to school. Then at midday, he'd often leave the bus parked on Seymour Avenue for a couple of hours to tinker on his cars and motorbikes in his garage.

He soon became a well-known presence on Seymour Avenue, chatting to his neighbors and often playing at their cookouts. He also played his bass on a rehearsal stage at the back of his uncle Cesi's grocery store.

"He became part of our lives," said Ariel's cousin Maria Montes. "He used to stop into my parents' store rather frequently. His daughters used to play with my sister."

"He was a good neighbor and good friend," said Jovita Marti, who then lived across the street with her mother, Aurora. "We saw him every day when his wife was there. We had parties, and he used to come over to my mom's house all the time for coffee on the porch."

Tito DeJesus was also a frequent visitor to the house, where he and Castro would rehearse together.

"I went to his house a few times," DeJesus recalled. "It

was in the early days soon after I met him. He'd let me through the living room toward the dining room, but I never went past there."

After rehearsing, the two Latin musicians would drink Corona beers together and gossip about the Cleveland music scene, before Castro would show him to the front door.

After Ariel Castro moved into 2207 Seymour Avenue, he unleashed a whole new reign of terror on his family. When Nilda became pregnant again Castro was furious, as he wanted no more children. So he started kicking and punching Nilda in the stomach, to make her abort the fetus.

"All hell started breaking loose," remembered her sister Elida. "I would go over to the house and be knocking at the door, and she was there and he wasn't. I'd say, 'Open the door!' and she'd say, 'I can't. Ariel has the key.' He locked her in."

Castro also ordered Nilda never to use the telephone, as he tried to cut her off from her friends and family. And he constantly spied on her to see if she was disobeying him.

"He would go creeping downstairs," said Elida, "spying on her. See who she's calling. Next thing you know he'll pop upstairs."

Frank Caraballo said Castro beat his sister-in-law Nilda relentlessly, pushing her down the stairs and breaking her nose again, as well as fracturing her ribs and dislocating both shoulders. Finally, Frank came to blows with him.

"I was hitting him too," he said, "because I was tired of [Nilda] being abused."

Their young son Angel Caraballo was terrified of his uncle Ariel, whenever he went to the house to play with his cousins. Angel remembers padlocks on every door, and the basement always bolted shut. When he and his parents arrived, Castro would make them wait outside the front door for thirty minutes or more before letting them in. No one was ever allowed to go past the living room.

Soon after he moved in, Ariel Castro acquired a creepy life-size mannequin with slanted eyes, which he clothed in a long dress and a black wig. He delighted in placing it in the backseat of his sports car, and then driving around Cleveland scaring people. He also would leave it propped up against a wall in the house as a warning.

"He threatened me lots of times with it," recalled Angel. "He would say, 'Act up again, you'll be in that back room with the mannequin.'"

On one occasion, Nilda came home with bags full of groceries. As she walked in, Castro leapt into the doorway in front of her, brandishing the mannequin. The poor woman was so terrified she fell down the stairs, smashing her head open.

One day their eldest daughter, Angie, managed to pick the lock on the basement door and sneaked downstairs.

"We went snooping," she recalled, "and I remember there being a fish tank down there, which is odd because there was nobody . . . to look at the fish."

She also saw the mannequin as well as a "porch-type, two-seat swing." After poking around she relocked the basement door, and her father never found out she had gone down there.

Ariel Castro had now joined the Roberto Ocasio Latin Jazz Project. And whenever he was away overnight playing out-of-town gigs, he'd lock Nilda and the children in the house.

"He would go out for days," said Chris Giannini, a private investigator who later interviewed Nilda. "He had the windows tinted, so you couldn't see inside, and the doors were padlocked. He would go out to play music and even her sister couldn't see her."

Tito DeJesus accompanied him on several out-of-town gigs, and will never forget a weekend trip to Youngstown, Ohio, in summer 1992. Castro had called him up, inviting him to come along, and Tito agreed. The following Saturday, Castro drove him to Youngstown in his blue Mustang. The gig went well and Castro had the bandleader call Tito up onstage to play a couple of numbers.

It was past midnight when they set off on the seventy-five-mile drive back to Cleveland. During the drive, Castro, who had been drinking beer all night, announced he needed to urinate. Tito said they should stop at the next rest area.

"He goes, 'No, it's late and I want to get home,'" Tito remembered. "I'm like, 'Well, park the car off the road.' He said, 'No, I don't want to stop. Grab the wheel.'"

Then, as his passenger nervously took the wheel, Castro opened the driver's door and started urinating out of the car, as they were traveling around ninety miles per hour up the Ohio Turnpike.

"What the hell are you doing?" asked a terrified Tito. "Are you crazy? We're going to get in an accident."

But Ariel Castro just laughed as he retook the wheel, and put his foot down hard on the accelerator.

On Wednesday, March 10, 1993, Ariel Castro called the Cleveland police, accusing two parents of physically assaulting him on his school bus. According to a police report, Castro claimed they had boarded his bus without permission, shoving him back into his driving seat when he attempted to stop them. He said he was uninjured and refused any medical attention.

Later that day, the parents explained to police that their

son was being bullied on Castro's bus, so they took him to the bus stop to protect him. After putting him on the bus that morning, they saw him being attacked by other boys.

"They got on the bus to stop it," read the police report. "However, [they] were shoved by the driver."

The case was turned over to the Cleveland School Security Department, but no charges were ever filed.

In October, Ariel Castro pushed Nilda down a flight of stone steps, cracking her skull and causing her permanent brain damage.

"[He] broke her skull from the front of her head to the back of her head," said her sister Elida. "Even after her injuries to her head he would still be mean to her."

Ariel, Jr., grew up in a battlefield, seeing his mother beaten and humiliated on a daily basis. He dreaded the sound of his father's car in the driveway at night, knowing he would have to protect his mother, and probably be beaten in the process. On one occasion his father dragged him down into the basement dungeon and whipped him with a dog chain. Afterward, he told his son how fortunate he was not to have a father who had abandoned him, like his own father had.

"I grew up in a house with a lot of fear and a lot of violence," Ariel, Jr., said in July 2013. "[My father was] incredibly strict. He had a temper. He wasn't a monster twenty-four/seven, but if you crossed him there would be consequences . . . physical consequences."

But for some reason, Ariel Castro never laid a finger on his daughters.

"He treated my sisters like daddy's girls," explained Ariel, Jr. "There was no abuse directed towards them. As a boy I sometimes resented it [when] I saw how they were treated differently than I was."

Castro's eldest daughter, Angie, agreed she and her sisters were never physically abused, although they often witnessed their mother's beatings.

"When Mom and Dad were fighting," said Angie, "I just wanted to melt into the ground. I've seen him basically stomp on her like she was a man."

Ariel Castro's violent behavior was an open secret on Seymour Avenue after Nilda came knocking on her neighbors' front doors for protection. But mostly neighbors turned a blind eye, not wanting to upset the unpredictable Castro.

"When he used to hit her," said Jovita Marti, "she used to come over here and ask for help. [Nilda] wanted us to call the police, but my father didn't want to get involved with the police . . . because Castro will get mad at him. So we helped her and let her stay in the house until Castro calmed down, and she could go home again."

At the end of November, a few weeks after he threw her down the steps, Nilda began suffering seizures and was admitted to the Cleveland Clinic for brain surgery. During the operation, doctors found she had a blood clot in her brain, which had hardened into a tumor.

"Dr. Hahn, who was doing the surgery, found meningioma," Nilda later testified. "It's a brain tumor."

When the surgeon asked later what could have caused it, Nilda told him how Castro had thrown her down the steps. Dr. Hahn said the timing definitely accounted for the size of the tumor, which was inoperable and would eventually prove fatal. The next day she was discharged.

On Sunday, December 26, at 7:20 P.M., less than a month after her brain surgery, a drunken Ariel Castro came home and attacked Nilda. He threw her to the ground and started kicking her head and body. When their terrified twelve-year-old son ran out the front door to summon help, Castro chased him along Seymour Avenue, as Nilda locked the front door and called the police.

By the time a squad car arrived at 2207 Seymour Avenue, Ariel Castro had disappeared. The police officers started searching for him, but a few minutes later a dispatcher ordered them back to 2207 Seymour, where a furious Castro was now trying to break in.

They pulled up to see Castro pounding on the front door, screaming for Nilda to let him in. But on seeing the police he fled.

"These officers chased the arrested male and caught him in the rear of 2117 Seymour," Lieutenant Caveit wrote in his official report of the incident. "At that time, the male was placed in ZC (zone car) and read his constitutional rights which he stated he understood."

A tearful Nilda then told the officers that she had recently undergone brain surgery and suffered seizures.

"The victim states that [Ariel Castro] threw her to the ground, hitting her about the head and face and kicking her body," read the report. "She had brain surgery a month ago. Her head is very sensitive. Victim refused medical attention at this time."

Nilda signed a misdemeanor complaint against Ariel Castro, who was then read his rights and taken to the Second District Police Station and booked.

The next morning, Nilda informed detectives that she had changed her mind, and wanted all domestic violence charges against Castro dropped. She then came into the detective bureau and signed a statement to that effect.

Later that day, the Ariel Castro case was reviewed by Cleveland City Prosecutor Richard Kray, who ordered it to go before a grand jury. A few hours later, Ariel Castro appeared in the Cuyahoga County Court of Common Pleas in front of Judge Shirley Saffold, who freed him on $25,000 bail.

In February 1994, a grand jury declined to charge him with domestic violence, after Nilda Figueroa denied that the beating had ever happened, saying it was all her fault. Ariel Castro was then discharged with a clean record.

Eleven years later, Nilda would admit that right before she was due to testify in front of the grand jury, Castro had met her in front of the courthouse. He offered her money and a new car and promised to treat her better if she did not testify against him. When she refused, Castro threatened to kill her and their children if she went ahead.

"He said, 'Look, bitch!'" Nilda would later testify under oath, "'If you do I'm gonna kill you, and I'm going to take care of the kids; I mean, kill the kids too.' So I was scared."

Frightened for her and her children's lives, Nilda then went into the courthouse and told the grand jury it had never happened.

"I said that," she said, "just so he wouldn't hurt me or the kids anymore."

A few days later, Ariel Castro moved out of 2207 Seymour Avenue and in with his mother, Lillian, and two brothers. But he would still arrive at the house without warning, demanding to see his children.

"He would show up uninvited," said Nilda, "although [he] was not living with me on Seymour Avenue. He attacked me again late one night after I had surgery. While I was down on the ground, [he] kicked me in the head. His son, Ariel, witnessed the attack and ran from the house to get help."

Nilda then walked out of 2207 Seymour Avenue for the last time, taking her four children to live with their grandmother on Corning Avenue.

Within hours, Ariel Castro had moved back into the house, and began fortifying it with chain-link fences, mortise locks and deadbolts.

* * *

On November 29, 1994, seventy-four-year-old Ernesto Santiago went to check on his rental property at 2211 Seymour Avenue, and discovered his chain-link fence was missing. He looked next door and saw an identical fence in Ariel Castro's garden. Then he knocked on Castro's front door to ask him about it.

"[Ariel Castro] became upset," read a subsequent police report. "He picked up a shovel and attempted to hit [Santiago] . . . and told him he was going to take care of him. Santiago was so afraid he left."

The police report was again referred to the Cleveland prosecutor, who took no further action.

4
BREAKING FREE

A few weeks later, thirty-one-year-old Nilda Figueroa had another brain surgery after suffering further seizures. Before the operation, she reluctantly asked Ariel Castro if he could look after their children while she recovered. He refused, saying they were not his problem anymore.

"He said he didn't have enough room in his house," said Nilda. "I mean . . . it has five bedrooms and two bathrooms."

After the operation, Nilda was put on a program of neurologic physical therapy, with regular outpatient appointments at Grace Hospital. One day in the waiting room, hospital security guard Fernando Colon saw her looking dazed, as she was recovering from yet another beating by Castro.

"I asked her if she would be able to walk to the X-ray zone," said Colon, "and offered to get her a wheelchair. She said yes, so I took her in."

Over the next few weeks, Nilda struck up a friendship

with the handsome thirty-year-old security guard, telling him how she had been beaten for years.

"When I saw her injuries," he said, "I offered my help. She paused for a little bit and said, 'Yes, I'm tired of this. I need to get out of this situation.'"

Colon told her that although she had moved out of his house and in with her mother, Castro still knew where she was.

"I said, 'He doesn't know me or where I live,'" said Colon. "So let's get you out of here. And that's what I did."

At the end of July 1995, Nilda and her four children moved into Fernando Colon's house on West Fifty-third Street. They soon became engaged, with Fernando giving her a diamond ring.

Ariel Castro found out only after his daughter Emily called him from Colon's landline one night. He was furious.

"So he got my number," said Colon, "and that night he just kept calling and calling and calling. And I let Nilda talk to him. I said, 'Look, tell him that you're done with him and to leave you alone. And if he doesn't we'll press charges against him, and this time they're going to go through.'"

When an angry Castro started berating her, Colon grabbed the phone.

"I told him, 'You need to leave her alone,'" recalled Colon. "He said that she was his wife, but I said, 'No, she's not your wife because you did not marry her. She doesn't want to be with you anymore. Don't call my phone again.'"

Then Ariel Castro swore revenge on Fernando Colon.

"He [said] he would get even with him," said Nilda in 2005, "for taking me away from him."

Castro also attempted to turn his son, now in his freshman year of high school, against his new stepfather.

"He constantly tried to undermine him," Ariel, Jr., later testified. "He told me, 'Yeah, he's gonna get his.'"

Soon afterward, Ariel, Jr., stayed the night at 2207 Seymour Avenue.

"[My father] took me to school the next morning," said Ariel, Jr. "We stopped near [Fernando's] house at a stop sign, and he looked over at the house and he said to me, 'You know what your mom's doing in there?' And I kind of looked over. He said, 'She's ho-ing in there.' He asked me if I knew what that meant, and I said, 'Yeah.'"

Over the next few months, Nilda began to get her self-confidence back. For the first time in years she was happy. Fernando Colon got on well with her four children, who gradually accepted him as their new stepfather. And Colon tried to provide them with a stable home life for the first time in their lives.

"Nilda and those kids were psychologically injured," said Colon. "He just had them all messed up with his threats. They'd seen him beat their mother, and he had the environment under his control for so long, nobody could do or say anything."

Ariel Castro now started showing up at Colon's house day or night without warning, demanding to take his kids out. When Colon refused to allow it and ordered him to leave, Castro would argue and threaten.

"I told him to his face," said Colon, " 'You're an abusive man. I don't know what you're going to do to these kids.' "

Finally, Colon told him to move on with his life and stop contacting Nilda and the kids.

"And he said, 'One day I'm going to get you back,' " Colon remembered. " 'I'm going to destroy your life.' "

On May 16, 1996, Fernando Colon filed a criminal complaint, accusing Ariel Castro of attempting to run him down with his car. A police report stated the incident happened at 7:45 A.M., while Colon was waiting in his car with the children for the bus to school.

"The children's father pulled up behind him," read the report. "He walked up the victim's auto [and] was very profane. He told the victim that he better watch himself."

When Colon tried to reason with Castro, he got back into his car and began to drive straight at him.

"Victim states that [Ariel Castro] would have run him over if he did not get out of his way," stated the police report. "This is an ongoing problem."

The case was sent to the Cleveland prosecutor, but once again no further action was ever taken.

After that incident, to everyone's relief, Ariel Castro backed off and had little contact with his children, staying out of their lives.

"He would call them about once a month," said Nilda, "and only saw them about three times a year."

Four months later, Ariel Castro came under Cleveland police scrutiny yet again, after his neighbor Ayana Sickes sued him over a property dispute. Castro then drove over to her house and stopped in the driveway.

"[Ariel Castro] screamed out of his auto window, 'I'm gonna get you, bitch!' " read the official report. "[He] then drove off."

A police report was sent to the Cleveland prosecutor, who took no further action.

On January 22, 1997, Cuyahoga Juvenile Court Division Judge Betty Willis Ruben awarded Nilda Figueroa full custody of the four Castro children, terminating their father's visitation rights.

"She told me it was not a good idea for Mr. Castro to

be around my children," said Nilda, "because of his abusive nature."

Ariel Castro did not even bother to turn up at the hearing, but when Nilda told him that from now on she wanted their children to use her surname of Figueroa, he flew into a rage and refused to allow it.

On March 16, 1998, a violent fight broke out on Ariel Castro's school bus, while he was taking pupils home from school. As he was listening to loud Latin music on his headphones, he had no idea what was happening and carried on driving.

When he finally realized, he stopped the bus, ordering everybody to sit down. He then handed one of the fighters a tissue, to wipe off the blood from a badly cut face and lip. After the crying student declined medical help, Castro carried on driving his route, without reporting the incident.

The next day, the Cleveland City School District found out about the fight, resulting in Castro being suspended for five days.

On August 12, 1998, Nilda gave birth to Fernando Colon's son, Ryan. They had just moved to West 110th Street, and were still engaged with no immediate plans to marry.

A year later, Ariel Castro, Jr., graduated from Wilbur Wright High School with honors, and was accepted by Bowling Green State University to study journalism. Before leaving, he said good-bye to his father and proudly showed off his diploma.

"Who cares about that?" Ariel Castro scoffed. "You don't do anything around here."

5

LILLIAN

In May 2000, Ariel Castro approached his fortieth birthday and was set up on a blind date by a musician friend of his. Lillian Roldan was a pretty brunette sixteen years younger, but she was immediately attracted to the stocky, now balding musician with a goatee. Lillian had known the Castro family since she was a little girl, and her parents came from San Lorenzo, a small Puerto Rican village eighty miles east of Yauco.

"It was love at first sight," recalled Lillian. "He was older than me and I liked that. He was very handsome and from the beginning he treated me so sweet."

After their blind date, Castro invited her to come hear him play on Saturday at Belinda's, and she eagerly accepted. That night he swept her off her feet and romance blossomed.

"We were like a normal couple," she said. "I used to stay over at his house some weekends, or I would cook at my home. He wasn't the kind of person to go to restaurants."

They soon became intimate and Lillian remembers Ariel Castro being a good and considerate lover.

"He was a normal man," she explained. "Nothing outrageous."

Whenever Lillian stayed over at 2207 Seymour Avenue, she would try to clean it up, as it was so filthy. Finally, she suggested they sleep at her place instead.

"I cleaned the kitchen, the living room and the dining room," she said. "The bath and the bedroom were filthy, so I told him I'd rather be in my place and you come over."

She soon got to know Ariel Castro's three daughters, who visited periodically, and saw how strict he was with them regarding clothes.

"He was jealous that they used to wear hot pants," Lillian recalled, "because of the boys or whatever."

One time over at his house, Lillian asked why there was a padlock on the basement door. Castro replied that he kept all his money down there, and didn't want his kids to steal it.

"So it was a good excuse, because they were really young," said Lillian, who later posed for photographs with Castro by the padlocked basement door.

Soon after they met, Lillian mentioned that a friend had some medical marijuana, and she was going to try it.

"He got upset," she remembered, "because I hadn't told him that I wanted to try some."

Then Castro said he had something to show her in the basement.

"So he unlocked the padlock," she said, "and we went into the basement. He had a real bag of marijuana, but it was all dried up. So I said, 'Okay, big deal. I'm not interested no more.' So we went back upstairs."

Soon afterward, Ariel Castro proposed marriage to Lillian.

"He asked me, 'Well, would you like to marry me?'"

she remembered. "And he did make a fuss about it. When I told him I don't believe in marriage, he asked me to move in with him. I told him no. That it was all right to carry on as we were."

Several days later, Castro took Lillian to a jewelry store in downtown Cleveland, telling her to pick out a ring.

"I wanted a red ruby," she said, "because it was my birthstone. He said, 'Well, I'm going to buy it for you.'"

After they left the store they walked over the Detroit-Superior Bridge, and when they reached the middle he stopped. Then he gave her a kiss and slipped the ring onto her ring finger.

"So he put it on and I never took it off," said Lillian, "I really thought that we were going to get married one day."

That night, he took Lillian to a salsa club, where he was playing bass. Suddenly, in the middle of the show, he walked to the front of the stage, ordering the musicians to stop playing. Then he took the microphone and addressed the audience.

"Today," he told them, "I gave my girlfriend Lillian a ring."

"So everyone clapped," said Lillian. "And he told the group that he wanted to sing 'La Bamba' for me. It was so romantic and I was charmed. It was such a special [night] and he really did show me love."

That Thanksgiving, Lillian introduced Ariel Castro to her family, who were much impressed. After the meal, he took out his guitar and played some traditional Puerto Rican songs, as Lillian's father, Angel Roldan, sang along. From then on he would be invited to every Roldan family birthday and holiday celebration.

"They treated him like my husband," said Lillian. "My father really got on well with him."

Castro also bonded with Angel Roldan over their love of motorbikes, and they often went out riding together.

"Ariel would say, 'Have fun on the motorcycle, let's go,'" said Lillian's sister Mildred. "Then he would take [Dad] on a ride. Ariel was one of the family. Well, [I thought] he was the perfect man for her. I saw the love they showed."

Lillian Rodriguez also approved of her son's new girlfriend, who shared a name with her, and often had them over to her house for dinner.

"His mother was really nice and made cookouts for us," said Lillian. "She told Ariel that I was a good woman, and why didn't we get married."

Lillian was best friends with Castro's neighbor, Jovita Marti, as they both worked for the same manufacturing company. Sometimes at lunchtime, Castro would park his school bus near their office and bring Lillian lunch.

"They were girlfriend and boyfriend for four years," said Jovita. "She really loved him and I think he [loved her] too."

On Friday and Saturday nights, Lillian helped Castro prepare for his shows, and was his biggest fan. He would play clubs and venues all over Cleveland, and once Lillian even saw him perform at the Rock and Roll Hall of Fame. Then on Sunday mornings he would take her to church.

"I thought they were the perfect couple," said Jovita. "We were best friends, so we talked about him all the time and how much they really loved each other. She would come to work on Monday morning . . . happy, because they had a great weekend together."

One day, when Lillian announced she wanted a tattoo of her favorite flower on her leg, Castro said he would get a matching one as a token of his love. But at the tattooist's, he insisted that she get a far bigger one than she had intended.

"I wanted a small tattoo," she explained. "And he said, 'No, I want that bigger.' So I did make it bigger and then he got one too. That was the only thing that I didn't like about him during our relationship."

Lillian often saw Nilda Figueroa, when she went over with Castro to pick up his daughters. And she had heard the rumors of how he had beaten Nilda when they were together.

"I couldn't believe it," Lillian said, "because I never saw that side of Ariel. I mean, he was such a mellow person, so I thought, she's probably [making it up]."

Meanwhile, a plan had slowly been forming in Ariel Castro's head. He had decided to kidnap a young girl and imprison her as his sex slave, to satisfy his lustful cravings. Since Nilda and his children had left, he had become obsessed with sadomasochistic sex and humiliation. His sexual fantasies had become darker and darker and his basement was now full of hard-core S-and-M sex videos.

Lillian Roldan knew nothing of this, later telling police their sex life was completely normal and he was always respectful of her. Ariel Castro liked that she shared the same first name as his mother, and put her on a pedestal.

Their relationship was the polar opposite of his with Nilda, where he had beaten and humiliated her, treating her like an animal. He had loved controlling and imprisoning Nilda, using her for sex whenever he felt like it. But after she escaped his clutches, he became obsessed with finding a replacement. And by the summer of 2002, he was ready.

TWO

THE VANISHINGS

6
MICHELLE

From the beginning, Michelle Knight had had the odds stacked against her. She was born on April 23, 1981, to Barbara Knight. Her father has never been named. According to Michelle's autobiography, *Finding Me,* her parents had identical twin sons, Eddie and Freddie two years later.

Michelle's first memories are of living in a car with her mother and two little brothers, fighting for space. As a small child she was fascinated by the fire trucks she saw driving to emergencies, and wanted to be a firefighter when she grew up.

Michelle's family was eventually housed by Cleveland Social Services in a bad part of town, with drug dealers and prostitutes on their street. Then they lived in a series of run-down houses, as Barbara Knight supported the family on welfare.

"[My mom] made sure I was dumber than a doormat," said Michelle in November 2013, "just to get the SSI money."

When she was five years old, Michelle was sexually molested by a family friend, who threatened to hurt her if she ever told anybody. The molestation continued almost daily throughout her childhood, and she never told a soul.

Her mother enrolled her at the Mary Bethune School, but Michelle rarely went to classes and was classified as slow. She struggled to keep up with the other children, who made fun of her, calling her an "ugly retard" or "Dopey."

"By the time I was twelve and going on thirteen," she said, "I had barely made it through the fifth grade! I was always the oldest kid in the class and it stunk."

But Michelle, who wore glasses, loved drawing and had a rare gift for it. She began illustrating her class books with butterflies, wolves and the big mansions that she hoped to live in one day.

In November 1994, at the age of thirteen, Michelle ran away from home to escape the sexual molestation. She slept rough on a park bench in downtown Cleveland, eventually finding a highway underpass, where she could sleep in a garbage can at night to keep warm.

Over the next few months, the tiny dark-haired girl survived on church handouts before being recruited by a local drug gang. They set her up in an apartment, paying her $300 a week as a drug runner. That lasted for a couple of weeks, before the gang leader was busted, leaving Michelle homeless again.

Soon afterward she was spotted on the street by a family friend, who called her father, who drove straight over.

"My father jumped out and dragged me toward the car," she said. "He shoved me into the backseat and hit me."

Then he drove Michelle home to her mother, who insisted she go back to school.

At seventeen Michelle became pregnant. She described the father as a handsome boy called Erik, with whom she had a brief affair. But it was later reported that the baby was the result of a gang rape by three boys, in a storeroom at her school. Although her mother wanted her to have an abortion, Michelle insisted on having the baby.

When she was five months pregnant her father left, and Barbara Knight found a new boyfriend, who was unstable.

On October 24, 1999, eighteen-year-old Michelle Knight gave birth to a baby boy she named Joey. She was now living with her mother on West Sixtieth Street, receiving social security checks to support her new son. Michelle was a devoted mother, and dreamed of finding a good job, earning enough money to move out and support her "Huggy Bear." But as she was just four feet seven inches tall and had never finished high school, her options were limited.

Soon after Joey was born, Barbara Knight invited her boyfriend to move into the house. He reportedly had a history of abuse and violence, and drank heavily. One afternoon in June 2002, Michelle came home and walked into a bedroom to find him lying on the bed with two-and-a-half-year-old Joey nearby. According to Michelle, her mother was supposed to be looking after Joey, but had gone out.

Then, the boyfriend began lunging at Michelle and making improper suggestions. Joey was so scared he began to wet himself, and the man drunkenly grabbed the little boy's leg, fracturing his knee.

"My mother's boyfriend [was] high and drunk," Michelle later told Dr. Phil, "and he decided to take out his frustrations on my son. He twisted my son's leg and I hear it crack. My son didn't scream. He didn't cry. He just looked at me and said, 'Mommy, help me.'"

Michelle then took her injured son to the nearest ER. When she was asked how Joey broke his knee, she said he had fallen in the park, as she was too scared to tell them the truth and risk having her son taken away.

While doctors were treating Joey, the boyfriend's sister called the hospital and told them what had really happened. Police were called and the boyfriend readily admitted it, later pleading guilty to child endangerment and felonious assault.

Joey was then placed in foster care until social workers could investigate the Knight home to see if it was a safe place to bring up a child.

"Then they tried to say that I never protected him," said Michelle. "I did all I could do."

In late June, Michelle Knight moved out of her mother's house, renting a bedroom at her cousin Lisa's house for $300 a month. She now devoted herself to getting Joey back, as well as finding a job to support him.

After Joey was taken away, Michelle, now twenty-one, fell into a deep depression. Lisa introduced her to friends around the neighborhood, so she'd have a social life. Soon she met Ariel Castro's fourteen-year-old daughter Emily Castro, who lived nearby.

"I got to know Emily," recalled Michelle. "She told me that her parents weren't together, but that she still saw her father on Seymour."

Over July, Michelle and Emily became friends. Although she was seven years older than Emily, Michelle was used to being with younger children, as she had always been a few grades behind at school.

Soon after they met, Emily showed Michelle a photograph of her father, whom she called "AC," on her cell phone. She said he drove a school bus.

Emily would often call "AC" while she was with Michelle, making plans to go out. One time she put him on speakerphone, so Michelle could hear his "silly hillbilly" accent, which he adopted for his daughter.

"Emily never actually introduced me," said Michelle, "yet I felt like I kind of knew him. He seemed like a pretty nice guy."

7

"I THINK I KNOW YOU"

On Thursday, August 22, Michelle Knight had a 2:30 P.M. appointment with Cleveland Social Services about her son, Joey. The office was in a part of downtown Cleveland that Michelle did not know, so her caseworker had offered to drive her there. But Michelle turned it down, as a relative had promised to take her.

At 11:00 A.M., the relative cancelled, so Michelle decided to walk there, as she did not have taxi fare. It was a sweltering hot day, and after putting on a white T-shirt, cut-off jean shorts and some sandals, Michelle set out toward downtown.

She soon got lost and with the appointment time fast approaching, Michelle went into a Family Dollar store on West 106th Street and Lorain Avenue, to call the social services' office for directions.

Ariel Castro was driving his old orange Chevrolet around Clark Avenue when he spotted Michelle Knight nervously asking people the way. He immediately recognized her as one of Emily's friends, thinking Michelle was probably around the same age as Emily.

He pulled up on the next corner and watched her walk into the Family Dollar store. Then he got out of his car and entered the store. As he walked toward Michelle, he overheard her asking an employee the way to the social services office. Suddenly, he realized it was a perfect opportunity to put his long-cherished plan into action.

He strolled up to Michelle with a friendly smile on his face, saying he knew exactly how to get there.

"[He] was right beside me," said Michelle. "He was like, 'Well, I know where that's at.'"

Michelle recognized "AC" from the photographs on Emily's cell phone. He looked harmless enough, with a goatee and a thick long-sleeved flannel shirt, his large belly hanging over his tight black jeans.

"I [said], 'I think I know you,'" said Michelle, "'your daughter's name's Emily, right?' He was like, 'This is a small world.'"

Then he offered to drive her to the social services office, saying his car was right outside. Michelle immediately accepted, and on the way out she told him about her fight to get her son Joey back.

Ariel Castro opened the passenger door and Michelle got inside. As he closed the door, she noticed there were no handles inside the car and wondered why. Then he turned on the engine and started driving. She saw a small sign on the windscreen, saying he had puppies for sale. Making small talk, Michelle mentioned that Joey loved puppies, and Castro said he had to swing by his house on Seymour Avenue to check up on them. He reassured her it was on the way.

At around 3:00 P.M., Castro pulled into the driveway at 2207 Seymour Avenue. Michelle said she'd wait in the car, as he got out and walked through the front gate and the back door of the house. A few minutes later he came out again, asking Michelle to come in and choose one of the puppies for Joey.

Michelle agreed and he led her into the house, through the back door. As they went upstairs, she wondered why it was so quiet and she couldn't hear any puppies barking. She saw a photograph of Emily on the wall, and Castro told her his daughter was downstairs in another room, and she'd see her soon.

Then he guided her up the stairs into a small pink bedroom, slamming the door behind him and locking it. Michelle screamed in fear, pleading to be let out so she did not miss her appointment.

As Ariel Castro came toward her, the smile had gone from his face. Then he put a strong hand over her nose and mouth, placing the other against the back of her skull and pulling off her glasses, which fell to the floor. Michelle was no match for her attacker, who weighed 180 pounds.

"I'll kill you if you scream again," he yelled, as he threw her to the floor and she passed out.

When Michelle came to a few minutes later, Ariel Castro was standing over her with a menacing look in his eyes. He ordered her not to move. Then he grabbed her pocketbook and threw it against the wall, and went into the next-door bedroom to look for something.

While he was gone, Michelle looked around the dark room, which had obviously been carefully prepared beforehand. There were two large metal poles set up on either side of the room, with a taut cable strung between them, several feet above the floor. Finally Castro reappeared carrying a stool and two orange electrical extension cords.

"Lie still!" he commanded, as Michelle attempted to stand up. Then he reassured her everything was going to be okay, promising not to harm her if she obeyed him and that he would free her soon.

Sitting down on the stool he grabbed Michelle's legs, as she desperately tried to kick him away. But he was far too strong for her. Then he started binding one of the cords around her ankles so tightly they went numb. When she tried to punch him away, he grabbed her wrists, pulling her arms behind her back and binding them together. He then wound the other end of the cord around her neck and tied it.

He then pulled down his pants, took out his penis and began masturbating over her, as she lay tied up on the floor. As he became more and more excited, he became strangely emotional. He told Michelle that he really wanted them to be friends, and how lonely he had been since his wife and kids had abandoned him.

"All I want is for someone to be here for me," he said breathlessly. "I need you."

Then he climaxed.

After finishing, Castro pulled up his pants and ordered her to stay still. Michelle screamed and started praying, thinking he was about to kill her. Then he punched her hard on the side of her head, telling her nobody could hear her screams, as he pulled out a gun and threatened to shoot her.

He rolled her over onto her stomach and tied the second orange extension cord around her hands, feet and neck, trussing her up like a chicken. After connecting her tiny body to the thick taut cable, stretched between the two poles, he hoisted her up about a foot above the floor, so she was hanging in front of the window.

"I was tied up like a fish," she would later say. "An ornament on the wall."

Finally, he stuffed a filthy gray sock in her mouth and wound duct tape around her head. Then, saying he was off to get some food, he turned on a radio and walked out, slamming the door, leaving Michelle suspended helplessly over the floor.

At 6:02 on Friday afternoon, Barbara Knight went to the Cleveland Police Department to report Michelle missing. She told Officer Westley Edrington that Michelle had last been seen the previous morning by her cousin Deanna, on West 106th Street and Lorain Avenue. She described her twenty-one-year-old daughter as four feet seven inches tall and weighing 160 pounds, with blue eyes and wearing glasses.

The missing-persons report classified Michelle as disabled, and noted that she went by the alias "Shorty."

"Reporting person states that missing person adult has a mental condition," it stated, "and that she is confused of her surroundings, a lot."

Investigators then checked local hospitals, a relative's house and the morgue, telling Barbara that they would let her know when her daughter was found.

Barbara would later claim that the police did very little to try to find Michelle.

"They figured that she had just left," she said, "because of the upset of the baby."

After Ariel Castro left Michelle Knight hanging like a wounded deer, he got in his car and started driving to clear his head. He would later say that he hadn't intended to kidnap a girl that day, but the opportunity had presented itself and he had taken advantage of it.

That night he went to his mother's house for dinner with his brothers and was his usual jovial self. Then, after having a couple of beers, he left to return to 2207 Seymour Avenue.

* * *

Michelle Knight could never be sure how long she was left trussed up in the bedroom, gagging with the dirty sock in her mouth. She spent agonizing hours staring out the window, as night fell and she could hear the radio upstairs, playing loud Spanish music. She wet herself several times, and her throat was sore from dehydration and her stomach aching from hunger.

Eventually, Ariel Castro returned with a McDonald's Egg McMuffin for her to eat. He ripped off the duct tape over her face and took the sock out of her mouth. When he pushed the sandwich into her mouth, Michelle screamed and tried to fight him off, but he grabbed her jaw and held her mouth open, ordering her to eat. When she refused, he threw the sandwich onto the floor.

Without a word, he untied the extension cord attaching her to the poles, so she fell hard onto the floor. Her arms and legs were numb. When she screamed and tried to sit up, he called her a "slut," telling her to stay still. Then he held her down as he untied the cord binding her wrists and ankles.

He told her to get up but Michelle sobbed, saying she was unable to as her legs hurt so badly. So he picked her up and slung her over his shoulders, carrying her into an adjoining white-walled bedroom.

After throwing her down on a filthy, stained mattress, he ripped off all her clothes and attacked her. For the next hour he raped her repeatedly, while she screamed in pain. Again and again she tried to fight him off, but she never stood a chance.

When he was finally satisfied, they both lay naked on the mattress, now covered in Michelle's blood. Composing herself, she tried to reason with her attacker, promising not to tell anyone what he had done if he let her go.

Suddenly, a change came over Ariel Castro. He began talking to Michelle as if she were his girlfriend, pouring out his heart to her. He spoke about being molested back in Puerto Rico when he was five, and how upset he was when Nilda had taken their kids and left.

"I didn't mean to beat her," he told Michelle, "but it's like I ain't got the power to stop myself."

Finally, he got off the bed and started to get dressed. Then he pulled some dollar bills out of his pocket and threw them at her, saying it was payment for her services.

After ordering Michelle to put on her blood- and urine-stained shorts and T-shirt, Ariel Castro dragged her down to the first floor, with her head hitting each stair on the way down. Then he took out a key and unlocked a heavy wooden door and opened it.

Michelle's heart froze as she saw a long flight of stairs leading into his basement. After dragging her down, he threw her onto a pile of dirty clothes on the concrete floor. Although it was dark and she had lost her glasses, she could make out a large white pole in the middle of the basement, reaching from the floor to the ceiling.

When he turned on a light, Michelle could see dirty clothes strewn everywhere. At one end of the room was an old washing machine next to a sink, and hundreds of X-rated pornographic videos stacked up against the wall. There was a small window covered in dirt, and an assortment of heavy rusting chains of various lengths, strewn around the floor.

"This is where you are going to stay," he told her, "until I can trust you."

Castro then picked up two lengths of chains and held them up to Michelle, who started crying uncontrollably. He ordered her to stop, picking up a dirty sock from the floor and thrusting it into her mouth.

Then he dragged her over to the pole in the center of the basement, wrenching her arms behind her back and fitting plastic restraints over her wrists. He wrapped a length of rusty chain around her waist to secure her to the pole, before winding another chain around her neck and head. Some of the chain went into her mouth, so she could taste the rusty metal.

Finally, he padlocked both chains together and placed a motorcycle helmet over Michelle's head to muffle her screams. Then she passed out.

That fall, Ariel Castro began a strict routine, keeping his life tightly compartmentalized. He would get up early and dress in his burgundy-colored uniform, and leave to pick up his yellow school bus. After dropping off the children at school on his morning route, he drove back to 2207 Seymour Avenue, parking his school bus outside for a few hours. Then he would feed Michelle stale McDonald's hamburgers before raping her.

Then, leaving Michelle chained up in the basement, Castro would get back in his bus in time for his afternoon route, driving the children home.

After finishing work, Michelle would hear him upstairs watching pornographic videos and smoking marijuana. She dreaded the sound of the key unlocking the basement door, knowing he had come to rape her again. When he had satisfied his lust, he would throw paper napkins at her to clean herself off with, and then "ram" them down her throat.

On weekends, he played the Cleveland salsa clubs with his various bands, and seemed happier than he had been in years.

Lillian Roldan still spent the occasional night at 2207 Seymour Avenue, and Michelle could hear them making love upstairs. Lately, Ariel Castro had been particularly attentive to Lillian, as they discussed their future.

"One night we were lying in bed," Lillian remembered,

"and he took out his guitar and sang to me. It was a Marc Anthony song called '*El Ultimo Beso*' ['The Last Kiss'], which we both liked. It was so romantic and became our song."

For the first few weeks of her captivity, Ariel Castro kept Michelle chained to the pole with a motorcycle helmet on her head. He raped her up to seven times a day, and if she ever complained he would beat her up.

"There's not a day that went by that I didn't get messed with," she said later, "or hurt in any type of way."

He brought in a plastic bucket for her to use as a toilet, placing it just close enough to the pole for her to reach. Most days he fed her only one meal, usually consisting of a McDonald's burger and a glass of orange juice.

"Most of the time I was hooked on a chain . . . in the basement," she said. "I was just passing out. That's how the time went."

Michelle managed to endure the endless days and nights lying chained up in the basement by thinking about her son, Joey. Whenever she wanted to die, she'd conjure his face in her mind. Thinking about being reunited with him one day gave her the strength to survive.

About a month after he kidnapped her, Castro brought Michelle out of the basement and back upstairs to one of the bedrooms, chaining her up naked to a bed. All the windows had been covered with sheets of gray wool with barbed wire across them, and the only way she could tell day or night was through the smells of her captor frying bacon for his breakfast every morning.

In late September, Michelle Knight became pregnant with Ariel Castro's baby. She recognized the symptoms, but was too scared to tell him, uncertain of how he would react. One day he noticed her nipples were leaking and asked if she was pregnant. Michelle said she thought she was and he attacked her.

"He punched me in my stomach . . . with a barbell," she said. "I fell to the floor."

Over the next few weeks he starved her and beat her. Chained to the bed, Michelle often fainted, had nosebleeds and vomited. Finally, after approximately six weeks, she had a miscarriage.

"And then when I did miscarry he blamed me," said Michelle. "He said I hated him [and] I killed his kid. He punched me in the face, saying that it was all my fault."

Castro then picked up the tiny fetus and placed it in Michelle's hands, asking if she wished it were alive and saying that she had caused its death.

As the weeks stretched into months, Michelle began to get some sense of time. On Sunday mornings she could hear the bells of nearby Immanuel Lutheran Church ringing. And one evening a drunken Castro came into the basement wearing flashy black clothes and a panama hat. He began boasting about his Latin band, and what a great bass guitarist he was. Soon afterward he warned Michelle, who was still chained up and wearing a motorcycle helmet, not to make a sound, as his band was coming over later to practice.

That night she heard voices downstairs speaking Spanish, and loud live music. This started happening regularly and Michelle deduced that the rehearsals were being held on Fridays or Saturdays.

Cleveland musician Rickie Sanchez regularly rehearsed with Castro, drinking beer and eating dinner afterward.

"I used to go there and cook," Sanchez recalled, "and being from Puerto Rico we like rice and beans."

One night, he heard some strange *boom-boom* noises coming through the walls, and asked Castro where they were coming from.

"And he said he had some dogs on the second floor," recalled Sanchez. "Then he took out the radio and cranked it all the way up. It was hard for you to hear him unless you were screaming, because of the music. It was always loud."

That winter, Michelle Knight almost froze to death. There was no heating in the house and it was a brutally cold winter. Castro refused to give her any blankets or clothes to keep warm.

"It was always very cold," said Michelle. "He didn't have heat and I only had one sheet. [It was] so cold that my lips would turn blue and you could see my breath."

Castro told Michelle that he would not give her blankets or clothes to wear until she had proved he could trust her. She was also filthy, as Castro had not allowed her to wash or use the shower since he had taken her, and he seldom emptied her toilet bucket.

If she disobeyed him in any way, he would stop feeding her. He would also show her his loaded .357 Magnum caliber revolver—the exact same firearm Clint Eastwood's Dirty Harry character talks about in the 1973 movie *Magnum Force*—threatening to shoot her dead if she ever tried to escape.

At Christmas, Castro gave her a puppy to keep her company. She named it Lobo and lavished it with love. But when Lobo came to Michelle's defense during one of his beatings and bit Castro, he picked it up and broke its neck right in front of Michelle. Then he carried Lobo's body out to the backyard and disposed of it.

On December 24, Ariel Castro celebrated the holidays with Lillian Roldan at her father's house. After dinner, he got out his guitar and began playing to entertain the family.

"He was playing and singing Christmas songs with my father," said Lillian. "And I said, 'Do you know what, it's the twenty-fourth and it hasn't snowed, so for me it's not Christmas. I need a white Christmas."

So Castro suddenly started strumming Bing Crosby's *White Christmas*.

"Suddenly, I looked out the window," said Lillian, "and it was snowing. I said, 'Oh my God, Ariel, you made it snow.' It was the best Christmas gift ever."

On Christmas Day, Ariel Castro raped Michelle Knight, and then started tormenting her because Joey was not there to celebrate with her.

"He rubbed it in my face that I wasn't with my son," recalled Michelle. "That I'm spending my holidays with somebody else. And he'd say, 'He's better off without you.' "

In early January, Michelle tried to escape. Ariel Castro had finally brought her downstairs to the bathroom for a shower, and while his back was turned she found a needle and hid it. After the shower, he brought her back to the bedroom and chained her up before leaving for work.

"I picked the lock," said Michelle. "But I didn't know he was in the backyard."

After getting free, Michelle was halfway out the window when she heard Castro running up the stairs.

"I'm panicking," she said. "I run back to the bed."

She then threw the chains back on, trying to pretend nothing was out of place. But Castro was suspicious and after searching the room, he found the needle under the pillow.

"What are you doing with this?" he demanded to know.

Michelle said she had used it to self-mutilate her arms, and Castro took the needle away, saying he disapproved of the practice.

"He figured it out," said Michelle. "The chain wasn't put on right . . . that's the last time that I had a chance to get out."

As punishment, he dragged her back to the basement and chained her to the pole. Then he told her that she was not the "only one" who had been down here, showing her a little shrine in a corner of the basement. Inside was a sign with the words REST IN PEACE, along with a girl's name that had been scribbled out.

"I couldn't really see," said Michelle, "because I didn't have glasses."

A few weeks later, he brought her back upstairs and gave her a battered old television to watch, so she would have something to occupy her time. She was still tethered to the wall on a three-foot chain, but at least she could pass the time watching her favorite shows.

In April 2003, Michelle Knight became pregnant again and dreaded what Ariel Castro would do when he found out. This time, he kicked her in the stomach so hard that she fell backward and hit a door. Ten days later she miscarried.

When Castro wasn't abusing Michelle, he would often talk to her. He constantly told her how he himself was a victim who had been abused as a child. He also spoke of his obsession with pornography and his hatred of African Americans. Once he confided that he regretted not getting to JonBenét Ramsey first, and that he would have loved to have kidnapped Elizabeth Smart.

He also told Michelle that he was now actively looking for another girl to kidnap, and this time he wanted a blonde.

"He had an obsession with blondes," said Michelle. "He would always say, 'I've seen this girl and I'm just sad I didn't get her in my car.' He would let me know what girl he was trying to abduct and where she worked."

8
AMANDA

Amanda Marie Berry grew up on West 111th Street, less than three miles north of Seymour Avenue. She was born on April 22, 1986, to Johnny Berry and Louwana Miller, who already had a daughter Beth, who had been born two years earlier.

Her father reportedly had a history of violence, serving jail time for sexual battery and aggravated assault. When Amanda was four years old, her parents split up and Johnny moved to Elizabethton, Tennessee, where he had family. Louwana remained in Cleveland, to raise her two daughters.

Every summer, Amanda visited her father and extended family in Tennessee, and was especially close to her grand-mother, Fern Gentry.

"Commando Amando," as her father nicknamed her, was a "real firecracker" and loved the rural countryside, where she played with her cousins in the Blue Ridge Mountains.

"We would play hide-and-seek [and] take showers in

the creek," said her best friend, Lisha Jacome. "It was her favorite place."

Amanda went to Wilbur Wright Middle School and knew Angie and Emily Castro, who were also pupils there. She was a good student with a reputation as a "girly girl," who dreamed of becoming a fashion designer when she grew up. She loved rap music and was a big fan of Eminem, putting his posters on her bedroom wall.

"She was always so smart," her cousin Tina Miller said. "Mandy was always in the magnet programs at school."

After spending a short time at John Marshall High School, where she was in the gifted student program, Amanda studied online at home. Her sister, Beth, had recently married a young man named Teddy Serrano, who had moved into the house.

At sixteen, Amanda got a job at Burger King on West 110th Street and Lorain Avenue, just three blocks away from her home. The petite five-foot-one-inch teenager had waist-length wavy blond hair, and had her left eyebrow pierced to keep up with the latest trend.

She loved Tommy Hillfiger and Nautica clothes, although she was careful never to mix them. She adored costume jewelry and collected necklaces, including a gold one spelling out AMANDA and another with a Playboy bunny.

Amanda loved to stay out late and party, drinking beer and smoking marijuana, but she always stayed clear of hard drugs.

In mid-March 2003, Amanda started dating Danizo Diaz, a tall, handsome sixteen-year-old Latino boy whom she first met after taking his order at Burger King's drive-through window. Diaz drove a white Dodge Intrepid convertible and was known to everyone as "DJ." Amanda told friends she thought the relationship looked promising.

* * *

At 2:00 P.M. on Monday, April 21, Amanda Berry kissed her mother good-bye and left for her shift at Burger King, wearing her maroon uniform.

"I love you," Louwana told her. "Have a good day at work."

It was the day before her seventeenth birthday, and her mother had organized a party. Before leaving, Amanda had carefully placed $100 in crisp new bills in her bedroom drawer to get her nails done later that night and buy a new outfit. A stack of gift-wrapped presents lay on her bed.

But there was something troubling Amanda that day. She had just heard that her brother-in-law, Teddy Serrano, who also worked at Burger King, was having an affair with a female worker there. The affair had started a month earlier, and when somebody told Amanda, she was devastated.

That afternoon, she tearfully called her mother several times for advice on what to do. Later, Teddy Serrano would tell police that he had seen Amanda "upset and crying," making calls on her new cell phone. Although her shift ended at 8:00 P.M., Amanda left half an hour early. She walked into the employee dining area and sat down next to Stephanie Torrence, who was waiting for her daughter to finish work. Amanda mentioned it was her birthday tomorrow and she was getting her nails done later. She was going to walk home, she said, as she had no money on her. Torrence offered to walk her home, but Amanda declined.

At 7:36 P.M. Amanda officially clocked out of Burger King, saying good-bye to Torrence a couple of minutes later. Then she started walking north on West 110th Street, still wearing her Burger King uniform with her black bag slung over her shoulder.

* * *

As Amanda Berry left the Burger King parking lot, Ariel Castro drove past her in his maroon Chevy van, with his youngest daughter, Arlene, in the passenger seat. Amanda had been on his radar for some time, as he had often seen the beautiful blond employee behind the counter.

Amanda too noticed when his van drove past her, thinking she recognized a girl she knew in the front seat.

After pulling into a driveway a few houses ahead and letting Arlene out of the van, Castro made a U-turn and drove back along West 110th Street.

Several minutes later, Amanda was talking to her sister, Beth, on her cell phone, as the maroon van pulled up alongside her. Then a smiling Ariel Castro opened the window, asking if she wanted a ride home. Amanda said yes.

"Gotta go, I've got a ride," she told Beth breathlessly. "I'll call you back."

Then Amanda Berry got into Ariel Castro's van and he sped off down West 110th Street.

As soon as Amanda was inside the van she realized Arlene was not there. But before she could say anything, the pudgy middle-aged driver with the porkpie hat and goatee introduced himself as Ariel Castro. He asked if she knew his son, Ariel, Jr., who used to work at that Burger King and his daughter Angie. Amanda said she knew both of them.

Then Amanda noticed that he had driven past her home on West 111th Street, and asked where they were going. Castro replied he was taking her to see Angie at his house.

A few minutes later they arrived at 2207 Seymour Avenue, and Ariel Castro pulled into the back of the driveway. He invited her inside to see his daughter, leading her in through the back door and into the kitchen.

"Angie could be in the bathroom," Castro told her, taking Amanda up some stairs. On the way, they passed a closed door with a large hole in it. Amanda looked in and saw a woman inside. She asked who it was.

"It's my roommate," he replied.

Then Castro led her into a bedroom with an en suite bathroom at the far end, edging her against the wall. Suddenly, Amanda became nervous and told him to let her go, or he'd be in trouble with the police.

When Ariel Castro suddenly grabbed her, she started screaming. He muzzled her mouth with his hands, threw her to the floor and raped her.

Afterward, he duct-taped her wrists and legs together and taped her mouth shut. He put a motorcycle helmet over her head, and carried her downstairs into the pitch-black basement, where he chained her around the waist to the large center support pole.

Then he went up the stairs and locked the basement door behind him, leaving Amanda helplessly chained with the motorcycle helmet over her head.

When Amanda Berry didn't arrive home after work, Louwana Miller immediately knew something was wrong. Her daughter was always punctual and was so excited about her birthday party the next day. She also knew that Amanda would never go anywhere without taking her phone charger or a change of clothes. There was also the hundred dollars in her bedroom drawer left untouched.

"Mandy waited all week for that party," said Louwana. "All her clothes are here. No way would she leave with her Burger King outfit on."

Over the next few hours, Louwana and Beth phoned around to all Amanda's friends, asking if they had seen her. Then at 12:33 on Tuesday morning, Louwana went to the First District Cleveland Police Department office on West 130th Street, to report her missing.

"Mom is concerned," read Amanda's missing person's report. "Mom claims there have been threats made against her at work. Cannot reach her on her cell phone. States this is unusual for her daughter."

The following morning, Detective Brent Scaggs interviewed Louwana and Beth at their home. They described Amanda as a "good kid" who had never done anything like this before. They were concerned for her safety.

In fact, Louwana had already printed up fliers with Amanda's photo and a brief description, which friends were now handing out around West 110th Street and Lorain Avenue.

"Mother also stated that [today] is Amanda's birthday and a birthday party is planned," wrote Detective Scaggs in his report. "Amanda took no money or change of clothes with her on the day that she left. She only had her Burger King work clothes. When ask[ed] about Amanda using drugs or alcohol they stated she does smoke weed and drinks beer but does not use any hard drugs. Mother and sister supplied me with info on Amanda's friends."

Louwana also told the detective that Amanda had called her from work before she disappeared, upset about her son-in-law Teddy Serrano's affair.

Detective Scaggs then interviewed Serrano. He readily admitted the affair, saying it had upset Amanda and "he was going to kick the ass" of the person who had told his wife about it.

"He and his wife have worked things out," the detective wrote. "He does not know who told on him."

After leaving the house, Detective Scaggs drove to West Ninety-ninth Street to interview Amanda's boyfriend, Danizo Diaz. DJ said he had spoken to Amanda several times on Monday, and they had arranged to meet at 10:00 P.M., after she had her nails done. Amanda was supposed to call him to arrange a meeting place, but she never had.

At around midnight, DJ said he had received a call from Amanda's cell phone, but his phone battery was almost dead and he could not hear anything.

"But he knows it was Amanda," wrote the detective, "because he had caller ID and it was her cell number."

He said that he had then gone out all night in his convertible, searching for Amanda.

"To be honest with you," DJ told the detective, "I think she was kidnapped."

From then on, DJ would become the prime suspect in Amanda Berry's disappearance.

Ariel Castro was now in possession of Amanda's cell phone, and was carefully listening to every message left for her by her worried mother, sister and boyfriend. Every day he would listen to their increasingly frantic calls. In time, he would even erase the messages to make room for new ones.

A few nights after she arrived, Amanda Berry tried to escape. But Ariel Castro easily overpowered her, holding her down as he taped her legs and mouth, savagely raping her again. Then he chained her back to the pole, placed a motorcycle helmet on her head and left her in the dark basement.

The next day he brought Amanda upstairs to the bathroom, where he raped her again, before bringing her into a bedroom and chaining her bound and gagged to a heater.

From now on, Ariel Castro would freely sexually assault Amanda whenever he felt like it.

9
"I HAVE YOUR DAUGHTER"

On Monday April 28, one week after Amanda Berry went missing, Cleveland's WEWS-5 led off its ten o'clock news with the story. A tearful Louwana Miller appeared on camera, pleading for any information to find her daughter.

"It's been a whole week and it's getting harder," she sobbed. "Somewhere between home and [Burger King] something happened. Nobody can figure it out."

A reporter called it "a mystery" and Cleveland police were completely baffled.

"Her sister is posting Amanda's picture," said the reporter. "She fears the worst but hopes for the best."

Then, as Amanda's face came up on screen, Beth Serrano appealed for her to come home, if she was watching.

"I'm hoping she's out there somewhere," said Beth. "I mean, I don't care. Just come home. I hope nothing happened to her [and] maybe somebody's got her, drugged her or something. Just bring her home."

Ariel Castro watched the newscast from his living room at 2207 Seymour Avenue. A few minutes later, he picked up Amanda's silver cell phone and dialed Louwana Miller's number on speed dial.

"I have your daughter," he told her. "She's healthy and okay." But when Louwana asked to speak to Amanda, he rang off. Two minutes later he called back.

"He said Mandy was going to be his wife," Louwana recalled in 2005. "He wanted to marry her. Mandy wanted to be with him. And then he hung up and that's the last I heard."

After dialing Amanda's number and leaving several messages, Louwana called FBI Special Agent Robert Hawk, who was leading the investigation. Hawk believed it might be a hoax and Amanda was part of it, as the caller had said she was fine and would be home in a couple of days.

Michelle Knight was also watching the news bulletin that night, with more than a little interest. Earlier, Ariel Castro had burst into her bedroom, where she was still chained, and turned on the television.

"If you watch the news tonight," he told her cryptically, "you might find there's a tragedy in Cleveland."

The moment she saw Amanda's face on the television screen, she realized that "the Dude," as she now called him, had kept his word and kidnapped another girl.

"The reason why he turned on the TV," Michelle said later, "is that he wanted me to know that there was another girl in the house."

But it would be several weeks before her captor brought a young blond girl, wearing a pair of boy's pajamas, into Michelle's room. Beforehand, Castro told Michelle to put a blanket over her naked body and hide the chains. Although he introduced the girl as his brother's girlfriend, Michelle immediately recognized her from the television news. She was embarrassed for Amanda to see the filthy conditions she was imprisoned in. The floor was covered with rotten sandwiches and pizza slices and it stank of urine.

"There were flies flying around the room," Michelle said. "It was pretty disgusting."

But as soon as Amanda saw Michelle she smiled warmly.

"I think she was happy to see there was another person there," said Michelle, "and she wasn't alone."

Michelle also noticed how clean and fresh Amanda looked and that she was wearing clothes, while she was naked in chains and had not showered in months.

Then Castro led Amanda out of the room and it would be months before the girls saw each other again.

On May 3, 2003, the Cleveland *Plain Dealer* ran its first story of Amanda Berry's disappearance in its "Law & Order" column. Under the headline CLEVELAND FBI SEARCHING FOR MISSING GIRL, it offered an unspecified reward for any information leading to her whereabouts.

"Authorities need help finding Amanda Berry," it began. "The FBI and Cleveland police said Amanda left work at 7:30 P.M. in a car with an unidentified driver. FBI agent Robert Hawk said the agency is treating the case as a kidnapping."

In the days following Amanda's disappearance, her mother embarked on a relentless campaign to keep her story in front of the Cleveland media. Nervous and chain-smoking Newport cigarettes, Louwana Miller aggressively courted local journalists to keep the story alive, praying that heavy media exposure would eventually lead to her daughter being found.

One morning, Louwana arrived at the *19-Action News* studios demanding to speak to investigative reporter Bill Safos. When he came out, she handed him one of her homemade missing person posters, with Amanda's photograph and description.

"And just seeing [Louwana's] face," recalled Safos. "The tears in her eyes and how desperate she was with that handmade poster. I thought a mother shouldn't have to go through this, so I paid a lot of attention to her."

Safos and a cameraman then drove to Louwana's house, where he interviewed her in Amanda's bedroom. It was exactly as she'd left it the day she disappeared. Her rosary was hanging on the doorknob and her Eminem posters on the wall by her CD collection. Her clothes were folded neatly on the bed.

Then Louwana opened a drawer, showing Safos the hundred dollars of Amanda's birthday money, lying untouched.

"That was *the* red flag to me," said Safos. "A kid's not going to run away without money."

Louwana also befriended *Plain Dealer* columnist Regina Brett, who would devote many of her columns to Amanda over the next few years, becoming personally involved in the search.

On May 11, three weeks after Amanda went missing, Brett wrote about Louwana's desperate battle to find her daughter.

"Louwana can't sleep or eat," read her column. "She lives on cigarettes and blind faith. Sitting on the couch in a cloud of smoke, she uses the coffee table as a desk, with two phones ready, a stack of business cards from detectives and FBI agents."

Brett described how Louwana avoided her daughter's bedroom, which lay untouched in suspended animation, as it was just too painful. And how every time the phone rings, she prays it's Amanda.

"I don't know if she's out there being held," said

Louwana. "I don't know if she's out there lying on the side of the road somewhere. Who gave her that ride?"

Three days later, FBI Special Agent Robert Hawk told the *Plain Dealer* that several people were now being interviewed in connection with her disappearance. He said investigators now believed that Amanda Berry had got into a white four-door sedan with three men inside. What he didn't reveal was that Amanda's boyfriend, Danizo Diaz, who owned a similar car, was now the prime suspect.

In the initial police report, Detective Scaggs had expressed some surprise that a sixteen-year-old would be driving such a flashy sports car. So investigators impounded DJ's four-door white Dodge Intrepid convertible for forensic examination and searched his home. DJ was also given a lie detector test, which he passed.

Agent Hawk also revealed that Louwana Miller had received a mysterious phone call from her daughter's cell phone a week after her disappearance. The FBI were still trying to determine if it was a hoax.

Louwana had now recruited a crack team of volunteers who pinned up MISSING posters and yellow ribbons to trees and telephone poles all over Cleveland. They also went farther afield, distributing the posters to truck stops and post offices all over the East Coast.

The poster, which had two photographs of Amanda, read:

MISSING
AMANDA BERRY
MISSING FROM CLEVELAND, OH
IF YOU HAVE ANY INFORMATION ABOUT AMANDA:
CALL THE CLEVELAND, OHIO FBI (216) 522-1400

Date Missing: 4/21/03

Date of Birth: 4/22/86

Age at Disappearance: 17 years

Race: Caucasian

Sex: Female

Height: 5'1"

Weight: 110 lbs.

Eyes: Brown

Hair: Sandy Blonde, long

Other: Surgical scar on lower

Abdomen and pierced left

eyebrow

Last Seen Wearing: Burgundy
Burger King shirt, black pants
And a black hooded jacket
Amanda was last seen walking
home from work at the Burger
King at W. 110th and Lorain in
Cleveland, Ohio on April 21,
2003. She has not been seen
or heard from since

AMANDA IS BELIEVED TO BE
ENDANGERED

Even though Ariel Castro now had two girls hidden at 2207 Seymour Avenue, he still had Lillian Roldan over to stay. One night, she heard Michelle Knight's television in an upstairs bedroom and asked him who was watching it.

"And my heart stopped beating," Castro later told detectives, "and I was like, 'Okay, she's probably catching on to something.'"

Castro then made an excuse and changed the subject. From then on he stopped inviting her to his house, saying he had more rehearsals to go to.

"When we first met he only played on weekends," said Lillian. "And then all of a sudden he had to rehearse Wednesdays and then play Fridays, Saturdays and Sundays. And the relationship was going down. I told him, 'Why don't I stay with you more?'"

Now Castro would stay over at Lillian's house and even had his own key. But he never gave her any money for anything.

"When he was living with me," Lillian said, "I used to pay for everything."

* * *

Ariel Castro was now a member of the Roberto Ocasio Latin Jazz Project, one of Cleveland's top Latin bands. But he was erratic and often failed to turn up for rehearsals or shows.

"He wouldn't call," said Daisy Cortes, who was engaged to the band's director, Roberto Ocasio. "He wouldn't show up."

At that time, Cortes was a news anchor for a Cleveland Spanish TV station, and often covered the Amanda Berry story. During set breaks Castro would seek her out, when she was sitting with her nine-year-old daughter, Bianca, asking for the latest news on the case.

"I was helping to find that girl," said Cortes in 2013. "I was sharing the story with him."

As Cortes told him what she had heard through the police grapevine about the Amanda Berry case, Castro would just say, "wow, wow," as he ran his fingers through Bianca's hair.

"No emotion at all," recalled Cortes. "Nothing."

Several years earlier, Emily Castro, now fifteen, had been diagnosed with manic depression and put on strong medication. The troubled girl had been expelled from Wilbur Wright Middle School in eighth grade and was now at a special school studying for her high school diploma. At times she would stop taking her prescribed medications and become unstable.

Nilda Figueroa blamed Ariel Castro for their daughter's problems, wanting him to have as little to do with her as possible. But in early 2003, Castro started taking more interest in his two youngest daughters, Emily and Arlene, and would arrive without warning to take them out.

"He was trying to make our lives miserable," said their stepfather, Fernando Colon. "He would just show up and ask to take the kids."

One afternoon, when Castro drove Emily back to her home on West 110th Street, Nilda confronted him in the street about taking her. As they argued, Emily went back inside the house.

A couple of minutes later, Fernando Colon came out to see what was happening. When Castro saw him coming he walked back to his van. But Colon came after him, ordering him to leave the children alone.

"At first he was arguing with my mother," said Ariel, Jr., who witnessed it. "And then Fernando came out . . . to back her up. So my father and my stepfather were also arguing."

Then, after swearing to get even with his rival, Ariel Castro drove off in a fury.

One day, Ariel Castro unlocked Michelle Knight's chains and took her to the bedroom, where he was holding Amanda Berry. Michelle told him that she didn't want to go inside, as she was naked.

"Basically I was embarrassed," said Michelle. "I didn't want to walk in front of [Amanda] being naked. And he was like, 'Well, she's got the same thing you have. You can come in the room.'"

When Michelle finally went in, she and Amanda hugged each other, as Castro left them alone for a couple of minutes. Michelle noticed Amanda had a chain around her ankle, although she had tried to hide it.

"I finally got to see where [Amanda] was at," said Michelle. "We're sitting there . . . and she told me, 'I think I remember you from school.' I was like, 'Yeah, I remember you.'"

Then Castro returned and took Michelle back to her room and chained her up again.

"It was like a big hug and bye," recalled Michelle. "He wouldn't let us stay in the same room for that long."

Although the two captives were chained up in adjoining bedrooms, they were too scared to talk to each other, even when Castro was out working.

"We weren't allowed," said Michelle. "If we did we would have got into trouble."

Over the first year of Amanda's imprisonment, they saw each other only a half-dozen times. On several occasions the teenager broke down crying, and Michelle would comfort her.

"I'd tell her everything will be okay," she said. "That one day we'll get home."

But Michelle could see how much better Amanda was being treated than she was. Castro provided Amanda better food and living conditions than he did Michelle, who was his "punching bag."

"He will always say," recalled Michelle, " 'I don't want to make her cry. I don't want to make her upset.' He would try and make her happy instead of sad. He treated her halfway decent . . . and let her have whatever she wanted because she was the new girl."

And whenever Amanda refused his sexual demands, Castro would go to Michelle's bedroom.

"[If] she wouldn't comply with him," said Michelle, "he'll come into my room and he'd be like, 'Well, she won't do it so you have to.' And if I didn't do it, he would force it on me."

That August, in the midst of a sweltering summer with no air-conditioning, Michelle Knight became pregnant for the third time. As she baked in the stifling heat in her tiny six-by-six-foot bedroom, it took several months for Ariel Castro to make her miscarry. Michelle later told police that he stopped feeding her for several weeks, as well as punching and jumping on her stomach.

"He would beat and starve me until I aborted," she said.

"He would kick me. He would punch me and jump on my stomach. He [took] a barbell and hit me right in the stomach."

On August 18, 2003, almost four months after Amanda Berry went missing, her mother held a prayer vigil outside Burger King on West 110th Street. Holding a homemade MISSING poster of Amanda, Louwana led one hundred supporters in a solemn walk from Burger King to her home.

Interviewed by a local TV crew, Louwana speculated that Amanda must have got into the car with somebody she knew. And she revealed that she had left numerous messages on her daughter's cell phone, which somebody had erased to make room for more.

"Somebody cleared [her phone] out twice," said Miller. "It was still taking messages. Then it stopped."

Louwana Miller was now often on the local TV news, and if ever Michelle saw her, she'd turn up the TV so Amanda could hear her mother's voice.

"If her mom was on TV, I would blast [it]," said Michelle, "so she can turn on hers. And then I'll quickly turn it down because you never knew when he's there."

On September 1, Ariel Castro made his TV debut, playing live in the Fox-8 studio in a pickup band on the morning news show. The smartly dressed bassist looked like he didn't have a care in the world as he smiled for the camera.

Twelve days later, eleven-year-old Shakira Johnson went missing on the East Side of Cleveland. The little girl was last seen at a block party, and over the next few days hundreds of volunteers searched the area looking for any signs of her.

The sixth-grader's disappearance shocked Cleveland and highlighted the other 2,700 missing persons reports so far in 2003.

A week later, community groups held a rally outside Burger King on West 110th Street to support Amanda Berry, now missing for five months. That same day Regina Brett wrote another column about the case.

"It's like she fell off the face of the earth," Louwana was quoted as saying. "I'm just about ready to crack up."

Louwana said that at first she thought that Amanda was being kept prisoner but now she feared the worst.

"I don't think my baby's coming home," she sobbed. "It's just been too long."

FBI Special Agent Robert Hawk said the case was still under active investigation, with agents tracking down new leads that were now coming in after Shakira Johnson's disappearance.

"We're working on it every day," said Hawk. "We haven't given up."

On October 20, Shakira's decomposed body was found in a field near East 71st Street and a murder investigation was launched.

The following day, Louwana Miller was interviewed on WEWS-TV news, in a story marking the six-month anniversary of Amanda's disappearance. And watching the news that night at 2207 Seymour Avenue were Ariel Castro and Michelle Knight.

"Tattered fliers are all that's left to remind us that Amanda Berry vanished six months ago," said a voiceover. "And that left her mother's dreams for a bright future in tatters."

Then a tearful Louwana Miller pleaded for anyone with any information about Amanda to call the FBI.

"It's just getting harder and harder," she sobbed, "to know that your daughter fell off the face of the earth and nobody knows where she's at. If anybody knows anything about my daughter [please] come forward, because somebody out there knows something."

At the end of the news segment, Ariel Castro laughed and started taunting Michelle.

"You see that?" he asked her. "At least somebody's looking for her. But who's looking for you? Not a soul. That's because you don't mean nothin' to nobody."

In late October, Ariel Castro broke off his three-and-a-half-year relationship with Lillian Roldan. He was now actively planning to take a third girl, and with his full-time job and playing gigs every weekend, he had little time left for traditional romantic entanglements.

One afternoon, Lillian arrived home from work to find a letter from Castro lying on her kitchen table.

"I opened the letter," she said, "and it said that he loved me, but not enough to have a long relationship."

Heartbroken, Lillian then called Castro, demanding that he come over and tell her they were over, face-to-face.

Then he drove over and explained how he now had too many commitments to have a proper relationship.

"But he told me not to hesitate," said Lillian, "if I ever needed anything from him. So I said, 'Okay.' "

Jovita Marti said her best friend was devastated after the breakup, and she spent many hours consoling Lillian.

"She was heartbroken," said Jovita, "because she really loved him. She was crying a lot."

On Saturday, November 15, the top-rated TV show *America's Most Wanted* featured a segment on Amanda Berry's disappearance. For months, Louwana Miller had been pitching the producers to run a segment on her daughter, and her persistence had finally paid off.

The day of the show, FBI Special Agent Robert Hawk told the *Plain Dealer* that investigators now believed the mysterious telephone calls to Louwana, the week after Amanda went missing, had come from her kidnapper.

"That leads us to believe she was not a runaway," he told reporters. "Someone had control of her cell phone."

Special Agent Hawk said the caller's voice sounded like that of a man between eighteen to thirty years of age. Initially, Louwana had thought it might be a prank, as the call came immediately after her daughter's photo was shown on television for the first time. But finally, seven months later, the FBI had confirmed it had definitely come from Amanda's cell phone.

"I would just hope that after this *America's Most Wanted* show, somebody out there will say something," said Louwana, "so I could see her for her eighteenth birthday."

Five days later, Cleveland police officially removed Michelle Knight's name from the FBI's NCIC (National Crime Information Center) database of missing persons. A Cleveland police spokesman would later explain it had been removed fifteen months after she went missing, as they had been unable to contact Barbara Knight to establish if she had been found.

On November 17, a twenty-five-year-old repairman named Daniel Hines was arrested for Shakira Johnson's murder. Thirteen months later a jury returned a not-guilty verdict and Shakira's killer has never been found.

On Christmas Day, Amanda Berry sat in her bedroom at 2207 Seymour Avenue watching the WEWS-TV news, when her mother was interviewed about her first holiday without her.

"Nobody tells me anything," said a frustrated Louwana. "I just sit here and if I don't figure it out myself, it don't get figured out. That's not right."

Louwana said it was going to be a lonely Christmas

without Amanda, as the camera panned in on a pile of gift-wrapped presents lying under the tree.

"We'll have a few gifts for her," she said, "hoping that she was . . . here to open them. To eat dinner with us. But it didn't happen. They're still waiting for her."

Then Amanda's grandmother Fern Gentry held up Amanda's missing-persons poster, appealing for anyone with any information about Amanda to come forward.

"We thought she'd be knocking on the door at Christmas," said Gentry, "and we were disappointed again. So I'm begging everybody out there, please, please help us find her."

On January 11, 2004, Ariel Castro's father, Pedro Castro, Sr., died, leaving behind an estate worth more than $260,000. The successful used-car dealer's money was split equally among his nine children, with each receiving $11,037. Ariel was also left a 1997 Chevy Malibu, valued at $1,500; Pedro, Jr., inherited a 1988 Buick, valued at $600; and Onil received a 1993 Ford Tempo, valued at just $150.

Two weeks later, Cleveland police arrived at 2207 Seymour Avenue to investigate Ariel Castro for abduction and child endangerment. That morning, Castro had picked up two elementary school children, who had to go to different schools. After dropping off one of the children, he drove to a Wendy's restaurant for lunch, ordering the remaining child, a four-year-old boy, to the back of his bus.

"Lay down, bitch!" he told the child, as he locked up the school bus and went into the restaurant. After eating his lunch, Castro returned to the bus and drove around for a while, before dropping off the student at the elementary school two hours after first picking him up.

After the boy's mother complained he had missed his class, two Cleveland police officers arrived at Ariel Castro's house to interview him about the incident. They knocked several times and when there was no answer, they left, never bothering to return.

The incident was also investigated by Cleveland's Child and Family Services, who found that the complaint against Castro for child abuse and neglect was "unsubstantiated."

"I didn't cause no near accident or anything," Castro told his supervisor in a letter.

However, he was later brought before a Cleveland School District disciplinary hearing, and suspended from work for sixty days without pay.

On the last day of January, Cleveland bandleader Roberto Ocasio was tragically killed in a car accident. On hearing the news, Ariel Castro telephoned Ocasio's fiancée, Daisy Cortes, to offer his help.

"He was the first person to call me for the condolence," recalled Cortes. "And he said, 'Well, I'm here for you if you need me.'"

At the end of February 2004, the body of a young girl was found near the Mexican border in El Centro, Texas. It bore similarities to Amanda Berry, and the FBI ordered forensic tests to determine if it was her.

Special Agent Hawk told Louwana Miller that her daughter's body might have been found, but it could take days before the tests could be completed.

"I've been up for two days, and I haven't eaten for two weeks," Louwana Miller told the *Plain Dealer* on March 5. "How long do I have to wait for an answer?"

Two days later, Special Agent Hawk informed Louwana that it was not Amanda's body, as the dental records did not match.

"We're still working the case," Hawk told the *Plain Dealer*, "and we remain optimistic."

* * *

In late March, Ariel Castro came into Michelle Knight's room and unchained her. He told her that a new girl would soon be arriving and she had to help him prepare another room.

"I had to help drill holes in the wall," said Michelle, "to put the chains through to hook us together. He had told me he was bringing somebody in the house . . . and to be very quiet."

10
GINA

Felix DeJesus had gone to school with Ariel Castro, and they were old friends. They came from two of Cleveland's most prominent Puerto Rican families, which went back a long way.

His fourteen-year-old daughter, Georgina, whom everyone knew as Gina, was also best friends with Arlene Castro. They were both in the seventh grade at Wilbur Wright Middle School, although Gina was taking special education classes and still learning to read.

At 2:30 P.M. on Friday, April 2, the two girls left Wilbur Wright together, walking toward West 105th Street and Lorain Avenue. It was a rainy afternoon and Gina was wearing a white coat, a sky blue sweater, jeans and white tennis shoes, her long curly brown hair tied in a ponytail.

They planned to go to Gina's house for a few hours to play, but first Arlene needed permission from her mother. They found a pay phone and Gina handed Arlene fifty cents for the call. But Nilda Figueroa said Arlene could not go over to Gina's, as Arlene had been grounded for bad behavior.

Gina good-naturedly said it was okay and she'd walk home instead, as she no longer had the $1.25 for bus fare. Then after saying good-bye to Arlene, she started home.

A few minutes earlier, Ariel Castro had arrived at Wilbur Wright Middle School in his maroon Jeep Cherokee, looking for Arlene. After getting permission from the security guard, Castro had gone into the school but could not find his daughter. Then he came out and started driving around looking for her.

Later he would tell police that sex had been on his mind when he first spotted Gina outside the school with his thirteen-year-old daughter Arlene. He said he had been "attracted" by Gina's "cleavage."

After driving past the girls, Castro made a U-turn a few blocks away and headed back.

"As I turned around," he said, "I noticed my daughter Arlene was now walking west on Lorain Avenue, and was by herself."

Then Castro saw Gina walking east on Lorain Avenue, and pulled up beside her. He wound down his window and asked if she knew where Arlene was. Gina replied she was walking home, and Castro asked her to help him find her.

Gina recognized the middle-aged man as Arlene's father, and got into the Jeep. Then as he started driving, he asked if she could help him move a speaker in his house. Gina agreed.

When they arrived at 2207 Seymour Avenue, Castro pulled into the driveway and led her in through the back door. Once inside the house, he took Gina upstairs, saying he no longer needed help with the speaker. He brought her into the bathroom and started looking at himself in the mirror. Suddenly, he asked Gina to show him "her privates."

She became very uncomfortable and told him she wanted to leave. Castro said she could, but it would have to be through a different door than the one through which they had entered.

He then tricked her into his basement, where he attacked her. After putting plastic ties on her wrists and chaining her to the pole, he raped her. Gina screamed, as she desperately tried to fight him off.

When he was finished, he placed a motorcycle helmet over her head and left her there, chained to the pole, sobbing.

Upstairs, Michelle Knight heard Gina's desperate screams for help and prayed. Earlier, he had come into her bedroom and told her that he had somebody in the house and to be quiet, so as not to scare her off.

"All I hear is fighting in the basement . . . and a girl screaming for help," said Michelle. "I could hear things crash and I could hear someone screaming, 'Get off of me! Get off of me!' And nobody helps her."

At 3:45 P.M., ten minutes after Gina usually arrived home, her mother, Nancy Ruiz, walked to the corner store to check if she had been there. Then she began calling around to Gina's friends, who had not seen her.

At 5:09 P.M., Nancy reported her daughter missing to the Cleveland police, saying Gina's behavior was out of character and she was concerned.

"Missing juvenile went to school and never returned home," read the Cleveland police report. "Last seen by School, Wilbur Wright, after school let out."

Nancy told police that her daughter was "normal and healthy" but "is mentally around the age of nine or ten years and attends special-ed classes." She then gave officers a photograph of Gina.

Meanwhile a detective called around to all Cleveland hospitals and the morgue, but there was no record of Gina.

An investigator also interviewed Arlene Castro, who was the last person to see Gina.

"[Arlene] states missing person told her she was walking home," read the police report. "Last seen by Castro, Arlene, of W. 110/Lorain. Unk. Destination."

On Saturday morning, police stopped traffic along Lorain Avenue at West 105th Street, showing motorists a photograph of Gina DeJesus. And police bloodhounds sniffed the pay phone where Arlene Castro had last seen Gina for any clues. One of the dogs tracked Gina's scent from the corner of West 105th Street to the end of the block on West 104th Street just past the pay phone, but then the trail went cold.

As Cleveland police blanketed the West Side searching for Gina, several police officers went to Seymour Avenue on Saturday morning to investigate a complaint of harassing telephone calls in an unrelated incident. They interviewed one of Ariel Castro's neighbors at 2202 Seymour Avenue before leaving.

Around midday, Amanda Berry's boyfriend, Danizo Diaz, left his house, to find it surrounded by Cleveland police. As police escorted him to a squad car for questioning, his neighbors applauded, thinking Gina's kidnapper had been caught. But a few hours later Diaz was released. For the next few years, he would be stopped and questioned periodically about Amanda and Gina's disappearances.

That afternoon, Gina's family and friends posted fliers with her photograph all around Cleveland's West Side, including one on a tree outside 2207 Seymour Avenue.

Community activist Khalid Samad said Ariel Castro helped in the search that day.

"He was friends with the [DeJesus] family," said Samad. "When we went out to look for Gina, he helped pass out fliers."

Late Saturday afternoon, Felix DeJesus was rushed to the emergency room with chest pains. He was kept in for observation and then released.

That night DeJesus family members gathered at Gina's house to help print fliers and offer her parents support. Local councilman Zack Reed also visited the family, saying Cleveland needed to devise a game plan to protect children.

At 10:00 P.M. WEWS-TV news broke the story of Gina DeJesus's disappearance, linking it to Amanda Berry's.

"The fourteen-year-old Wilbur Wright student was last seen in the area Friday afternoon," said a reporter, "this same neighborhood where Amanda Berry vanished almost one year ago."

One of Amanda's classmates said that she and her friends no longer walked around the West Side alone.

"I'm usually always with somebody," said the unnamed friend. "I don't go out at night by myself. Before I didn't worry, but now I do. Scary, really scary."

On Sunday, the FBI joined in the search for Gina DeJesus. That afternoon her parents set up a command post at their house. They distributed fliers to friends and family, who then left to hand them out in the street or staple them onto trees and utility poles. FBI agents searched Gina's bedroom and questioned her parents. An FBI agent also interviewed Arlene Castro, who claimed to have been almost kidnapped three times, at her stepfather Fernando Colon's house.

On Sunday afternoon Gina's mother gave her first interview to *Plain Dealer* reporter Joan Mazzolini.

"I gave her the dollar twenty-five to catch the bus," said Nancy, "because it was cold outside. But she has the tendency to walk home and use the money for [snacks]."

Ariel Castro began to grow paranoid in the weeks after Gina's disappearance. He was convinced that one of the security cameras at Wilbur Wright Middle School had photographed him lurking around before he snatched Gina DeJesus. And he believed it was only a matter of time before police came to search 2207 Seymour Avenue.

Late Sunday night, he wrote a four-page handwritten confession, with numerous crossings-out. In it he claimed he was a "sexual predator," while accusing his three victims of being responsible for their kidnappings.

CONFESSION AND DETAILS

Page 1   Date 4-4-04

To the best of my knowledge, I was born in P.R. I was abandoned by my father and later my mother. My grandma raised me. I was abused sexually by the son of Luis and Filia, his name is Pucho. He penetrated my rear a couple of times. I was 5 or 6 years old. I soon learned how to masturbate. I was interested in sex at a very young age. Sex has always been a too big part of my life. I married at age 20. I lived a normal life with my wife and children, but my marriage was a failure from the beginning. My mother was an abusive parent. Her ways of discipline were very bad. For this made me grow hatred for her. There were times I wished she would die. Anyway, my marriage was abusive also. My wife would hit on me and push me to the limit. I hit her back. She put me in jail only to go get me out and apologize to me. This happened a couple of times, but the name calling and arguments were always there. I tried to reason with her that the kids did not need to see or hear the arguments or fights. I felt bad to see my children frightened and scared. My wife always said she didn't give a shit if they were [indecipherable] or not. The marriage lasted about twelve years. I always loved and still love my children.

Page 2

About six years ago my wife left for [another] man. I didn't mind as long as my kids . . . And in a good home. This man did nothing [for the] children. <u>I kept taking this in,</u> but [they were] better off with their mother. I [can't] Understand why this man took the [trouble] To finish raising my kids when he knew [I was] In a relationship as a father. My ex wife has many problems with this [man and] just can't get out of the relationship. I lived alone for the most part after my . . . Marriage. I had a good sex drive. I was in a relationship with a [indecipherable] woman I cared [indecipherable]. I met a woman at Family Dollar on Clark. The woman needed a ride somewhere. I [indecipherable] brought her to my home. Michelle has been there ever since, about two years. I got another opportunity to get another woman [indecipherable] in my van. This girl is Amanda [indecipherable]. On West 110 walking home a (short distance). I asked her if she needed a ride home and she said yes. I [indecipherable] brought her to my house. She has been there for about a year, smoking her pot cigarettes that I provide [indecipherable] These two women accepted [money] for sex. I treat them well and make sure they eat good.

I don't understand why I keep looking for women out in the street, as I already had two in my possession. One day I was driving down Lorrain Ave and near 105 a woman was walking. I asked her if she needed a ride. She agreed. I calmly drove her to my house. This girl is Georgina. I asked her to come inside, she said Yes. These women are here against their will because they made a mistake by getting in a car with a total stranger. I had no idea Gina was so young, she looks a lot older. Also not knowing she is the daughter of Felix, a school classmate of mine. The bottom line is, I am a sexual predator who needs help, but I don't bother to get it. I live a private life. I function around others like a normal person. I've been having problems with my head for a long time. I feel depressed, dizzy and short term memory loss. I really [indecipherable] know what's wrong with me. To the parents of these three women, I would like to say <u>I'm very sorry</u>. *I am sick. Five years ago I was diagnosed with a cyst in my brain. I don't [know if] this is what made me behave the way I do, not have any feelings for the bad things I have done. I can [indecipherable] the public, these three women are the only ones I have [done] harm to, holding them against their will. [indecipherable] When I wake up in the morning, I don't feel like I'm really hear [sic]. For some reason I feel ????trate. This is a big problem in my every day life. I want to put an end to my life and let the devil deal with me.*

I feel so bad about the age of Gina. I will admit I did molest her but did not rape her. I actually feel the closeness to her and her parents. I do not have the urge to touch her. I feel its [sic] wrong.

Anyway, my intentions are to let these women go, when I feel I have arranged everything, so my family knows what to do after I take my life. I have a <u>Dollar Bank Account with about $10,875.21</u> (Ten Thousand Dollars. And I have cash—about Eleven Thousand in cash, 11,000, under the washer machine. That's it. Do not look for any more money, Their [sic] isn't anymore. (My family will need to know this.) I would like the money to go to the 3 victims. For they deserve every red cent of it. Again, I apologize (sorry) to every one this whole ordeal has affected.

To my children. Please be strong and make the right decisions. Just because you may think you know someone, do not get into their vehical [sic]. This was the case of Amanda and Gina.

Nilda, please do your best to insure my babies are safe. If possible move away, (far away).

As I write this letter on 4-4-04, 2:05 PM, my simptons [sic] are clearly bothering me (Dizzyness and not really feeling like I'm hear [sic]. Also Depression. <u>I know I am sick</u> (Mentally).

After finishing his confession, Castro folded it up and placed it in a drawer in his kitchen, where it would stay for the next nine years.

11

THE SEARCH

On Monday, April 5, more than fifty people marched to Cleveland City Hall in support of the DeJesus family. Then, at a city council meeting, the subject of Gina De-Jesus and Amanda Berry's disappearances was raised.

"You should be concerned," declared Councilman Matt Zone, who represented the district where both girls went missing. "We've had three abductions in recent months. Something needs to be done."

Councilman Zack Reed called for council members, the police and school leaders to work together on a plan to make the streets of Cleveland safer for children.

"We must . . . get more eyes on the children as they walk to and from school," he said. "And we must teach young people to walk in pairs or to find safe houses, if they feel they are in danger."

Fifteen FBI agents were now working the Gina De-Jesus case full-time, and the agency offered a reward for any information leading to her being found.

Special Agent Robert Hawk, who had led the search for

Amanda Berry, was again in charge. He told the *Plain Dealer* that his men were now running down hundreds of leads, as well as interviewing Gina's classmates and neighbors.

Back at West 71st Street, Felix DeJesus had turned his home into an unofficial search headquarters, as he and his wife Nancy coordinated scores of volunteers in the hunt for their daughter. They worked around the clock, feeding and handing out fliers to the helpers who were blanketing Cleveland with them.

One afternoon, Ariel Castro arrived at their house and hugged Nancy, offering his sympathy and help. He then left with a handful of fliers.

Gina DeJesus's disappearance was now front-page news, leading off every local news program. And there was real fear on the streets of the West Side that no child was safe.

"They called it the Bermuda Triangle," remembered Michelle McDowell, who lived nearby. "It was really awful just to think about, and I was very scared because of my stepdaughters."

West Side resident Lupe Collins said the whole community was living in terror.

"There was a fear," she said. "It was hard for us. [Everyone] was afraid to let their daughters walk to school. We didn't know what was going on. Where did they go? How did they just vanish?"

The two girls' disappearances had also become a hot political issue. On Tuesday morning, Cleveland Mayor Jane Campbell and a deputation of city leaders arrived at the DeJesus house to comfort Gina's parents. Outside on the lawn was a shrine to Gina, bedecked with photographs, yellow ribbons and religious symbols.

The mayor met with Felix and Nancy, who then joined

her for a news conference at the First District Police Head-quarters.

"I have a fourteen-year-old daughter myself," Mayor Campbell told the press, "and I know a little bit about what fourteen-year-olds are like. Nobody's going to get into any trouble. Just tell us what you know."

A weary-looking Felix DeJesus then thanked the community for all its help and prayers to find his daughter.

"It's been hard," he said.

After the conference, the media were given a photograph showing the clothing Gina was wearing the day she disappeared.

That night, the six o'clock news led off with the latest on the search for Gina.

"By air. On ground. Every inch of Cleveland's West Side is under the microscope," said a reporter, "as investigators along with bloodhounds work around the clock to track this missing girl."

An unnamed female volunteer was then interviewed, echoing the feelings of so many others moved by the terrible plight of the DeJesus family.

"I knew I had to come out," she said, "because I know what they're going through. [I] just hope this case ends with a safe return of a precious life."

The search was also being closely followed at 2207 Seymour Avenue. Michelle Knight had immediately recognized Gina as the younger sister of her high school friend Mayra. But when she asked Ariel Castro if he had taken a fourteen-year-old girl, he denied it.

"He would come to my room [and] tell me, 'I didn't take her,'" said Michelle. "And I'll look up at him and [say], 'You're a damn liar. I know you took that girl.'"

* * *

On Wednesday morning, Cleveland police rounded up every known sex offender living on the West Side, questioning them about Gina's disappearance. Seven men were arrested on warrants for other offenses.

"We're just trying to shake some trees," Cleveland police Chief Deputy Charles Corrao told reporters. "I'm personally tired of these animals taking our children."

Cleveland police also combed through desolate wasteland and parks, looking for clues. And the FBI collected security videos from stores near where Gina had last been seen, studying them frame by frame. But they did not examine video from security cameras in and around Wilbur Wright Middle School, as Castro had so feared.

That night more than five hundred worried parents packed the Wilbur Wright Middle School auditorium for a public meeting, where they were addressed by Cleveland police, and city and school officials.

"We have followed up every possible lead," said Mayor Jane Campbell, "and will continue to do so. We still do not have a grip on where Gina is. We have to have every bit of information."

At one point, several angry parents were ejected by police, after heckling the mayor for ignoring other cases of missing girls, including that of Amanda Berry. When the meeting continued, police officials appealed to parents to question their children closely for any information that could help the investigation.

In the days following Gina's disappearance, there had been a flood of ghoulish rumors that Gina's body had been found. These had so upset the family that Gina's cousin Sylvia Colon made a public appeal for them to stop.

"We're hearing them daily," she told the *Plain Dealer*. "It's been very difficult. Help us by not perpetuating those rumors. Stop spreading them."

* * *

On Thursday, April 8, Gina DeJesus turned fifteen, and the DeJesus family organized a candlelight vigil the following night, at the corner of West 105th Street and Lorain Avenue, where she was last seen.

At 6:00 P.M. on Good Friday, more than a hundred Cleveland residents gathered at the intersection to pray for Gina, many clutching her photograph. Among them was Ariel Castro, who had also joined the search earlier that day and handed out fliers.

Police blocked off West 105th Street from traffic, as the crowd surrounded Gina's parents and her siblings, who were all holding large burning candles, to pray for Gina's return. Yellow ribbons and MISSING posters had been posted to telephones poles around the pay phone and intersection where Arlene Castro had called her mother, before Gina had left to walk home.

News reporters and local TV camera crews covered the vigil, which was led by West Side community activist Khalid Samad.

"We believe in total community involvement," he told the crowd. "We know that without the community this situation will not be solved. We just want to bring this baby home."

An emotional Nancy Ruiz also addressed reporters, the stress of losing her daughter visibly taking its toll.

"I can feel her near me," she said. "I know she's out there somewhere and close."

Earlier that day, a man had been arrested in Dayton, Ohio, in connection with an attempted abduction on Cleveland's East Side. And a buzz went through the crowd that maybe he had taken Gina. Police were careful not to raise expectations.

"There was a man arrested," a Cleveland police spokesman told a WEWS-TV reporter. "We're just pursuing a lead, but right now there's nothing connected to what's going on [here]."

At the end of the vigil, as the crowd held hands, a friend of the DeJesus family appealed for everyone to carry on the search for Gina.

"Continue to pray," she said. "Continue to take out the fliers and hopefully we're going to get Gina back very, very soon."

Earlier on Friday, after an anonymous tip believed to have come from Ariel Castro, the FBI picked up Fernando Colon for questioning. Colon, who had recently graduated from the police academy, was now working security at the Westown Plaza. On Friday morning, special agents arrived at his house and brought him downtown to FBI headquarters. For the next few hours, Colon was interrogated about Gina's disappearance, undergoing a polygraph test, which he passed. His security patrol car was also forensically examined for any evidence linking him to Gina DeJesus.

"I had nothing to hide," said Colon in 2013. "I said, 'I'll tell you whatever you want me to tell you, because when that girl disappeared I was working.'"

As an FBI agent was driving him home later, Colon advised him to take a close look at Ariel Castro as a possible suspect.

"I told them to investigate Ariel Castro," recalled Colon. "Because he knows Gina and her parents and where they live."

But the FBI ignored Colon's advice, never once questioning Ariel Castro about Gina's disappearance. Years later the FBI would vehemently deny that Colon had ever told them to investigate Ariel Castro.

At nine Saturday morning, more than two hundred people assembled at the Zone Recreation Center on Lorain Avenue to spend the day searching for Gina DeJesus. Before they fanned out in groups through the West Side of Cleveland, Mayor Jane Campbell told them she was praying for an "Easter miracle."

For the rest of the day the volunteers handed out fliers to passersby, and knocked on doors asking for any information. That afternoon, Felix DeJesus canvassed Seymour Avenue, speaking to residents outside Ariel Castro's house, where MISSING posters for Amanda Berry and Gina De-Jesus hung together on a pole.

"Gina's father came round," said Daniel Marti, who lived directly opposite, "and I remember talking to him and telling him how sorry I felt."

On Saturday night, millions of viewers coast to coast saw Arlene Castro on *America's Most Wanted,* in a segment about Cleveland's two missing girls, Gina DeJesus and Amanda Berry. Arlene described the last few minutes before her best friend disappeared, and calling her mother to see if Gina could spend the afternoon at their house.

"I decided to call my mom and ask her," Arlene told reporter Tom Morris. "So [Gina] gave me fifty cents to call. My mom said no, that I can't go over to her house, and so I told her I couldn't. And she said, 'Well, okay, I'll talk to you later,' and she just walked."

The program also featured Amanda Berry, who'd disappeared just across Lorain Avenue almost a year earlier.

"Two attractive teenaged girls," said Morris. "They disappear in similar circumstances along the same busy avenue. What does it mean? A lot of the local people around here are talking about it, and how they're getting a little bit scared for their children as well.

"Whether or not these cases are connected, police and the families of these two girls need your help."

Ariel Castro had turned down playing a gig that night so he could stay at home and watch Arlene on the top-rated

FOX TV show. He must have felt smugly satisfied that he had gotten clean away with his third kidnapping, and Cleveland police and the FBI were absolutely clueless.

Indeed, he felt so confident he had outsmarted law enforcement that right after taking Gina, he congratulated himself by buying a sports utility vehicle with the money his father had left him.

Michelle Knight first met Gina DeJesus a couple of weeks after she arrived in the house. In the days leading up to it, Ariel Castro kept telling Michelle that his daughter was coming over and he wanted them to meet.

At their first brief meeting, Castro put them in the bathroom together for a couple of minutes while he went to the kitchen.

"I whispered into her ear, 'You're Gina DeJesus,'" recalled Michelle. "And she looked at me and she was like, 'You know who I am?'"

Then Michelle, who had now been in the house almost two years, gave Gina some advice on dealing with their abductor.

"I told her not to tell him that I know who you are," Michelle said. "That there will be consequences to you telling him."

Then she promised to tell Gina more when they next saw each other.

Then Castro came into the bathroom and told Gina to put Michelle's hair into twists, and stayed to watch. But when Michelle thanked Gina for making her hair look so beautiful, Castro became incensed. He then took both of the girls upstairs, chaining Michelle to the bed in the pink bedroom, before bringing Gina back down to the basement.

A few days later, he moved Gina upstairs into one of the bedrooms, where he'd pinned up one of her MISSING posters on the wall.

* * *

One night a drunken Ariel Castro brought Michelle Knight downstairs and offered her some shots of rum. She refused, and after her captor took a large swig from the bottle, he told her how he used to follow a young girl home from Wilbur Wright Middle School every afternoon. He said she looked like Gina, and he had gotten them mixed up.

"He said he didn't know that he'd kidnapped his daughter's friend," said Michelle, "until he saw Gina's name on the news."

After Gina's disappearance, Arlene Castro fell into a deep depression and started self-cutting. Nilda took her to a psychiatrist, who diagnosed post-traumatic stress disorder.

"She was Gina's best friend," her mother would later explain, "and she was with her when she disappeared. So it traumatized Arlene because she felt responsible for [Gina's] disappearance."

12

"SOMEBODY KNOWS WHERE AMANDA IS"

Wednesday, April 21, 2004, marked the one-year anniversary of Amanda Berry's disappearance, and the day before her eighteenth birthday. That morning, Cleveland *Plain Dealer* columnist Regina Brett wrote a column about the tragic case, headlined, SOMEBODY KNOWS WHERE AMANDA IS.

"One year ago today," wrote Brett, "Amanda Berry fell off the face of the earth and her mother landed in hell. Louwana Miller hasn't heard her daughter's voice in a year. Hasn't seen her face in 365 days. Hasn't slept a single night without worrying, without wondering, Where is she?"

Since Amanda's disappearance, Brett wrote, Louwana has been tormented by images of her daughter, as a drugged-out sex slave or being dead and buried. She was now afraid to leave home in case she missed a call from Amanda, and scared of answering the phone to hear about yet another sighting of Amanda "pregnant, prostituting herself or prancing happily around in Florida."

All the sleepless nights had taken their toll on Louwana,

now forty-two, who had visibly aged since Amanda disappeared.

"As the months passed," wrote Brett, "the posters faded, the yellow ribbons fell down, and the media lost interest. No one seemed to care about Amanda—until another girl disappeared two weeks ago."

Since Gina DeJesus went missing, there had been renewed interest in Amanda by the media, with new MISS-ING posters of Amanda suddenly appearing all over Cleveland.

In the article, Louwana criticized Cleveland police and the FBI for taking so long to admit that Amanda was not a runaway. She also questioned whether her daughter might have been found if the FBI had traced the two strange phone calls she had received from Amanda's cell phone.

"If she's dead," said Louwana, "can somebody out there tell me? I'm living in hell."

On Saturday, FBI Special Agent Robert Hawk updated the Cleveland *Plain Dealer* on the search. Since Gina's disappearance, more than five hundred tips had been followed up without any success. Police had questioned around a thousand people, and given polygraph tests to seven people close to her. But Hawk admitted they were no further forward than they had been on day one.

That weekend, the DeJesus family and their supporters canvassed the West Side yet again, hoping for any scrap of information that might lead to her. And on Sunday night, Gina's parents attended a prayer rally for Amanda Berry at West 110th Street and Lorain Avenue, where she disappeared. From then on Felix, Nancy and Louwana Miller would become close, working together in a common mission to find their daughters.

* * *

Four days later, Ariel Castro assisted in a Cleveland police investigation, after an angry mother boarded his school bus, threatening to kill a nine-year-old student. Castro had then contacted the student's parents, who called in police.

The mother denied all of Castro's allegations, saying she was merely protecting her daughter, who was the victim of bullying. The police report said Castro had described how the mother had lashed out at the student on his bus.

"She told him she would 'Fuck him up' and 'Kill him,'" Castro told police, "[if] he ever hit her daughter."

There is no record of any further criminal action taken against the mother.

The first week of May, the FBI's Quantico-based Behavioral Analysis Unit arrived in Cleveland to build a psychological profile of who might have taken Gina. The unit, which specializes in missing-children cases, advised that Gina's MISSING posters should be in English and Spanish, and an aerial map of the path Gina took from Wilbur Wright the day she disappeared should be given to the media. A special tip line was also established for any anonymous information that might lead to Gina.

"They are confident that there is someone out there who has information that would resolve this investigation," FBI Special Agent Hawk told the *Plain Dealer*.

Felix DeJesus was becoming increasingly frustrated with the lack of progress. Each night since Gina had gone missing, Felix and several friends went out scouring the streets for her. And when police asked him to stop, he refused.

"I will not give up," Felix declared. "As long as she's out there missing, I'm going to be out there with her."

He was also actively investigating sex offenders living on the West Side. One night he and some friends reportedly broke into the apartment of a known sex offender, just a block away from where Gina disappeared.

Police were called to the apartment on West 104th Street and Lorain, but although no criminal charges resulted, Felix was again asked to stop this line of inquiry.

"I'm not a vigilante," he told the *Plain Dealer*. "I'm desperate to find my daughter."

While Felix was out searching, Nancy lit candles on her porch and prayed for her daughter's safe return. She had also constructed another shrine in their living room, full of Gina's photographs, toys and tchotchkes.

On June 1, 2004, a $20,000 reward was offered for any information leading to the discovery of Amanda Berry or Gina DeJesus. A couple of days later, a twenty-two-year-old Bowling Green University journalism student named Ariel Castro, Jr., wrote an article for the Cleveland *Plain Press* community newspaper.

Headlined GINA DEJESUS' DISAPPEARANCE HAS CHANGED THE NEIGHBORHOOD, the article, bearing the byline "Ariel Castro," focused on how radically his old Cleveland neighborhood had changed since Gina had disappeared. Castro interviewed Gina's mother, Nancy Ruiz, as well as several parents and a community organizer.

"Since April 2, 2004," his article began, "the day 14-year-old Gina DeJesus was last seen on her way home from Wilbur Wright Middle School, neighborhood residents have been taken by an overwhelming need for caution."

Castro noted that everybody in the neighborhood felt deeply connected to the DeJesus family, and had come together for a single cause.

"You can tell the difference," Nancy Ruiz was quoted as saying. "People are watching out for each other's kids.

It's a shame that a tragedy had to happen for me to really know my neighbors."

Ariel, Jr., also interviewed parents waiting for their children to be let out of Wilbur Wright Middle School, where Gina had left that fateful day with his sister Arlene.

"I really believe there needs to be more security," Vaneetha Smith told Castro, as she waited for her niece. "We have too many kidnappings and they should crack down on all the sex offenders in the area."

Castro noted how the Ohio Electronic Sex Offender Registration and Notification database listed 133 sex offenders living or working near Gina's home.

"I have been notified of only one sex offender," Ruiz told him, "and he lives only about 1,000 feet away from here."

Around this time, Ariel Castro brought Gina into the pink bedroom with Michelle. Several days earlier he had removed the bucket Michelle had been using as a toilet, replacing it with a larger white plastic portable one.

He then ordered Gina onto the dirty queen-size mattress with Michelle, padlocking a long rusty chain around Michelle's neck, and attaching the other end to Gina's ankle. When Gina asked how they were supposed to use the toilet if her leg was chained to Michelle's neck, Castro unlocked the chains and shackled their feet together instead. Then he threw some T-shirts and sweatpants on the bed for Michelle, who was still naked, leaving the girls on the bed chained together.

13

REVENGE

At the beginning of June, Ariel Castro started buying his daughters Emily and Arlene expensive presents for no apparent reason. He now visited them every day, paying them more attention than he had ever done before. Although suspicious, Nilda allowed him more access to their daughters, hoping he might have changed for the better.

"He was bringing them a lot of stuff," she said later. "Putting too much attention on them."

Over the next few weeks, he bought them expensive cell phones, iPods and perms, even promising to buy them cars when they turned eighteen.

"He began having a lot of contact with Arlene," said Nilda. "He would pick her up from school or from my home, or contact her by telephone quite often. He purchased Arlene a lot of clothing. Some of the clothing is inappropriate for her age and I will not let her wear it."

When he gave each of the girls a thousand dollars from his father's will, Nilda insisted on taking the money on their behalf, so they wouldn't waste it.

He also began probing into the most intimate parts of his daughters' lives, quizzing them about their periods, to the embarrassment of their mother.

"Are you sure you started your period," he asked each of his daughters, "or did somebody stick their finger up your vagina?"

As Ariel Castro insinuated himself into his daughters' daily lives, he began turning them against their stepfather. In the seven years since Nilda had become engaged to Fernando Colon, he had become the disciplinarian of the family. And his strictly enforced rules against smoking, hanging out in bad company and maintaining curfew did not endear him to Emily and Arlene.

"I was [strict] with them," said Colon, "because I didn't want them to get into drugs or become pregnant."

In June 2004, after a fight with her stepfather, sixteen-year-old Emily walked out of the house, moving in with Colon's sister, Sonia Lebron. Her mother was powerless to stop her.

"She would push me around," said Nilda, "and do what she wants to do. She used to stay up all hours of the morning [and party]."

Then, on July 4, Arlene was grounded for several weeks for breaking her curfew. She was furious, complaining that her stepfather had no right to order her around.

"[Fernando] wanted the rules of the house followed," explained Nilda. "[Emily and Arlene] didn't like the rules. They told me, 'He's not my dad, so why should he ground me [and] tell me what to do.'"

Now being treated for depression, Arlene Castro was regularly playing truant from Wilbur Wright Middle School.

"Sister Caroline called me from the school," said Nilda, "and told [me] that she wanted to expel Arlene because she's constantly lying. She's always saying she has a baby at home and that's why she couldn't attend school. Other children told me [Arlene] was pregnant."

In late July, Ariel Castro told Nilda he still loved her, asking her to dump Fernando Colon and move back in with him.

"He'll put his arm around me," said Nilda, "or he'll come in the house to try and kiss me. Because I'm his property. He says it all the time."

But Nilda told him she would never return to 2207 Seymour Avenue because of "his abusive nature."

"I don't love him," she would later say. "I don't want him. I'm scared of him."

That summer, as Michelle Knight and Gina DeJesus lay chained together in the pink room, they bonded into a sisterhood. They told each other their life stories and discussed their most intimate secrets. They regularly endured terrible indignities together, inflicted by Castro, including sharing the same filthy plastic portable toilet, which he rarely emptied.

When he was out working, they watched the ancient TV he had given them, and it was their only window to the outside world. Michelle warned Gina never to let "the Dude" catch them watching any programs with African Americans in them, or they'd be punished.

"We liked *The Fresh Prince of Bel-Air* and *Friends*," Michelle later told *People* magazine. "At least we were looking at the same things the rest of the world was looking at, even if we were locked up in a prison."

He also gave all three of his captives spiral notebooks, so they could keep journals and draw pictures. He would sometimes sneak a peek in them to see what they were saying about him, and be hurt if they ever criticized him.

"I wrote every day," said Michelle. "Poems. Songs. Dreams of how I wished everything could be different."

Michelle even made a list of what she needed for an imaginary camping trip, including: underwear, sleeveless T-shirt, long sleeves for when it's cold, shorts, long johns, socks, compass, hiking boots, peanuts, chocolate-chip cookies and pegs.

The most prolific writer was Amanda Berry, who used her journals to mark the passage of time, carefully chronicling her everyday life as a prisoner, as well as the horrible sexual abuse she suffered.

Amanda kept three distinct journals: the "Blue Journal," detailing her molestation by Ariel Castro; the "Miss Shady Hand Crafted Items," containing her personal notes and drawings; and a black journal titled "Love," in which she described herself as a "prisoner of war."

She also wrote daily letters to her mother about her ordeal, and her hopes for them to be reunited one day.

"The journals have extreme detail," said attorney Craig Weintraub, who would later read them. "And parts of them are very graphic about what occurred inside the house. The journals describe their relationships [with each other and Castro], the food, the clothing, the bathroom, the shower, the television and the chains and sex."

Most nights, Ariel Castro would come into the pink bedroom and rape Michelle or Gina, as they gripped the other's hand for comfort. He would also beat them in front of each other, although Michelle would always be hit harder.

"Hers were more like a smack," said Michelle. "Mine was more like a fist. There were times that he would hit her too . . . and I would jump in front of her and take the hit."

On Wednesday, July 15, Ariel Castro brought Emily and Arlene into the Cleveland Police Department's First District Station, where they accused Fernando Colon of sexually molesting them. But as Castro no longer had custody of his daughters, Nilda was called in to sign a release form.

"The first I knew of any criminal allegations against Fernando," she said, "was the day I was asked to sign a release form so that my daughters could talk to the detectives."

When Nilda arrived at the police station, she was greeted outside by Ariel Castro.

"He was laughing and excited," Nilda later testified. "He told me to go along with the complaints against Fernando, and he would buy me a new car. I told him I don't need anything from [you]."

Then Castro suggested that after Emily and Arlene talked to the police, they all go out to dinner.

"Castro believes that we will be together again," she said. "He told me that [Fernando] would know what it's like to be on the other side of the badge."

Six days later, Ariel Castro drove his daughters to the Justice Center, where they repeated their allegations to Detective Arthur King. With their father looking on encouragingly, they told the detective how their stepfather had been touching them for years.

"I was about eight or nine years old," Emily said in her statement, "and I woke up to him touching me under my clothes. We slept upstairs and they had a bedroom downstairs. And every night around twelve or one he would go into our room and just feel on me under my clothes."

Arlene told the detective how she had been molested by Fernando too.

"The first time . . . I was seven or eight," Arlene said in her statement. "Me and my sister was sleeping in the living room. He came downstairs and . . . started touching on me and started feeling on me. And I don't remember him penetrating me. I woke up and he said, 'If you ever tell anybody this I would hurt you.' He went back upstairs and I went back to sleep."

Arlene said her stepfather next touched her when she was asleep on the couch.

"He started feeling on my chest," she said. "I got up and went to my room and locked the door."

The third incident she alleged happened when she was sleeping on the couch, and he came in to clean the living room.

"He started touching on my butt," she told the detective. "Then I looked up and went to my room."

A few hours later, police arrested Fernando Colon on suspicion of kidnapping and rape as he protested his innocence. When he was later released on bail, he moved out of his house into a nearby hotel, until a grand jury could meet to decide whether the case would go to trial.

Two weeks later, Emily Castro was hospitalized for three days, after taking a drug overdose at her aunt Sonia's house. After she was admitted to Lutheran Hospital, Nilda telephoned Ariel Castro to let him know. He told her he did not care. But the next morning, he arrived at the hospital with breakfast for Emily.

The doctors told Nilda that Emily had overdosed on methamphetamine and marijuana. When she asked Emily about it, she replied that her father had given her the money to buy the drugs.

After she was discharged from the hospital, Emily moved back in with her mother, while Fernando Colon moved into his sister Sonia's house, until the molestation accusations could be resolved.

By the fall, everything seemed to be going according to plan for Ariel Castro. Not only had he successfully kidnapped three women, but his vendetta against Fernando Colon was well under way.

His job was also going well, and despite his suspension for leaving the young boy on the bus, the Cleveland School District had just given him a raise to $17.26 an hour. He also had the summer off while the schools were out.

Inside 2207 Seymour Avenue, Castro now began referring to Amanda Berry as his wife, and gave her a new color television. Most evenings, Michelle and Gina would hear Amanda going downstairs to his room, where they spent hours watching television together.

"I had no idea if he still had her chained up or what," said Michelle.

After informing Michelle and Gina that he and Amanda were now "married," he started taking them outside into the backyard, which was littered with barbwire, rusty chains and plastic tarps, where he would rape them.

"This made me wonder," said Michelle, "if, in his twisted mind, maybe he thought he should try to hide from her all the sex he was still having with me. He kept on raping Gina too."

With everything running smoothly with his three prisoners, Castro settled into a daily routine. Every morning, he would carefully lock the bedroom doors and leave the house by the back entrance to pick up his school bus at the depot. Then he would drive it to the Burger King on West 110th and Lorain Avenue, where he had snatched Amanda Berry, for his morning coffee.

"He used to park his bus down on the hill," recalled Ashley Bright, who served him. "He came in his uniform and the black leather hat. 'Hi, how are you doing?' Then he'd have his coffee and leave."

Around nine-thirty, after finishing his morning route,

he would park his yellow school bus outside his house with the engine running, and go in carrying large bags of McDonald's and sodas.

"What brought that to my attention," said Israel Lugo, who lives three doors away, "is that my daughter at the time was taking the school bus, and it would pick her up in front of the house."

On several occasions, Castro parked the bus outside Lugo's house after his morning shift, so his young daughter's bus had to stop in the middle of the street, blocking traffic.

"I would get upset," said Lugo, "so I started watching his movements. And sure enough, every morning he had a bag of McDonald's and he'd park his bus there and leave it for at least forty-five minutes to an hour. He went in the house and came back out. Clockwork. He did this every day for a long time."

Over the next few years, Castro's yellow school bus became a well-known sight on Seymour Avenue.

"He used to park the school bus here all the time," said Jovita Marti, who lived opposite. "He'd go in [to his house] and stay maybe half an hour, forty-five minutes, and then go. Every day. Sometimes twice a day. We saw him plenty of times with a big bag of McDonald's. I thought, he's a single man and probably eats from McDonald's all the time."

Then in the evening, Castro would come home and be very visible.

"He'll jump on his motorcycle," said Lugo, "and take off for a little bit. Then he'll come back and switch his clothes and jump in his car and take off. It was Ariel doing Ariel."

Castro also drove his school bus over to Tito DeJesus's house, picking up musical equipment for gigs.

"I'd walk out the door and [say], 'Dude, you're bringing a bus over here in front of my house?' He'd say, 'Do you want to go for a ride?' I'm like, 'No, Ariel, I bussed when I was a kid. I don't want to go on a school bus again.'"

On hot summer nights, Castro would often hang out at his neighbors' barbecues, strumming Latin songs on his guitar.

Neighbor Juan Perez had known Ariel Castro since he was six years old and liked him.

"He was a nice guy," said Perez. "He gave the kids rides up and down the street on his four-wheeler."

But some found it strange how Castro never entered his house through his front door, and had all his windows boarded up.

"His windows were always closed," said Altagracia Tejeda, who lived opposite. "I never, ever saw a window open or the curtains drawn."

Every night he would turn on his porch light, although he never sat outside. And no one was ever allowed in the house, except his brothers Pedro and Onil and the few musicians that came over to practice.

"You can't even put a foot on the step," said Lugo, "he didn't like that. He was very protective."

Castro kept his growing collection of cars, motorcycles and his red pickup truck in his garage, where he would often work on them.

A few times a week, Castro went over to his mother's house for a family dinner. After eating he would suddenly leave without a word, before returning later as if nothing had happened.

"He would disappear for an hour or so and then come back," said his eldest daughter, Angie. "And there would be no explanation where he went."

According to Michelle Knight, Pedro and Onil Castro regularly visited the house, while she, Amanda and Gina were chained up.

"The brothers never knew about us," she said, "and they were too drunk to know. They'd have a six-pack before they came over to the house, and they wouldn't recognize the noise because the radio was on."

On weekends, neighbors would often see him carrying his double bass out of the house, to take it to shows.

"He was a sharp dresser," recalled Daniel Marti. "On Friday and Saturday nights he would dress up and go out and do his little gigs. He was a clean, very representable guy. He was popular because he played an instrument."

Ariel Castro often played Belinda's Nightclub, where he always came alone and was usually late.

"He would bring his instrument in and his amp," said club owner Bill Perez. "Shake my hand and then have a beer and whatever."

Tito DeJesus says Castro always dressed up for a gig, and fancied himself a ladies' man.

"He would be suited up," said Tito, "playing the bass and smiling. He would always wear these hats, because his hair had started thinning and he was very self-conscious. One day he shaved his head. He got a razor all the way down."

After a couple of beers, Castro always wanted to dance.

"He would go pick out a stranger and say, 'Want to dance?'" recalled DeJesus. "And many times they would say no."

But the arrogant bassist always refused to take no for an answer, and pestered the women to dance with him.

"He would come back very mad," said DeJesus, "because they didn't want to dance with him. I would say to him, 'You shouldn't do that, you're going to embarrass yourself.'

"But he'd say, 'Yeah, but still look who I am. I'm a bass player. I'm onstage.' I told him, 'Who cares. You can be

Liberace. You can be the president; if they don't want to dance with you, you can't force them to dance with you.'"

Daniel Marti also saw him harassing women on the dance floor.

"If he liked a girl he'd be bothering and bothering her," he said. "And the girl would say, 'No. No.' But he would keep insisting and trying to go out with her. And women just blew him away. Women just didn't like being around him."

Then after the audience left at around 3:00 A.M., Castro would buy large amounts of fried *pastelillos,* shish kebabs or fried pork left over at the concession stand, to take home.

"So at the end of the gig on Saturdays," said Perez, "Ariel would buy twenty-five to thirty dollars' worth of food. We all knew he was single and has no one to take care of, so we all wondered why is he buying so much food?"

That fall, Lillian Roldan's mother died and she asked Ariel Castro to lend her the fare to Puerto Rico for the funeral.

"I called him," Lillian recalled. "I said I needed a favor as I want to see my mother. And he lent me a thousand dollars to go to Puerto Rico."

When she returned she repaid him, as he told her he did not want to see her anymore.

In mid-September, Ariel Castro, Jr., moved to Fort Wayne, Indiana, after graduating with a degree in journalism from Bowling Green State University. He had spent a year living in Rochester, New York, where he had interned on the *Democrat and Chronicle* newspaper. He had recently gotten married, and had been hired as a reporter on the Fort Wayne *Journal Gazette.*

On the way there, he brought his new wife, Monica, to

2207 Seymour Avenue to meet his father. Monica had heard horrendous stories about Ariel Castro, and how he had abused the family growing up.

"They were like hostages in their own house," she said. "[My father-in-law] always gave me the heebie-jeebies. I don't think we were there more than twenty minutes."

While she was there, Monica did not see anything suspicious.

"I had always heard how he locked everything, like, obsessively," she said. "So if I'd seen a lock, I'm not sure I would have thought it was out of the ordinary."

While they were in Cleveland, Nilda Figueroa told her son about his sisters' allegations of sexual molestation by Fernando Colon.

"She didn't believe them," Ariel, Jr., would later explain, "as she talked to my sisters and talked to Fernando. But she . . . didn't want to be in the middle at the same time."

On November 1, 2004, a grand jury indicted Fernando Colon on twenty-eight charges of rape, kidnapping, and molestation. Detective King's case to the grand jury was based solely on Emily and Arlene's statement, although they could not give specific dates when the alleged molestations had occurred.

14

"SHE'S NOT ALIVE, HONEY"

On Wednesday, November 17, 2004, Louwana Miller appeared on *The Montel Williams Show,* asking TV psychic Sylvia Browne what had happened to Amanda. A year earlier, Louwana had first seen Browne on the show, and was convinced she could help find her daughter. So she'd enlisted the help of WOIO-TV reporter Bill Safos, who had arranged for her to appear on the nationally syndicated show.

"Louwana was so excited," recalled Safos. "It had been nearly a year of asking me and here we were, the moment she's waiting for."

At the start of the show, Montel Williams ran a brief videotape about Amanda Berry's disappearance before introducing Louwana, to the applause of a studio audience.

"It's been a year and a half since I've heard anything from my daughter," Louwana told Williams. "I need to speak with Sylvia to see if she can help me find out where my daughter is."

After asking several questions about her daughter, the

TV psychic said she saw Amanda's black hooded jacket in a Dumpster with DNA on it. Louwana then told her that it was believed that Amanda had got into a white car with three people inside.

"There was only one person," said Browne. "Now the thing that gets me is this sort of Cuban-looking [man], short, kind of stocky build, heavyset."

"Can you tell me if they'll ever find her?" asked Louwana, close to tears. "Is she out there?"

"She's . . . ," began the psychic. "See, I hate this when they're in water. I just hate this. She's not alive, honey. And I'll tell you why. Your daughter is not the type that wouldn't have checked in with you if she was alive."

"Right. Right," Louwana agreed.

"But I'm sorry they didn't find the jacket . . . because that had DNA on it."

"Is there any way . . . this case will be solved?" asked Louwana.

"I think it will," said Browne, "especially if they look for this person."

"So do you ever think I'll get to see her again?" Louwana sobbed.

"Yeah, in heaven. On the other side," replied Browne.

"Let me take a little break," said Montel Williams. "We'll be right back."

After Sylvia Browne's grim prediction, Louwana finally lost hope that Amanda would ever be found alive. She went home and cleaned out her daughter's bedroom, took down her pictures and gave away her computer. She told friends she was now "98 percent" sure that Amanda was dead, and was not buying "my baby" any more Christmas presents.

On December 15, Nilda Figueroa swore out an affidavit, accusing Ariel Castro of manipulating their two daughters to frame Fernando Colon on rape and kidnapping charges.

In the nineteen-point sworn affidavit, Nilda outlined the terrible injuries and abuse she'd suffered at his hands.

"Ariel Castro and I were never married," read her affidavit. "During our relationship he was very abusive. He was arrested and convicted of domestic violence in Cleveland."

She also outlined how in June, Castro had suddenly started taking an interest in Emily and Arlene, after ignoring them for years.

"He would pick [Arlene] up from school or from my home," she wrote. "Mr. Castro has also purchased Arlene a lot of clothing, compact discs, a Walkman and a cell phone with North Coast PCS service. Some of the clothing is inappropriate for her age, and I will not let her wear it. Emily recently told me that her father was going to give her the new SUV that he had just bought."

Nilda said the first she knew of her daughters' allegations came after their being summoned to the First District police station to sign a release form so they could talk to detectives. Then Castro had confronted her outside, offering to buy her a new car if she supported her daughters' allegations. She had refused.

"I have never seen any inappropriate conduct between Fernando Colon and any of my children," she wrote. "If anything inappropriate had occurred, my daughters would have been quick to tell me."

Soon after her stepfather's arrest, Emily Castro was expelled from Wilbur Wright High School, and found a job as a cashier at Dave's Supermarket. She was now back living with her aunt Sonia, in the same house as her stepfather Fernando Colon. And for the next three months they would live together under the same roof, as he awaited trial.

Saturday, April 2, 2005, marked the first anniversary of Gina DeJesus's disappearance. That morning the Cleveland *Plain Dealer* ran a front-page story with the headline

FAMILY WAITS, HOPE FOR GIRL'S RETURN HOME—ONE
YEAR AFTER DISAPPEARANCE, NO TRACE OF GINA DEJESUS
FOUND.

"When Nancy Ruiz woke this morning," began the
story, "her daughter's bed was empty. The Cleveland
mother doesn't know where to find the teenager who fears
the dark. She doesn't know when the finicky eater who dis-
likes ketchup, mayonnaise and mustard last ate. She
doesn't know whether her daughter is alive or . . . the al-
ternative, which makes the mother's eyes tear."

The story said that in the year since Gina went missing,
Cleveland police and the FBI had interviewed hundreds of
people and searched the city, coming up with nothing.

"The best hope they give me," said Nancy, "is that they
haven't been here to tell me they found a body."

That night, the DeJesus family held a first-anniversary
vigil on West 105th Street and Lorain Avenue, where Gina
had last been seen.

A week later, the FBI released a sketch of "a person of
interest" wanted for questioning in connection with Gina's
disappearance. The green-eyed Latino man with a goatee
had been seen near Wilbur Wright Middle School shortly
before Gina went missing. He was described as being
between twenty-five to thirty-five years old, weighing between 165 to 185 pounds, and about five feet ten inches tall.

The sketch looks uncannily like Ariel Castro.

On April 21, the second anniversary of Amanda Berry's vanishing, Louwana Miller led a vigil march from the
Burger King at West 110th Street and Lorain to her home
on West 111th Street. When the marchers reached her
home, Louwana led them in singing "Happy Birthday" to
her daughter, who would turn nineteen a few hours later.

Since losing hope of ever finding Amanda after TV psychic Sylvia Browne's reading, Louwana had changed her
mind and now believed she was alive.

"Please make a phone call," Louwana told her missing daughter in a TV interview. "Don't be scared. If you have to disguise your voice, do that. Give an idea where [you're] at."

That night Amanda Berry was watching coverage of the vigil on her TV with Ariel Castro. To celebrate the second anniversary of her abduction, Castro served her and his two other prisoners birthday cake. It would begin a ghoulish ritual of his serving a celebratory dinner and a cake on the anniversary of each abduction.

Over the next few months, Ariel Castro started giving his captives a little more freedom in strictly controlled doses. He no longer kept them chained up all the time, and they were free to roam around their darkened rooms. But they could not see daylight, as he had boarded up the reinforced Plexiglas windows with wooden strips.

There was only one bathroom downstairs in the house, and Castro never allowed his prisoners to use it. Instead they had to make do with plastic toilets in their rooms, which he rarely emptied. Michelle and Gina, who shared the pink bedroom, were seldom allowed to take showers, and conditions were so filthy they suffered from painful bed sores.

Castro also employed "psychological restraints" by repeatedly raping and beating the girls in front of each other, and employing cruel mind games as well. He would tell them he was going out, and then wait outside their doors. Then, if one of them tried to open her door, he would beat her and chain her to the pole in the basement again.

"He used to play tremendous dumb games," said Michelle Knight. "He'll leave the door unlocked and he'll sit there and say, 'Well, if you try [anything] I'll hang you upside down,' or he'll threaten [to hurt] somebody else in the house."

Withholding food and drink and taking away their portable toilets were also used as punishments. Other penalties included putting them in the freezing basement during the bitter winters, or in the boiling attic in the summer.

Castro had also installed a series of mirrors inside and outside the house, so he could monitor everything. And he drilled little peepholes in the bedroom doors, so he could spy on his prisoners.

"He can see directly into your rooms," said Michelle, "to see what you're doing."

He carried his Luger revolver around at all times, warning that he wouldn't hesitate to shoot them if they ever tried to escape. And he also played Russian roulette with his terrified captives, as a demented game of trust. He would hand his revolver to one of the women, ordering her to put it to his head.

"Pull the trigger," he'd say. "If it's God's will that I die, I die. I'll say my prayers."

The girls never knew his gun was always empty, and it was his way of finding out whom he could trust.

Castro kept the victims in a state of powerlessness, making them believe that their physical survival depended on him.

Several times he told them that they were not the first girls he had taken, with some making it home and others not. These continual threats and humiliation terrified the women into complete subservience.

But perhaps the cruelest weapon of all was allowing them to watch the rest of the world go by on their televisions, as they were held in captivity.

"I felt like everything was frozen," said Michelle. "Nothing was moving at all. The only thing that was moving was the outside world and we were at a standstill."

15
FRAME-UP

In early June, as Fernando Colon's trial loomed, Emily and Arlene Castro had second thoughts about testifying. Nilda Figueroa would later claim that Arlene had broken down one night, admitting that she had made it all up.

"Arlene told me . . . that this didn't happen," said her mother. "That Mr. Colon never put his finger inside of her. I confronted her sister Emily about it the next day. Emily got loud with Arlene and told her, 'Don't say that! Don't say that!'"

Then Emily had stormed out of the house, calling Ariel Castro on her cell phone.

"Emily spoke to her father first," said Nilda "and then gave the phone to Arlene. And [he] started talking to Arlene and she went really quiet."

The next day, Nilda brought Arlene to Cuyahoga County Prosecutor John Kosko's office to repeat her story that her stepfather had never molested her.

"I told Arlene to tell them the truth," said Nilda. "She kept her head down and wouldn't look at me."

Once inside the prosecutor's office, Arlene insisted she had been telling the truth and had been molested by Fernando Colon.

"She didn't change the story," said her mother. "She was scared to look at me."

In early July, Emily Castro, now seventeen, discovered she was pregnant. The father was a young man named DeAngelo Gonzalez, who had recently moved in with her. Terrified of what Ariel Castro might do if he found out, Emily and Gonzalez relocated to Fort Wayne, Indiana, moving in with her elder sister, Angie, who was now married with children.

"[I wanted] to get away from everything," Emily later explained. "Just get away from Cleveland to start over."

On July 25, private investigator Chris Giannini, who was gathering evidence on Fernando Colon's behalf, interviewed Ariel Castro in his van outside Castro's uncle Cesi's bodega, after serving him with a subpoena.

"He would not meet me at his house," said Giannini. "We met down the street at his uncle's store, but we couldn't talk there so we sat in my van."

During the interview, Castro was "very polite," and the seasoned private investigator felt he was being manipulated. Castro denied ever assaulting Nilda, saying he did not know why she had called the police and had him arrested. And he accused her of striking him, saying he had been defending himself.

"He recalls that she did have to go to hospital one time for a laceration," wrote Giannini in his notes. "He does not remember how she got the laceration. He thought she hit herself or hit a door jamb."

Castro described himself as "a family man," who had a good job and had always taken responsibility for his four children. He denied any "hard feelings" toward Fernando

Colon, although he admitted being "hurt" when Nilda and the kids had moved in with him.

He told Giannini that he had first discovered Colon had been sexually molesting Arlene, when she had mentioned he was "touching her behind." When he questioned her about it, Arlene said she did not want him "getting mad."

"According to Ariel," wrote Giannini in his notes, "Arlene told him that Fernando penetrated her vagina with his finger."

Castro said he had then asked Emily about her sister's allegations.

"Emily said that there was never any penetration," wrote Giannini, "but he touched and spanked her behind."

Castro said he had had "discipline problems" with both his daughters for years, and Emily did drugs and smoked marijuana. He denied ever threatening to ruin Fernando Colon's life.

On Monday, August 29, 2005, the day before Fernando Colon's trial, Nilda Figueroa swore out a restraining order against Ariel Castro. She claimed that he threatened to kill her and her two daughters if Emily didn't return from Fort Wayne to testify against Fernando Colon.

The previous Friday, Nilda had filed a police report, accusing Castro of threatening their lives. That afternoon, a tearful Emily Castro had called her, complaining that her father wanted her back in Cleveland immediately, to testify at Fernando Colon's trial. Emily did not want to go, but he was insisting on driving to Fort Wayne to collect her.

"[Emily] was upset," said Nilda, "she said her dad wants her to come over here, but [she] didn't want to. She thinks she's pregnant and she doesn't want anybody to know. And plus the stress. I just didn't want Mr. Castro to pick her up, because I know what he's doing to them."

Nilda then phoned Castro, asking why he was pressuring

their youngest daughter so hard about coming back to testify.

"I asked him why he is making her cry," said Nilda, "and why he is making her come back. He told me, 'Look, bitch! If [you] don't make her show up, I'm gonna beat the shit out of you . . . in front of her to see how you like it.' That's his words."

Then Nilda called her son, Ariel, Jr., concerned about how Emily would get to Cleveland.

"My mom called me distraught," he said. "She said because she has custody, if anyone's picking [them] up it would be her."

Late Friday night, Nilda called Ariel Castro, telling him not to go to Fort Wayne to collect Emily.

"[I said] I would make the arrangements," she said, "and he started cussing me out."

Later it would emerge that over the last week before the trial, Ariel Castro had been in close touch with Cuyahoga County Prosecutor John Kosko, who had "begged" him to go to Fort Wayne to pick up his daughter, so the molestation case would not fall apart.

Early Sunday morning, before it got light, Ariel Castro rounded up his three hostages and brought them downstairs. He gave them brown wigs and sunglasses to put on, before leading them out of the back door in chains. Then he walked them across the backyard and into his garage.

"I'm moving you into my van," he told them, " 'cause my family is coming over here soon." Then he forced them into his large maroon Chevy van, which he had previously equipped with chains and padlocks.

"It smelled really bad in there," said Michelle Knight. "He locked Gina and me together on the seats, and he chained Amanda by herself in back."

He left just enough slack on the chains so his prisoners

could use a portable pot as a toilet, but not enough so they could look out of the windows.

"If I hear a sound," he told them, "I will come out here and kill all three of you."

Then Ariel Castro got into his sports car and drove 227 miles west along I-90 to Fort Wayne, Indiana, to bring Emily back to Cleveland.

On arrival, he drove straight to his daughter Angie Gregg's house and collected Emily, taking her to a dress shop in Glenburg Square mall and giving her $60 to buy clothes.

"I asked her, 'Do you need clothes for court tomorrow?'" said Castro. "She says yes. So I took her there."

While Emily was trying on clothes, Castro met up with Ariel, Jr., and Angie. Later that night they all had dinner, before he drove Emily back to Cleveland, where she and Arlene spent the night at 2207 Seymour Avenue, without telling their mother.

The next morning, Nilda Figueroa appeared before Cuyahoga County Domestic Relations Judge Timothy Flanagan, to apply for a restraining order. She accused Ariel Castro of repeatedly threatening her and their daughters' lives. Castro, who had taken the week off from work for the Fernando Colon trial, was in court with his counsel, Jose Torres-Ramirez.

Nilda told the judge that Castro had repeatedly beaten her over the years, twice breaking her nose, her ribs and dislocating each of her shoulders. His violent attacks had caused an inoperable blood clot on her brain, she claimed. Although she had full custody of their children, Castro frequently abducted his two daughters and kept them from her.

Judge Flanagan granted a temporary protection order, forbidding Ariel Castro from contacting Nilda or his children, and requiring him to stay five hundred feet away from them. Castro was also ordered to appear at a Domestic Relations hearing in September.

Straight after the hearing, Ariel Castro walked across the street to the Cuyahoga Court of Common Pleas for the start of Fernando Colon's trial. But the trial was delayed after Arlene Castro failed to show up. Her father spent the rest of the day looking for her, finally tracking her down at a friend's house.

That night Emily and Arlene Castro spent their second night under their father's roof, as his three prisoners lay chained up in a van a few feet away.

16
WITNESS FOR THE PROSECUTION: ARIEL CASTRO

On Tuesday, August 30, Fernando Colon went on trial, accused of twenty-eight criminal charges of rape, kidnapping, and sexual molestation. Colon, now forty, had pleaded not guilty, and the trial would be in front of Judge John J. Russo, without a jury.

That afternoon, a visibly nervous Emily Castro took the stand to testify. Under direct examination from Cuyahoga County Prosecutor John Kosko, Emily said she had first met Fernando Colon ten years ago at the age of seven, when her mother became his girlfriend. After briefly living with him at her grandmother's house, Colon had bought a house, moving her mother and three siblings there.

Under oath, Emily testified that her stepfather had first molested her when she was eight or nine years old.

"I was laying on the sofa," she told Judge Russo, "and I woke up to him feeling on me . . . touching my breasts. He had his hand in my shirt just feeling my breast area."

Then Kosko asked her to describe the next time the defendant had behaved inappropriately. Emily said she was in her room sleeping in bunk beds with her two sisters, Angie and Arlene.

"And he was in our room," she said, "and I woke up and he was touching my older sister. And when he turned around to look at me I just closed my eyes. He noticed that I was awake and just walked out of the room."

When the prosecutor asked her to describe the next incident of molestation, Emily looked lost.

"I don't . . . my mind is going blank," she replied.

"Your Honor," said Colon's defense attorney, Robert Ferreri, "I notice that the witness is unable to answer the question."

"So we'll let her gather her thoughts," said Judge Russo.

"Was there ever another incident that happened . . . where you were touched by the defendant?" asked Kosko.

"I know there was," said Emily, "but I can't remember anything."

Growing impatient, the prosecutor asked her to describe what had happened.

"No," Emily replied.

"Why can't you describe it?"

"I don't know."

Then Kosko had her read the two-page statement she had given to Detective Arthur King a year earlier, before asking her again about the third incident.

"It was the day before my last day of school in sixth grade," she told the court, "and I was sleeping on the sofa. And I woke up to him French kissing me."

"French kiss is what?" asked the prosecutor. "What does that mean?"

"I was laying down and he had put his tongue in my mouth," she said. "I can taste the Black & Mild?"

"The what?" asked the prosecutor.

"He smoked Black & Milds at the time."

"All right. Go ahead. What happens next?"

"I woke up and looked at him, and he just walked away."

Then Kosko asked about other occasions he had molested her, but Emily could not remember any specific details.

"I know there were other ones," she said, "but I can't . . . tell you when it was. Would wake up to it [and] just turn over so I wouldn't have to deal with it."

Then the prosecutor asked her exactly what would be happening when she woke up.

"He would have his hands in my pants," she testified. "You just come to your senses, like wake up, and he would just like, you know, remove his hand and just walk away."

"Okay," said Kosko, "hand in your pants where?"

"My vagina."

"How many times do you remember that happening, approximately?"

"Remembering it, like, about three times."

"On your vagina?"

"Yes."

"Was that skin touching skin?"

"No, I had panties on."

"And what age are you this time?"

"Probably from eight to nine to about ten."

Emily testified that after the French-kissing incident she had told her mother, who had then confronted Colon. According to Emily, her stepfather explained it was dark and he thought she had been her mother.

Kosko then asked if she had ever told her father about it.

"He always asked us," she replied, "but we always said no."

Emily said that she had finally told her dad about being molested in July 2004, on the way to McDonald's.

"He told me that he wanted to talk to me," said Emily, "so I left with him. He told me, your sister [Arlene] told me something . . . and I just wanted to ask you what do you know about it? I told him I believe her, because he did it to me too."

Then Castro had picked up Arlene and taken them both to the district police station to file a report.

After the prosecution finished its questioning, Judge Russo recessed for the day, turning his attention to the sealed protection order against Ariel Castro, ordering him to have no contact with Nilda or his daughters.

"Judge, this is a very sensitive issue here," said Prosecutor Kosko. "That's why I wanted [Emily and Arlene] to stay with Mr. Castro. I don't know if it's going to do any good, [but] I'd like you to tell Mrs. Figueroa that she needs to bring both girls back 9:00 tomorrow morning."

Then Judge Russo brought Nilda into the courtroom, telling her to make sure her two daughters were in court early the next morning.

"[Emily] is not done testifying," he told her, "and in fact your second daughter will begin to testify tomorrow."

On Wednesday morning, Emily Castro was cross-examined by defense attorney Robert Ferreri. He asked if she had ever told her mother that she did not want to testify.

"No," replied Emily.

Then Ferreri asked if her father had promised her money and presents to testify against Fernando Colon.

"No," she replied.

"All right," continued the defender. "If I were to tell you that I've had information that Mr. Castro, your biological father . . . gave you $1,000 to testify, would that be a true or false statement?"

"Objection," said Prosecutor Kosko, but the judge allowed her to answer.

"When his father died," Emily said, "he gave us all $1,000, my brother and sisters."

"Did your father ever promise you an SUV if you would

go along with this story of Fernando sexually molesting you?"

"No," replied Emily, resolutely.

Then, as Ferreri had Emily read out her police statement to the court, she began hyperventilating. The judge called a recess.

After a short break, Emily retook the stand and Ferreri asked if she had ever seen her father striking her mother.

"Yes," she replied.

"How many times were you a witness to an assault between your father on your mother?"

"One time."

"Only once?" asked the defender.

"Yes."

"Do you know if your mother, as a result of this assault, was hospitalized?"

"No."

"Did you ever hear of your mother having sustained broken bones as a result of your father's assaults?"

"No."

"How about teeth knocked out of her mouth?"

"No."

"How about shoulders being dislocated?"

"No."

"How about being kicked in the head?"

"No."

"Did you ever hear of your father hitting your mother with a hand weight in the head?"

"No."

On Wednesday afternoon, Arlene "Rosie" Castro took the stand and was sworn in. Just a week away from her fifteenth birthday, Arlene told the court that Fernando Colon had first molested her at the age of seven, by putting his finger in her vagina.

"I was real scared of him," she told prosecutor John Kosko, under direct examination. " 'Cause he had told me that if I said anything, he'll hurt me."

Arlene testified Colon had touched her again during Thanksgiving 2003, but she had never told anyone about it. Then a year later, she had mentioned it to her father, during a restaurant meal.

"I just told him," she said. "He said, 'What?' and so he got my sister Emily, and we went to go make a police report."

In cross-examination, defense attorney Ferreri asked her about the expensive cell phone he had seen her using in the lobby.

"How did you get the money to pay for this cell phone?" he asked. "Who bought it for you?"

"My father had bought it for me."

Then Ferreri asked Arlene about her depression and being under medication to treat it.

"Do you remember a young lady by the name of Gina DeJesus?" he asked.

"Yes," she replied.

"Okay," said Ferreri. "She was your girlfriend?"

"Yes."

"More than a girlfriend, she was like your best friend?"

"Hold on. Hold on," interrupted the prosecutor. "What was the name?"

"Gina DeJesus," said Judge Russo, before calling a sidebar.

Back on the record, the judge said he would allow the line of questioning to continue, as Arlene and Gina DeJesus had been best friends.

"Arlene," asked Ferreri, "have you ever been diagnosed with post-traumatic stress disorder?"

"No," replied Arlene, "I have never been diagnosed."

"Did you talk to a psychiatrist about you being . . . bummed out?"

"Yes."

"Partially about your friend?"

"Yes."

Arlene then said she had stayed over at 2207 Seymour Avenue on Friday and Saturday nights.

"I stayed over at my father's house," she said.

"Was that his idea, or was that your idea?" asked the defender.

"His idea," she replied.

She then denied her father had bribed her to testify, with money, presents and the promise of a car when she turned eighteen.

"Did your father ever ask you to go along with the story about Fernando, so [he] would not be around any longer?"

"He told me," said Arlene, "like when I go to court, to tell the truth."

Arlene said she couldn't remember her mother ever being beaten by her father, or being hospitalized for injuries.

"And do you remember your mother ever going to court," asked Ferreri, "on more than one occasion about your father's violence?"

"No," she replied.

On Thursday, September 1, Ariel Castro took the stand to testify against Fernando Colon. Dressed in a smart suit and tie, he looked relaxed and confident. After he was sworn in, Prosecutor John Kosko began his questioning.

"Are you employed?" he asked.

"Yes," replied Castro. "I am a school bus driver."

"And how long have you been doing that?"

"This is my sixteenth year."

"Do you have . . . another job?"

"I am a musician," he stated.

"And what instrument do you play?"

"Bass guitar."

Castro said that he had been a member of the Roberto Ocasio Latin Jazz Project, until the bandleader's death a couple of years earlier. Since then, he had played for various bands around town, two or three nights a week.

Kosko then asked his witness about his relationship with Nilda Figueroa, whom he called the "girl next door."

"You went out on a date," said Kosko, "and you ended up taking her home permanently?"

"That's correct," said Castro.

Castro said Nilda had borne him four children, although they had never officially married. Then the prosecutor asked him about a 1982 incident, when they were living in Nilda's mother's house and Ariel, Jr., was just a baby.

"One day I came home and I noticed something suspicious," Castro testified. "My son was downstairs. She was upstairs taking a bath. Something gave me the gut feeling that something's wrong."

Castro said he had then gone upstairs to the attic and found his half brother hiding, immediately suspecting Nilda of being unfaithful to him.

"Well, I asked him, 'What are you doing here?'" said Castro. "And he says, 'I think you know. You caught me.'"

Castro testified he had then ordered his half brother downstairs, demanding that he unzip his pants and show him his penis.

"I just wanted to see if there was some kind of visual evidence there that they were having sex," Castro explained.

"What happened to Nilda?" asked Kosko.

"Well," he continued, "when she came out of the bathroom, I confronted her about it. I asked her what is he doing here? What are you doing? Why is the baby down-stairs?"

Castro said he was so upset after catching her cheating that he left her for a day or two.

"Did you get violent with her?" asked the prosecutor.

"No," said Castro.

"You did not hit her, whack her out, nothing like that?"

"No."

Ariel Castro testified that after that incident, Nilda had become more and more difficult to live with.

"We were always arguing," he told the judge. "She always waited for me to have a beer or two before she would start stuff. She always started fighting. I couldn't understand why."

"Now, did it ever get physical?" asked the prosecutor.

"There were times when she did get physical with me," Castro replied. "She would throw herself on me, striking me. One time, yes, we struggled together and we fell and she . . . hit her head on the doorjamb."

Castro acknowledged that it had resulted in his arrest, but pointed out he had never been convicted of anything.

"She dropped it," he explained.

The prosecutor then asked how he had first become aware of Nilda's relationship with Fernando Colon.

"The defendant used to come to my house to pick her up for hospital visits," said Castro, "because she's always been in and out of hospital [for] chronic headaches. So this is how they met."

He said the first he knew of the relationship was when Nilda announced she and the children were leaving him and moving in with Colon.

"Well, she basically left," he said. "And I said, 'That's fine.'"

According to Castro, it was Fernando Colon who had started menacing him.

"Because he's a security guard and he carried a weapon," Castro explained, "he tried to intimidate me with it. He basically told me to stay away."

Then the prosecutor asked how he had found out his daughters were being molested. Castro said he had been driving Arlene and her friend Tabetha for a meal, when he overheard them talking about Fernando acting inappropriately.

"I questioned [Arlene] right there and then," he told Judge Russo. "After talking to her I tried to remain calm and proceeded to [McDonald's]."

After lunch he dropped Arlene back at her mother's house.

"I gave her a kiss and told her I love her and left," he said. "I just drove home and I was thinking about it [and] the very next day I went to the police department with Arlene and Emily."

"And did you put the girls up to doing this?" asked the prosecutor.

"No," replied Castro firmly.

"Do you want to get back with Nilda?"

"Never."

Then Robert Ferreri stood up to cross-examine Ariel Castro, warning him not to "play games" with the court.

"Last Thursday Nilda called the Cleveland Police Department about you," he began. "Do you know why?"

"She called me on the phone," Castro replied, "and told me that she's gonna go downtown and file a restraining order against my children."

"Okay," said Ferreri, "and against you as well?"

"She did not say that," said Castro.

Then Ferreri showed him the restraining order against him, which had been marked as Exhibit F. Castro said he had not seen it yet, and only knew he had to appear at a Domestic Court hearing in ten days' time.

"Did you have a conversation with Nilda," asked Ferreri, "because your children were unavailable to testify against Fernando?"

"I had a short conversation with her," he said. "She says, 'Listen, I'm going to go downtown and file a restraining order . . . so you don't get near the kids.' I hung up the phone because I knew she wanted to argue."

"Okay," Ferreri continued, "did you ever have a conversation within the last week with your daughters, Emily or Arlene, threatening them if they did not come to testify against Fernando?"

"No," replied Castro.

"Did you ever make offers of reward to them about testifying against Fernando?"

"No."

"Did you tell Nilda that you would punish her and get even with her for testifying on Fernando's behalf?"

"The answer is no," replied Castro resolutely.

Ferreri then asked if he had ever threatened to "beat the shit" out of Nilda in front of Emily, so their daughter would see what would happen if she refused to testify.

"I never made that statement," replied Castro angrily.

"Okay," Ferreri continued. "Have you ever beaten Nilda?"

"Never," snapped Castro. "No."

"Have you ever struck Nilda in such a way that she was required to get medical attention?"

"No."

"Did you ever hit Nilda in such a way that you knocked a tooth out of her head?"

"No."

Ariel Castro then denied ever shattering Nilda's ribs, dislocating her shoulders or breaking her nose several times.

"Did you ever hit her in the head with a hand weight,"

asked Ferreri, "when she was eight months pregnant with one of your daughters?"

"No," said Castro.

"Did you ever hit her with a piece of metal that resulted in her having a hemorrhage and a blood clot on her brain?"

"No."

Castro also denied that his beatings had ever led to Nilda being hospitalized, saying he was not responsible for her brain tumor.

"Have you ever threatened to kill Nilda and the children?" asked Ferreri.

"No."

"You've never done anything to Nilda, or to the children, to make them afraid of you?"

"No," he replied. "I'm a good father to my children. I love my children."

Then Ferreri questioned Castro about Emily's recent drug overdose.

"Did you ever give your daughter Emily money so she could buy marijuana?" asked the defender.

"No," replied Castro.

"Did you ever tell Emily what to tell the doctors when they were treating her for her drug overdose?"

"No."

"Is it your testimony that you don't know exactly what type of drug she ingested?"

"I don't have the information to that."

In redirect, Prosecutor Kosko asked Ariel Castro about driving to Fort Wayne the previous weekend to collect Emily.

"And would it be fair to say," said the Cuyahoga County prosecutor, "that you and I were on the phone last Saturday and Sunday quite a bit, right?"

"That's correct," replied Castro.

"In fact," continued Kosko, "at the risk of embarrassing myself, I begged you to go to Fort Wayne, right?"

"Yes," replied Castro.

"You didn't want to go, right?"

"If I had to send her a [Greyhound] ticket I would have done that, but I wanted to pick her up personally."

"Now when we got here to court Monday, Arlene was missing, right?" asked Kosko.

"That's correct."

"You found Arlene Monday night?"

"Yes."

"And those girls spent the night with you on Monday night, right?"

"Yes," said Castro. "Well, Emily spent the night Monday, and then Tuesday, Arlene did."

"Anyway, the night you got Arlene," continued the prosecutor, "you were calling my house again, right?"

"Yes."

"About what?"

"Oh, about the mother making threatening phone calls to me about the restraining order."

Then Ferreri objected when the prosecutor asked what Nilda had told him in the phone calls. The judge then asked him to rephrase the question.

"All right," said Kosko. "In any event, at some time this week you had both girls at your house?"

"That's correct," replied Castro.

"And [if] you had not gone to get Emily, and if you had not found Arlene, neither one would have been in court this week, would they?"

"That is correct. Yes."

Then the prosecution rested its case.

That afternoon, the defense called Ariel Anthony Castro, Jr., as its first witness. The bearded twenty-three-year-old, who now closely resembled his father, told the court that he worked as an editor for the *Journal Gazette* in Fort Wayne, Indiana.

"Have you ever been around your father," asked defender Robert Ferreri, "when he made any disparaging remarks about Fernando Colon?"

"Yes," replied Castro, as prosecutor John Kosko objected and Judge Russo called a sidebar.

When they went back on the record, Judge Russo allowed Ferreri to continue.

"Did you ever hear your father make any statement relative to wishing . . . revenge against Fernando Colon?"

"Yes," he replied.

"Tell the judge what those statements were, and the circumstances in which they arose."

"Well, my parents broke up in the freshman year of high school for me," said Castro. "And soon after that my mother got together with Fernando. For the first year or so, there were a couple of times [my father] told me, 'Yeah, he's gonna get his.' He constantly tries to undermine him."

Then Castro told the judge how his father had once collected him from school when he was thirteen and driven past his stepfather's house, telling him his mother was "ho-ing" in there.

Then Ferreri asked if he believed his two sisters were being sexually molested by their stepfather.

"No," he replied.

Ariel, Jr., said he had witnessed several verbal arguments between his father and stepfather, although he had never seen them get violent.

"Have you ever seen [your father] be physically violent with your mother?" asked Ferreri.

"Yes," Ariel, Jr., replied. "Well, he used to beat her."

"And you saw those things?"

"Yes."

"And do you know the extent of the injuries sustained by your mother?"

"I know my mother was hospitalized more than once," he replied. "I mean, some of the incidents were, you know, too young for me to remember now, but yeah."

"It's difficult to talk about?" asked Ferreri.

"Yes."

Then, as the prosecution had no questions for Ariel Castro, Jr., he stepped down.

The final witness for the defense was Nilda Figueroa, who told the court how she had left 2207 Seymour Avenue because of Ariel Castro's horrendous abuse. She outlined some of the terrible beatings she had suffered over the years. Once, she said, he had beaten her while she was pregnant, when she told him she was too tired to do the dishes.

"So he just punched me in the mouth," Nilda told the judge, "and took my teeth out."

When she was nine months pregnant with Emily, Castro had hit her hard in the stomach with an exercise weight.

Nilda told the court that she had been repeatedly hospitalized after his beatings, suffering two broken noses, broken ribs and dislocated shoulders. Once he had hit her on the head with a metal pipe; forty stiches were required to close up the wound.

"Did you receive a scar from that activity?" asked Ferreri.

"Yes," she replied.

"Is it visible?"

"Yes."

"Show the judge."

Then Nilda walked over to Judge Russo and showed her the scar on her head.

She also recounted another savage beating.

"He came at me full force with his fist," she said. "He punched me in the eye. There's a lot of nerve damage."

"And you told me," said the defender, "that one of your eyes is round and the other eye is squinty, and both at different levels?"

"Yes," she replied.

Nilda then told Judge Russo that she had undergone brain surgery at the Cleveland Clinic, because of all Ariel Castro's beatings. She had suffered seizures, and doctors had diagnosed meningioma, or a brain tumor.

"Is your brain tumor operable?" asked Ferreri.

"No," replied Nilda.

"Can they fix it?"

"No."

"Do you know the term prognosis?" the defender asked.

"Yes . . . your outcome. How are you."

"Your future?"

"Umm-umm."

"And what is yours?" asked Ferreri.

"I have none," replied Nilda. "I mean, there's nothing they can do for the tumor. They tried. But they couldn't do anything."

"Would it be fair to say that the prognosis is, in medical terms, terminal?"

"Yes," she replied.

Ferreri then asked if Ariel Castro had started buying Emily and Arlene lavish presents in the weeks leading up to their allegations against Fernando Colon. Nilda said that he had bought them each expensive cell phones, iPods, and clothes, and given them cash.

"He's buying them," she said.

Nilda also testified how Castro had threatened to kill her and the children, if she went before a grand jury and testified against him, when he faced charges of criminal domestic violence.

"I was scared," she told Judge Russo. "I said that . . . nothing happened, just so he wouldn't hurt me or the kids anymore."

Then Ferreri asked if she believed Fernando Colon had ever sexually molested her daughters.

"No," she replied.

"Why is that?" asked Ferreri.

"Because I know my daughters. My daughters tend to lie to me a lot."

Finally, the defender asked Nilda about Ariel Castro's unusual behavior when their daughters started having periods.

"When [Angie] started her period," she said, "Mr. Castro, in front of me, [asked her], 'Angie, are you sure you started your period, or did somebody stick their finger up your vagina?'"

"Did [Emily] have a similar situation with her first period?" Ferreri asked.

"Yes, he asked her the same question."

"How about Arlene?"

"Yes, the same situation."

"So, with every female child who experiences her first transition from little girl to woman, Ariel Castro says, 'Did somebody finger you and that's why you're bleeding?'"

"Exactly," replied Nilda.

"And these kids, Angie, Arlene, Emily, they never complained to you about any inappropriate touching from Fernando, did they?"

"Right. Never. They never did."

In his cross-examination, Prosecutor John Kosko asked Nilda why Ariel Castro would want to frame Fernando Colon.

"Mr. Castro is, like, I'm his property," she replied, "and he thinks I'll come back with him. He thinks we're going to be happy together again. That's why he has never re-married. He's sort of waiting for me."

"And you think the girls all went along with this to help him out?" asked Kosko.

"Yes and no," she replied. "The girls are probably mistaken about something that happened. That's what I think."

Then the prosecutor asked if she was trying to help the defendant be found not guilty.

"I'm trying to make sure the truth comes out," she replied. "I mean, it's obvious he's not guilty."

Then the defense rested without calling defendant Fernando Colon to the stand.

In Friday's closing arguments, Cuyahoga County Prosecutor John Kosko, asked what possible motive Emily and Arlene Castro would have to lie on the stand.

"And the motive that's been brought forward by the defense," he told Judge Russo, "is that this is some sort of frame-up that's orchestrated by the girls' father, so that he could get rid of [Fernando Colon]. I don't know if you saw Mr. Castro testify. What reason would he have to do this to this guy?"

The prosecutor said Fernando Colon's defense relied solely on Nilda Figueroa's testimony that her two daughters were lying, because she had not wanted to believe her fiancé had sexually molested them.

"Everything was directed at making Mr. Castro some kind of bad guy here," said Kosko. "How is Mr. Castro a bad guy? He's told this by his daughters. He does exactly what he's supposed to do. He goes to the police station [and] has them make a report."

The prosecutor told the judge it was "nonsense" that Castro had given his daughters expensive presents and money, just so he could move back with their mother.

"That's the part that's not credible," he told Judge Russo.

"And I'm going to ask you to make a finding of guilty in this case."

Then Robert Ferreri stood up to address the judge.

"It's difficult for me to sit here," he began, "and listen to my colleague say that Mr. Castro's being made to be a bad guy. The fact is, Mr. Castro is a bad guy."

The defense attorney then called Ariel Castro's sworn testimony "outrageous."

"How do we know he was lying?" Ferreri asked. "His lips were moving. He said he had no idea why he would be brought into the court process. He never touched Nilda. He never threatened her. He never threatened the girls."

Ferreri said Emily and Arlene Castro had not wanted to testify, and had only done so out of fear for their father.

"This case had a peculiar odor about it from the very beginning," he told the judge.

Ferreri said there was no evidence they had even been molested by their stepfather, questioning why they had suddenly come forward with their story after so many years.

"What we do have in way of evidence," he continued, "is that the dad was obsessed with their sexuality. Obsessed with Fernando. Asked them point blank, even to the point of being so bizarre and so intrusive and so violative of personal self-respect of saying, 'Well, you have your period. Is it your period or did somebody put their finger in there?'

"Can you imagine your own father doing that? I can't imagine mine. I mean, to me that [is] crude, unbelievable behavior on the part of Mr. Castro."

Ferreri then described Ariel Castro's family life at 2207 Seymour Avenue, prior to Nilda and her children moving out, as shocking.

"They're so bizarre," he said. "It was like one of those strange reality shows. I mean, this family and family dynamics [are] pretty bizarre. But the reality is that's their reality. That's their life. That's the way their family traditions and customs operate.

"Do I think a frame-up took place? I think that is a derogatory statement. I think what happened here is that everybody gets something with Fernando out of the way."

He then asked Judge Russo to acquit Fernando Colon on all charges, and let him walk out a free man.

In his rebuttal, Prosecutor Kosko condemned the defense for attacking Ariel Castro's good character.

"This demonization of Mr. Castro has no basis here," he said angrily. "He's obsessed with their sexuality? I didn't see any evidence of that."

Once again, Kosko admitted "begging" Castro to bring Emily back from Fort Wayne, as her mother was making "no effort" to bring her back to Cleveland.

"And what happens when Emily shows up?" he asked the judge. "Suddenly we're running to domestic relations court and getting a restraining order."

On Tuesday, September 6, Judge John Russo convicted Fernando Colon of four counts of gross sexual imposition, relating to Emily and Arlene Castro. He acquitted him of the remaining nine counts. Judge Russo found that Colon was not likely to engage in future acts of sexually violent offenses, deleting the "sexually violent predator" specifications from the guilty counts.

"This court," said Judge Russo, "after careful and deliberate review of all the evidence, finds that the State of Ohio has presented evidence that this court believes rises to the acceptable legal standard of guilty beyond a reasonable doubt."

Two months later, Judge Russo sentenced Colon to three years of supervised community control, ordering him to register as a sex offender.

That same day, Nilda Figueroa told Fernando Colon that she and Arlene were moving to Fort Wayne, Indiana, and their relationship was over.

After hearing the guilty verdict, a triumphant Ariel Castro drove back to 2207 Seymour Avenue to celebrate his victory. That night, under cover of darkness, he unchained his three prisoners from his van and brought them back into the house, disguised in wigs and dark glasses. It would be the last time they would leave the house for almost eight years.

In September, Cleveland Domestic Relations Court officers arrived at 2207 Seymour Avenue to serve Ariel Castro with a summons to attend a court hearing about Nilda Figueroa's protection order against him. After three unsuccessful attempts to get an answer, Castro came to the court and picked up the summons.

The hearing was held in November, with Castro and his attorney both attending. But Nilda's attorney Robert Ferreri did not show up, as he was in juvenile court that day. Nilda then decided not to proceed and the judge dismissed the case, leaving Ariel Castro with a clean record.

17

"SHE DIED OF
A BROKEN HEART"

In late October, Gina DeJesus's parents appeared on a *Maury Povich Show* segment focusing on missing children. After Felix and Nancy made a national plea for any information about their daughter, Povich introduced Long Island psychic Jeffrey Wands, who had studied their case.

Wands said that he believed Gina's kidnapper was a sexual predator, who had spoken to her several times. He told them their daughter was still alive, and her abductor knew the area from where she was taken very well. He described him as a black man with facial hair in his late twenties to early thirties, around five feet nine inches tall.

That Christmas, Louwana Miller was hospitalized for pancreatitis and other serious health issues. Two months later, on March 2, she died of heart failure at a rehabilitation center in Lakewood, Ohio.

Friends said that after TV psychic Sylvia Browne had declared Amanda dead, Louwana lost hope of ever finding her daughter alive.

"She died of a broken heart," said Louwana's sister Theresa Miller. "After all the stress, she would say, 'I can't eat. I don't know if Mandy ate.' My sister was a very strong person, but it took a lot out of her."

Her friend and missing-persons activist Art McKoy said Louwana went downhill after *The Montel Williams Show*.

"[She] was never the same," said McKoy. "I think she had given up."

WOIO-TV news reporter Bill Safos agreed that she died of a broken heart.

"And people ask me, 'How do you know that?'" he said. "Because I was listening to her heart break for three years."

That afternoon, Michelle and Gina learned of her death on the TV evening news. They were shocked when the reporter said Louwana had died of heart failure, as Michelle remembered Castro boasting of calling her on Amanda's cell phone.

A few hours later, Castro unlocked Michelle and Gina's chains, and let them walk around the second floor. Michelle wandered over to Amanda's white bedroom and went in, saying she was so sorry about her mother. Amanda looked puzzled and asked what she was talking about. Then, Michelle realized she did not know and broke the sad news that her mother had passed away. Amanda began to cry.

"I backed out of the door," recalled Michelle, "wanting to give her some peace and quiet. When I was back on my mattress I could hear her sobbing. I felt so terrible for Amanda—and so furious this man had stolen her from her family."

Several weeks later, Ariel Castro became a grandfather for the second time after Emily gave birth to a baby girl she named Janyla. She was now living in a house in Fort Wayne, Indiana, with her boyfriend, DeAngelo Gonzalez, and her mother and sister Arlene. It was a very turbulent relationship and Emily would often accuse Gonzalez of having affairs.

At around the same time, Amanda Berry became pregnant with Ariel Castro's baby. She started suffering morning sickness and throwing up in her room. One morning, when all the women were having breakfast in the kitchen, Amanda complained of feeling nauseated.

That night, Castro told Michelle that he thought Amanda could be pregnant. Michelle replied she probably was and Castro smiled and seemed pleased. Michelle then told him to take better care of Amanda during her pregnancy than he had with her.

But Michelle suspected that, as Ariel Castro considered Amanda to be his wife, he would want to keep her baby.

As Amanda's belly swelled over the next few months, she never acknowledged that she was pregnant to the other girls. Michelle was dying to ask her if she wanted the baby, and if Castro had ever threatened to make her abort it, but she never did.

During her pregnancy, he kept Amanda away from Michelle and Gina, who rarely saw her.

"I could only guess what must have been going through her head," wrote Michelle later. "I kept thinking about my babies—the one I was trying to get back to and the ones this monster had killed."

Ariel Castro now started treating Michelle Knight worse than ever. He fed her only once a day on stale leftovers, and she was allowed just one shower a week. She was his "punching bag," suffering his fists at the least provocation.

"I was the only one he physically hit," Michelle later told *People* magazine. "I was the one being told I was ugly."

At one point, Amanda asked her why he treated her so badly, and Michelle said it was because he disliked her.

"He was the type of person who wanted to break everyone in the house," explained Michelle, "and I was considered unbreakable."

Whenever Michelle stood up to him, Castro would threaten to cut open her uterus end to end, showing her the black rubber chain he would tie through it.

"And he would hang it right in front of the door where I was sleeping," she said. "And he would [say], 'Remember that.'"

Chained together on the bed in the pink room, Michelle and Gina forged a uniquely close relationship.

"Gina and I had that bond like I never had," Michelle said. "It was not normal for me to ever have a friend."

Michelle always tried to rally Gina's spirits and protect her against Castro.

"I would hold her hand," Michelle remembered, "so she could squeeze when she was in pain."

Amanda was always treated far better than his other two prisoners. As his "wife," she enjoyed better food, clothes and blankets. And it set her apart from them in the house.

"She got basically whatever she wanted," said Michelle. "She was the wife-type of person. I was the punching bag."

And the ruthless manipulator used this to distance the women from each other.

"[Amanda] was like one of those girls that really didn't get it," said Michelle. "She would see it but she wouldn't believe it. She wants to think that it wasn't happening. He treated her totally different, so she looked at the situation in a different way."

On July 4, Cleveland police cars converged on Seymour Avenue to break up a street fight, just a block away from Ariel Castro's house. More than twenty people fought with baseball bats, sending a pregnant woman to the hospital.

A few days later, Michelle and Gina were sweltering in

their pink bedroom, writing in their journals, when they heard a little child's voice downstairs. A few minutes later Ariel Castro came into their room, saying he was taking care of his eldest daughter Angie's young son, and wanted to bring him upstairs. He told them to conceal their chains, as he didn't want to scare the baby, threatening to shoot them if they tried anything.

The girls were baffled, as Castro had never brought anyone upstairs to meet them before, secretly praying the little boy would tell his mother about them later. First, Castro brought his grandson into Amanda's room and proudly introduced him. Then he brought him into the pink bedroom to meet Michelle and Gina.

"This is my grandson," he said with a smile on his face, as the girls waved to the little boy.

Suddenly, the toddler burst into tears and screamed for his mommy, and Castro put a hand over his mouth and took him downstairs again.

Several weeks later, according to Michelle, Ariel Castro's two eldest daughters, Angie and Emily, arrived at 2207 Seymour Avenue to search the house. They had brought along Angie's husband and Emily's boyfriend to help them. Michelle believes that they had become suspicious that something bad was going on in the house.

Shortly before his family arrived, Castro unchained all the women and marched them downstairs into the basement. He then chained them to the large pole in the middle, winding duct tape around their heads and stuffing dirty socks in their mouths. He told them that if anyone made a sound while his family were there, he would shoot her.

A few minutes later, Michelle heard voices upstairs, and a woman demanding that he unlock the basement so they could go down there.

"Then one of the younger boys came to the basement

door," recalled Michelle, "saying, 'They're down there. I hear music.'"

Castro told them they couldn't go down, as it was under renovation and it was flooded. The three girls held their breath, afraid to scream for fear of what Castro would do to them.

After his family had left, Castro came back into the basement, took off the duct tape over their mouths and fed them a meal. Then he went back up and left them all together in the basement.

For the next three weeks they remained chained in the basement. Every night he would come down and take one of the girls upstairs for sex, and then bring her down again. While they lay chained in the dark basement, they exchanged stories about how they had been kidnapped, and what Castro had done to them. But Amanda was always vague, just agreeing that she had also suffered the same indignities.

"I figured Amanda was too scared or exhausted to talk," wrote Michelle. "I felt sorry for her."

Finally, Castro brought them back upstairs, putting Amanda by herself in the white bedroom and Michelle and Gina in the pink one.

On Thursday, September 21, Cleveland police arrested two men on suspicion of the aggravated murder of Gina De-Jesus. After an anonymous tip that her body was buried under a concrete garage floor on West Fiftieth Street, detectives arrested thirty-five-year-old registered sexual predator Matthew Hurayt and John McDonough.

At 10:00 A.M., after Gina's parents had been briefed, dozens of police and FBI agents began searching the suspects' four-bedroom colonial house. As helicopters hovering above shot TV news footage, CSI specialists began cutting the recently poured concrete floor in the garage into sections, before a backhoe moved in and dug five feet deep into the foundations, looking for Gina's body. A cadaver dog was led around the garage, sniffing for human remains.

During the search, many family members and friends arrived at the DeJesus house to comfort them, including one of Amanda Berry's aunts and Shakira Johnson's mother. Ariel Castro also came to offer his support.

At a midday news conference, carried live on all Cleveland TV stations, a police spokesman said they had found "a dungeon" in the house, and a police dog had picked up the scent of a dead body.

The search finally ended at 7:30 P.M. when police announced it was a false alarm and the two suspects would be released the next day.

After hearing the news, the DeJesus family supporters burst into cheers and offered a communal prayer for Gina's safe return.

Nancy Ruiz told a TV reporter she was certain Gina was still alive, appealing to whoever took her daughter to release her immediately.

"Just let her go," she sobbed, "so she can come home."

18
MIRACLE AT CHRISTMAS

In early December, as Amanda Berry entered the final stages of her third trimester, Michelle Knight became pregnant for the fourth time. After missing a period, Michelle told Gina that she was pregnant and was terrified about what Ariel Castro would do to her this time, now that Amanda was also expecting.

"Michelle was pregnant most of the time," Gina later told investigators. "She had stuff coming out of her breasts."

When Castro found out, he starved her for three weeks and forced her to drink soda pop.

"I started to throw up and couldn't keep anything down," said Michelle. "I would try and steal food just to eat."

Castro kept her upstairs and stopped her from going into the kitchen, ordering Gina not to feed her.

"She'll do it anyway," said Michelle, "because she didn't want me to hurt."

Michelle vomited continually during this pregnancy,

enduring three weeks of agonizing pain as she starved. Every night, as they lay chained together in bed, Gina would rub Michelle's stomach to reassure her and try to ease the pain.

Finally, losing patience, Ariel Castro punched and kicked Michelle in the stomach, until she aborted their baby.

On Christmas Day, Amanda Berry went into labor and Ariel Castro brought her into the basement to give birth. As her contractions became stronger, Castro ordered Michelle, who was still recovering from losing her own baby, into the basement to deliver Amanda's. In preparation he had bought a black plastic children's swimming pool for Amanda to sit in, so there would be no mess.

Down in the filthy basement, Castro and Michelle were sitting on either side of Amanda as the baby started to emerge. Suddenly, Amanda pushed and the baby's head became stuck. The baby began turning blue from lack of oxygen.

Michelle, who had no medical training, told her to stop pushing, as the baby could not breathe. But Amanda said she couldn't help it.

"And I told her, 'Oh, I see the baby's head,'" said Michelle. "And the baby is blue."

Michelle said they had to get the baby out right now, grabbing Amanda's arms to support her.

"When I say, 'One, two, three,'" Michelle told her, "I want you to push as hard as possible and grab onto my hands."

Finally, as Amanda held Michelle's hands, the baby came out but was not breathing. When Ariel Castro saw this he screamed at Michelle, telling her it was her fault and threatening to kill her if his baby died.

"So I laid the baby flat on her back," said Michelle, "and lifted her head up."

Michelle began breathing into the baby's mouth and doing compressions with two fingers, as Castro kept threatening to kill her. Then the baby started screaming.

It was a baby girl and Ariel Castro named her Jocelyn, keeping the placenta in his refrigerator as a memento.

Soon after Jocelyn was born, Ariel Castro took off Amanda's chains, so her baby would never have to see them. But it would be another two years before he would remove Gina and Michelle's. The tiny baby moved into Amanda's bedroom and she took care of it.

The new baby in the house raised everyone's spirits. Ariel Castro now saw his three hostages and his new daughter as a family, although he didn't hesitate to beat them at any opportunity.

After seeing four of her pregnancies brutally terminated, Michelle was delighted that something positive had finally come out of 2207 Seymour Avenue.

"It was just so amazing to bring a new life into the world," she said, "but it was also traumatic at the same time. I knew that if I didn't get her to breathe, that he would have killed me right then and there."

Three months later, on April 4, 2007, nineteen-year-old Emily Castro repeatedly slashed her eleven-month-old baby's throat with a knife. Emily had recently stopped taking her medicine for manic depression and become delusional. She believed that her boyfriend, DeAngelo Gonzalez, had slept with her two sisters and mother, who all planned to kill her and take her baby.

The previous day, Gonzalez had moved out of their apartment, leaving their baby, Janyla, behind. Emily had called her mother, who came over and hardly recognized her.

"Her eyes didn't seem the same," said Nilda. "She was not there."

At around 6:30 P.M. the next day, Emily picked up her infant daughter and carried her into the garage. She then slashed the baby's throat four times with a sharp knife, before carrying her back into the house, covered in blood and struggling for breath. Nilda grabbed her granddaughter out of Emily's arms and ran into the street, screaming for help.

After they left, Emily tried to commit suicide using the same knife she had tried to kill her baby with. She slashed her wrists and stabbed her neck, before staggering outside to a creek behind her home, where she tried to drown herself.

Meanwhile in the street, Nilda desperately flagged down a young student named Heather Powell, showing her the baby, who was bleeding from deep cuts to the throat.

"The bitch tried to kill the baby," Nilda told Powell, who misunderstood, thinking Janyla had been bitten by a dog. She then called 911, reporting that a baby had been attacked by a dog.

As they were waiting for medics to arrive, a nurse who was passing by tried to stop the baby's bleeding with a towel.

When Fort Wayne police arrived, they found Nilda Figueroa holding her granddaughter, who was covered in blood. A few minutes later, Emily gave herself up to police, drenched in blood, mud and water.

She was then arrested for attempted murder and battery, as she and her daughter were taken to the hospital for emergency treatment.

The next day, Emily Castro was interviewed in the hospital by Fort Wayne Police Detective Taya Strausborger.

Wearing a hospital gown, her wrists heavily bandaged from her suicide attempt, Emily told the detective that she had been hearing voices and believed her boyfriend was cheating with her sisters and mother.

"It really spaced me out," Emily told the detective. "They were going to kill me and take my daughter."

In the ninety-minute videotaped interview, a tearful Emily said that if she was going to be murdered, she wanted to take her baby with her.

Later, Fernando Colon would say that he was not surprised what had happened to Emily, after Ariel Castro had cut him out of their lives.

"Everything went down the drain," he said in 2013. "They started using drugs. They got pregnant. Everything that I tried to prevent happened right after Ariel made those accusations, because they didn't have me there to stop it."

On Saturday, April 22, Amanda Berry celebrated her twenty-first birthday, one day after the fourth anniversary of her abduction. At seven that night, her family organized a "Mandy's Birthday Prayer Vigil," outside the Burger King where she was last seen.

"Let's stand in for Louwana and pray for Mandy's safe return," read the flier, with a photograph of Amanda and her late mother. It also invited supporters to choose a biblical passage and post it on Amanda's newly inaugurated website at www.amandaberry.net.

The official flier for her vigil quoted Isiah 54:17, saying, "No weapons formed against (Amanda Berry) shall prosper!! The word becomes flesh. Wherever she is Jesus is! God is the word!!"

On July 9, fourteen-year-old Ashley Summers went missing. The pretty Cleveland teenager, who bore a striking resemblance to Amanda Berry, disappeared in the same West Side neighborhood as she and Gina DeJesus had.

Detectives investigating the case at the time believed it might be connected to Amanda and Gina's disappearances.

That summer, Ariel Castro was highly visible on the Cleveland Latin music scene. Most weekends he played at clubs all over the city with his various bands.

"He wanted to be in the spotlight," recalled Belinda's Nightclub owner, William Perez. "He wanted to be *the* kid."

Pianist Tito DeJesus, who often played with him, said Castro loved attention.

"Ariel would stand in the middle of the stage playing," said Tito. "I mean, that's a weird spot for a bass player. Often when he was playing he would go into a daze. We'd tell him to pay attention, but he would close his eyes and just drift off. We used to always make fun of him."

Castro was now playing with Grupo Fuego, one of the top Latin bands in Cleveland. He was usually late for practices and gigs, offering such lame excuses that they ended up firing him.

He also played sporadically with Grupo Kanon over a fifteen-year period, at various clubs, churches and cultural events. Bandleader Ivan "Popo" Ruiz later described him as weird and crazy.

"He could do the job," Ruiz told the *Plain Dealer*, "but he became increasingly defensive and unreliable. It was like he couldn't leave the house."

Ruiz, who owns a restaurant and is a pillar of Cleveland's Latin music scene, thought it strange the bassist rarely allowed anyone into his house, to help carry out heavy amplifiers and musical equipment.

"He wouldn't let me pull up the driveway," recalled Ruiz. "Said there were nails or something."

Ruiz also wondered why Castro never stayed overnight in hotel rooms with the other musicians when they played out of town.

"He would say, 'I have to get home,'" recalled Ruiz. "He was the only one who never stayed. It was weird."

After Jocelyn was born, Ariel Castro stopped going into his uncle Cesi's Caribe bodega, as questions might have been raised if he bought diapers and baby food. Having a new baby in the house gave the three hostages hope that one day things would improve. Amanda was a natural mother and nurtured Jocelyn from the beginning, while her father was always careful to treat the girls better when the baby was around.

"It brought a joy into the house," said Michelle Knight, "even though there was sadness. It was like having a beautiful light [and there were] smiles and laughter. It made [us] hope that there would be a brighter day."

On Tuesday, January 15, 2008, Emily Castro went on trial for the attempted murder of her baby daughter. Waiving her right to a jury trial, Castro, who had been found competent, was pleading an insanity defense. She faced twenty to fifty years in prison if convicted.

Since the attack, Janyla had made a complete recovery and was living with her father, DeAngelo Gonzalez.

On the first day of the three-day trial, Allen County Deputy Prosecutor Stacey Speith briefly outlined the state's case to Superior Court Judge John F. Surbeck, who would be deciding the outcome. She told the judge how Emily had tried to kill Janyla after her boyfriend broke up with her.

Then defense attorney Zachary Witte said that Emily had suffered from depression since she was thirteen, but she had become paranoid after her daughter's birth. Witte told the judge that Emily's maternal instincts had succumbed to her depression.

The prosecution then called student Heather Powell, who described dialing 911 after Nilda ran toward her in the street with her bleeding granddaughter. Emily Castro's friend and neighbor Shamona Howard told the judge that she was "a caring and compassionate mother," whom she never thought would harm her baby.

Fort Wayne police officer Christopher Reed then described how Emily Castro had walked up to him, after trying to commit suicide, soaking wet and covered in mud and blood.

On the second day of the trial, prosecutors reviewed Emily's hospital interrogation. Still recovering from her wounds, with a blanket over her hospital gown, she said she heard voices. And she had believed her mother and two sisters were having an affair with Gonzalez, and wanted to kill her baby.

Watching the video from the defense bench, Emily wept throughout it.

Then Nilda Figueroa testified, telling the judge that her daughter was "paranoid."

"She didn't think straight," Nilda said. "She would think things about people that wasn't true."

Nilda said her daughter seemed emotionally distant when she saw her the night before the attack.

"She was so withdrawn," she said. "That was not my daughter that was there."

Then Deputy Prosecutor Patricia Pikel asked Nilda why Emily had tried to kill Janyla.

"There's no way my daughter [would] do that," Nilda replied.

The prosecutor also asked why the Castro family had not had Emily committed to a psychiatric hospital earlier, if she had posed a danger to herself and other people.

Nilda said the family had been worried Emily would hurt herself, taking her to the Parkview Behavioral Health facility a few months before the incident.

On the final day of the trial, Judge Surbeck heard testimony from court-appointed psychologist David Lombard. He testified that Emily was sane, and had deliberately exaggerated symptoms of mental illness when he had examined her. He acknowledged she did suffer from manic-depressive disorder, but that would not affect her knowing the difference between right and wrong.

Several other Castro family members testified on Emily's behalf, supporting her insanity defense.

In his summation, Judge Surbeck said that her family had "exaggerated or ignored what happened in the past to support their family member."

He then convicted Emily Castro of attempting to murder her daughter, saying mental illness did not equal insanity.

"[Emily] exaggerated issues to create an insanity defense where none exists," he said. "She does suffer from significant mental illness, but not such that it keeps her from knowing right from wrong."

Then, as Emily wept at the defense table, the judge added that although it defied human nature that a mother would try to kill her baby, it did not mean she was insane.

"Frequently things don't make sense," he said. "And in no sphere of experience does this make sense."

A month later, at her sentencing, Ariel Castro, Jr., read out a statement to the judge on her behalf.

"What happened to Janyla was serious, unthinkable and irreversible," he said. "What happened to my sister is no less serious."

He said the family had observed Emily's mental illness every day, and it was regrettable that it did not meet the legal definition of insanity. He described Emily as a "proud mother," who had started a scrapbook in preparation for Janyla's first birthday.

"[She is not an] animal who tried to kill her daughter out of revenge," he told the judge.

Then Emily Castro stood up to address Judge Surbeck before he passed sentence.

"I don't know how this happened," she sobbed. "I want you to know I am a very good mom."

The judge then sentenced her to thirty years in prison, suspending the last five years to be served as probation. She was also ordered to seek mental health treatment as part of her probation.

"It's certainly a mystery," said the judge, "as to how this happened or why this happened."

19

A NARROW ESCAPE

At 8:35 P.M. on Thursday, June 12, 2008, Ariel Castro was stopped by Cleveland police for driving his motorcycle without a license or a helmet. Officer Jim Simone was patrolling the West Side when a motorcycle whizzed past him at high speed with its license plate tilted sideways. The seasoned cop knew it was an old trick, used to obscure the plates, and quite illegal. In fact, the plates did belong to another vehicle.

Officer Simone then pulled him over at a nearby gas station. Castro, wearing a sleeveless white T-shirt, looked visibly nervous as Officer Simone approached him—his dash-cam video filming the entire incident.

"Your driver's license, please," demanded the patrolman.

"Excuse me?" replied Castro.

"Let me see your driver's license, please."

"What's wrong?" asked Castro defensively.

"First off," replied Simone, "your plate is improperly displayed. It has to be displayed left to right, not upside down or sideways. You have to be able to read them from behind."

"I just got it out, sir."

"Can I see your motorcycle license?"

"That, I don't have," said Castro.

Then as Castro ran his fingers through his hair nervously, the officer asked why he was not wearing a helmet or carrying a driver's license.

"And you subject yourself to being arrested," Simone told him. "Is that what you want?"

"No, sir. I don't," Castro replied.

"You're getting deeper and deeper," the officer warned. "Just stand by your bike and take out your insurance documents."

"I know," said Castro. "But I just got off work. I'm a school bus driver. I'm going to get all this taken care of."

Then Castro asked Officer Simone to give him a break, explaining he could lose his job if he was arrested.

"Normally I would arrest people for that," explained Officer Simone in 2013, "but he was very polite and explained to me he was a school bus driver."

Officer Simone then ran a background check on his patrol car computer, as Castro waited by a gas pump anxiously combing his hair.

"He only had a few traffic violations," said Simone, "and no criminal background."

Then Officer Simone let him off with just a warning and a couple of tickets.

"You gotta get the plates changed over," he told Castro. "You gotta get all the things that are required by law. This is an arrestible offense. You could be going to jail over something silly, you know."

The officer ordered him to push his motorbike the mile back to his house, following in his patrol car. Then, as Ariel Castro wheeled his motorbike through his front gate of 2207 Seymour Avenue, Officer Simone drove off without giving him another thought.

As Jocelyn grew into a toddler and began to talk, Ariel Castro gave his prisoners aliases. He ordered them never to use their real names again, in case his daughter ever realized who they were with the ongoing TV coverage.

"I'm going to give you different names," he told Michelle one day. "I don't want her to know your real names."

He renamed Michelle, "JuJu," after Jujubes candy, and Gina became Chelsea, but Amanda appears to have been allowed to keep her real name.

Soon afterward he removed their chains, after Jocelyn started pulling on Michelle's, saying, "JuJu lock?" Now, he occasionally allowed them to roam around the house under his strict supervision, satisfied that they were too terrified to try to escape. But just as a reminder, he always had his Luger service revolver on his hip as a warning.

"He didn't do it out of the kindness of his heart," said Michelle. "It was because Jocelyn was getting old enough to understand what was happening around her."

Each evening after work, Castro would bring everybody into the kitchen for dinner. Michelle would hold Jocelyn and gently rock her to stop her crying, while Gina cooked a meal. Castro would chat away to Amanda about his day, as if she were his wife.

Occasionally, they would all gather in the living room to watch his favorite TV show, *Keeping Up with the Kardashians*, while he made obscene comments about Kim Kardashian.

During the interminably long days, while they were locked inside the boarded-up pink bedroom, Michelle and Gina could hear Amanda playing with her new daughter in the adjoining bedroom.

Everybody loved the innocent little toddler and pitied her for being born into slavery. Michelle and Gina spent hours making baby clothes from dirty old T-shirts, using needles and thread that Castro provided. He also brought in old toys for Jocelyn to play with, promising to buy proper clothes for his daughter, but never did.

After years of intense emotional and physical abuse by Ariel Castro, all three women were suffering from Stockholm syndrome. The condition was first identified in 1973, when a gang of bank robbers took employees at the Kreditbanken in Stockholm, Sweden, hostage for six days. During that time they became emotionally attached to their captors, resisting rescue attempts by the police and later refusing to testify against their kidnappers. The term was first coined by Swedish psychiatrist Nils Bejerot, who had advised police during the incident.

A year later, American newspaper heiress Patty Hearst went even further, after being kidnapped by the radical Symbionese Liberation Army. She joined the group, participating in several bank robberies, subsequently serving a two-year jail sentence, later commuted by President Jimmy Carter.

Dr. Frank M. Ochberg, a clinical professor of psychiatry at Michigan State University, who helped define Stockholm syndrome, says Ariel Castro's three victims are classic cases.

"He degraded, demeaned and diminished them," said Dr. Ochberg. "Some acts terrify, others degrade. To be bound, gagged, deprived of a toilet—to be treated in a less than human way—causes not only fear, but profound shame and humiliation."

And when this is done relentlessly over a period of many years, it drastically changes a victim's sense of self.

"We become bonded to the person who aggresses

against us," said Dr. Ochberg. "And that's the Stockholm syndrome."

As the days turned into weeks, and the weeks into months, and the months into years, the three captives did whatever they had to do to survive. Ariel Castro held the power of life and death over them all, robbing them of their basic humanity.

"You're made like an infant," explained Dr. Ochberg. "And when you're treated so you can't eat, you can't sleep, you can't use a toilet, you can't move without explicit permission, you are . . . infantilized.

"But then little by little, you are given what it takes to survive. And in your mind, unconsciously, you deny that this is the person who did all of this to me. And you start to feel the way you did as a little baby with your mother, who is the first source of nourishment—of life itself."

Castro also practiced a barbaric barter system. After raping the women, he would throw money at them, telling them he was paying for their sexual services as if they were prostitutes. Whenever they needed something special from the store, he would then demand payment out of the cash he had given them.

After Jocelyn's birth, they became a bizarre travesty of a family, with him as the father, constantly telling them to respect their elders.

"In his own demented mind," explained Michelle, "he loved all of us because he thought we were all family. That goes back to his fake world where he wanted a family and he didn't have it. He always complained how his family had . . . abandoned him."

Castro now began taking his infant daughter to church every Sunday, telling people that it was a girlfriend's baby. He would also shoot home videos of himself playing with Jocelyn, acting out the part of devoted father.

Meanwhile, the only one in the house that dared to

stand up to Ariel, and refused to play into the happy family charade, was Michelle Knight, who suffered the consequences. He would spit in her face, punch her and try to humiliate her in front of the others, calling her worthless and continually telling her that no one was even looking for her.

"What's wrong with you?" he'd scream at her. "You're supposed to be happy."

In early 2009, Arlene Castro posted a photograph of Gina DeJesus on her MySpace page. Now reinventing herself as hardcore rapper, Cheri Alize, Arlene captioned the photograph, "This is gina Dejesus. she is now 19 years old. she has been missing since April 2, 2004. i pray in my heart that she is okay!! i love u gina."

At around 4:00 P.M. on April 3, Ariel Castro made an illegal U-turn in heavy traffic, outside Robinson G. Jones Elementary School, as he couldn't be bothered to drive around the block. Several teachers watched in horror as he put his busload of students in danger, immediately reporting him to the Cleveland School District. Two weeks later, Castro stood in front of a disciplinary board, on two charges of disregarding his passengers' safety and negligence.

"[It] was not only dangerous to the students and other motorists," his boss Ann Carlson wrote to the disciplinary board, "it was totally unnecessary. I recommend a sixty-day suspension."

Castro persuaded the school's principal, Joshua J. Gunvalsen, to write a letter on his behalf.

"I did not witness what occurred," he wrote, "but I do want to say that I have known Mr. Castro to be an effective bus driver. I have witnessed him trying to work with students, families and myself to handle student issues. If you have any questions about the kind of service that Mr. Castro has provided to my school, please contact me."

Nevertheless, his bosses ordered a sixty-day unpaid suspension. A few months later, Castro's Teamsters Local 407 representative appealed the sentence, and it was reduced by five days.

During his suspension, Ariel Castro drove to Fort Wayne, Indiana, to visit his son and two daughters. Before leaving he had warned them that he could not stay the night, and would drive straight back to Cleveland.

While he was in Fort Wayne his car broke down and he became very upset. Despite his family's pleas to stay over and get it fixed the next day, Castro told them he "needed to get home and feed the dogs."

20
AMINA'S LAW

In late August 2009, Jaycee Lee Dugard suddenly reappeared in Antioch, California, eighteen years after she had gone missing. Now grown up, she told a chilling tale of how Phillip Garrido and his wife, Nancy, had held her captive since 1991, when she was eleven. Jaycee was repeatedly abused and raped by Garrido, who married her in a bizarre wedding ceremony and had two daughters with her. Over the years of imprisonment he brainwashed her into becoming his devoted wife, as Nancy was relegated to the role of housekeeper.

Jaycee's story captured the world's attention and made headlines for weeks. It also gave renewed hope to Amanda and Gina's families that their daughters might also be found one day.

In October, Oprah Winfrey devoted a special show to Cleveland's missing children, concentrating on Amanda Berry, Gina DeJesus and Ashley Summers.

"We're on Cleveland's West Side," FBI Special Agent

Phil Torsey told Oprah's global TV audience. "Three girls have disappeared from the area within blocks of one another."

Also featured in the show were Amanda's sister, Beth Serrano, Gina's mother, Nancy Ruiz, and Ashley's mother, Jennifer Summers.

"Jaycee's story gives me hope," Summers told Oprah, "because it makes me believe that Ashley will come home."

The DeJesus family had also been participating in a new docudrama about Cleveland's missing children called *Where's Gina?—A Look at Missing Children*. Directed by local filmmaker Ruben Reyes, professional actors worked with Gina's parents to re-create how she had gone missing five years earlier.

On Saturday, October 24, the film premiered at the First Spanish Baptist Church, and the WOIO-TV news team interviewed Gina's parents about it.

"The family of Gina DeJesus will never give up the search for their daughter," said a reporter. "This documentary is another way to keep the search for Gina alive and raise awareness about the eight hundred thousand children who go missing each year."

Felix DeJesus said he and Nancy had participated in the movie to raise awareness of the missing children in Cleveland.

"I am the voice for them now," he said. "It doesn't get any easier."

Felix said he had never given up hope that his daughter was still alive and would come home one day.

"I don't have that empty space in my heart saying that she's gone across that line," he said. "She's out there somewhere and I want her if she sees this to know that her father is still searching and fighting."

* * *

A few days later, on October 29, a fifty-year-old Cleveland ex-marine named Anthony Sowell was arrested on suspicion of murdering eleven women. Police had first gone to his Imperial Avenue house on Cleveland's East Side, after a young woman had accused him of rape. When police arrived with an arrest warrant, the convicted rapist was nowhere to be found. But police did find a freshly dug grave, containing two dead bodies.

Over the next few days they would discover more rotting bodies in the living room, in crawl spaces, under a basement staircase, and in the back garden, as well as a woman's skull in a bucket. For months neighbors had complained about the putrid smell on the 12200 block of Imperial Avenue, which many blamed on Ray's Sausage Company next door.

Sowell, a registered sex offender, was finally arrested and the media dubbed him the Cleveland Strangler. He was by far the city's most prolific serial killer, and over the next few weeks cold-case detectives pored over missing-persons files looking for more possible victims, including Amanda Berry and Gina DeJesus.

"When I first heard about the bodies on Imperial Avenue," wrote Cleveland *Plain Dealer* columnist Regina Brett, "I felt sure that Amanda and Gina would be unearthed. But no, this serial killer didn't go for young girls."

Anthony Sowell's subsequent high-profile trial and conviction for murdering the eleven women raised many disturbing questions about the way the Cleveland authorities handled its hundreds of missing-persons cases. Most of Sowell's victims were black and impoverished, either homeless or living alone with severe drug and alcohol problems. And their families questioned how these unfortunate women had been allowed to disappear, without any questions being asked.

In the wake of the Cleveland Strangler, the City of Cleveland appointed a commission to examine how police handled missing-persons cases. And the DeJesus family joined forces with Amanda Berry's family to campaign for what they called "AMINA's Law," to improve the handling of missing-persons cases across America. They wanted missing-persons' parents to be given a written explanation of police responsibilities and their rights, plus an outline of the investigative process.

Nancy Ruiz said that when Gina had gone missing, a simple pamphlet to show her how to help the investigation would have been invaluable.

"It's so sad," explained Nancy, "you have nowhere to go, nowhere to turn to and nobody to speak to, because there's nothing there available to guide you."

On Wednesday April 1, 2010, the day before the sixth anniversary of Gina DeJesus's disappearance, Mayor Frank Jackson, who had been elected in 2006, unveiled a nine-hundred-page report at city hall, detailing more than two dozen problems with how Cleveland's police handed missing-persons cases. It recommended setting up a special unit to deal with them. The mayor vowed to adopt all the commission's recommendations, including Felix DeJesus's suggestion of an information guide.

The next day, the DeJesus family attended an emotional vigil to mark the sixth anniversary of Gina going missing. As Ariel Castro mingled in the large crowd of supporters, Nancy Ruiz addressed reporters about the commission's scathing report.

"They should have done it a long time ago," she said. "But it's a start. A step forward."

That night, WEWS-TV news ran coverage of the vigil, which Castro made sure Gina and the other hostages watched on their televisions.

"I don't know how you've made it through six years," a reporter told Nancy. "Talk to me about that. How does a mother get through even six months, let alone six years, not knowing what happened?"

"At first it was very hard," said Nancy. "I wouldn't even give interviews at the beginning. Now, I'm fighting. I'm coming out. My daughter's out there somewhere. Somebody knows something. I need them to step up to the plate and start speaking. Tell me where my baby's at so I can bring her home."

Felix DeJesus said he still went out searching for Gina every night after work.

"I have that hope that we're going to bring her home," he said, "so I don't have to come back out here another year looking for my daughter."

Three weeks later, Beth Serrano led a small group of supporters in a march past the Burger King on West 110th Street, commemorating the seventh anniversary of her sister Amanda's disappearance.

"I feel somebody did see something," Serrano told WEWS-TV news. "Maybe they're scared but they could be anonymous. Because maybe that one piece they hold could pull it together."

In November, Anita Lugo heard a pounding sound coming from her neighbor Ariel Castro's house. She looked up to see a woman and a baby at a window, half boarded up by a piece of wood. She immediately called Cleveland police.

"That was me," Michelle Knight would later explain. "I was trying to get out."

When police arrived at 2207 Seymour Avenue, an

ABOVE LEFT: The mountain in Duey, Puerto Rico, which was owned by the Castro family. **ABOVE RIGHT:** The shack in Duey where Ariel Castro was born. *(Both photos Courtesy John Glatt)*

ABOVE LEFT: Ariel Castro was one of the top Latin bassists in Cleveland and often played with his best friend Tito DeJesus, who is pictured bottom left. **ABOVE RIGHT:** Ariel Castro and other Latin performers at a show in Cleveland. *(Both photos Courtesy Tito DeJesus)*

ABOVE LEFT: When he started going bald, vain Ariel Castro shaved his head. *(Courtesy Tito DeJesus).* **ABOVE RIGHT:** Most Saturday nights Castro would perform with various salsa bands at Belinda's Club. *(Courtesy John Glatt)*

Castro's house at 2207 Seymour Avenue, where he kept his three prisoners for more than a decade. *(Courtesy Dan Callister)*

RIGHT: Lillian Roldan pictured inside 2207 Seymour Avenue in 2002 with Castro, who she dated for more than three years. *(Courtesy Lillian Roldan)*

ABOVE LEFT: Lillian shows off her matching tattoo that she got with Castro as a show of their love. *(Courtesy Lillian Roldan).* **ABOVE RIGHT:** During their three-year relationship, Lillian often spent the night at 2207 Seymour Avenue, totally unaware that Michelle Knight was imprisoned there. *(Courtesy John Glatt)*

Amanda Berry before she was kidnapped. *(Courtesy The Cuyahoga County District Attorney's Office)*

ABOVE: Castro kidnapped Gina DeJesus after seeing her outside school with his youngest daughter Arlene, who was her best friend. *(Courtesy The Cuyahoga County District Attorney's Office)*

LEFT: Ariel Castro's aunt Monserrate Baez, who knew him as a young boy, still lives in Duey. *(Courtesy John Glatt)*

Just days after abducting Gina, Castro wrote out a confession letter, describing himself as "a sexual predator." *(Courtesy The Cuyahoga County District Attorney's Office)*

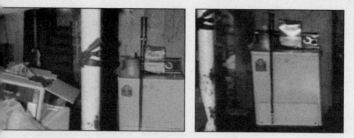

ABOVE LEFT: The pole in the basement where Castro chained up his three terrified victims after he kidnapped them. **ABOVE RIGHT:** The washing machine in the basement which contained thousands of dollars in cash, that Castro threw at his victims after raping them. *(Both photos Courtesy The Cuyahoga County District Attorney's Office)*

The motorcycle helmet which Castro made his victims wear for days at a time to muffle their screams. *(Courtesy The Cuyahoga County District Attorney's Office)*

Investigators found more than 99 feet of rusty chains in 2207 Seymour Avenue, which had been used to restrain the three women. *(Courtesy The Cuyahoga County District Attorney's Office)*

Cleveland Councilman Brian Cummings outside the Burger King where Amanda worked. *(Courtesy John Glatt)*

Fernando Colon incurred Ariel Castro's wrath after Nilda Figueroa took their four children and moved in with him. Later Castro took his two youngest daughters to Cleveland Police, where they accused Colon of sexually molesting them. *(Courtesy John Glatt)*

ABOVE LEFT: Castro's Uncle Cesi's bodega, just a couple of blocks away from 2207 Seymour Avenue. *(Courtesy John Glatt)* **ABOVE RIGHT:** Amanda and Jocelyn's bedroom was full of toys. *(Courtesy The Cuyahoga County District Attorney's Office)*

ABOVE: Amanda taught her daughter Jocelyn in their bedroom and put up her artwork on the wall.
RIGHT: Gina DeJesus's missing poster. *(Both photos Courtesy The Cuyahoga County District Attorney's Office)*

MISSING
Georgina "Gina" DeJesus

Age: 14
Sex: Female
Race: Hispanic
Hair: Brown   Eyes: Brown
Height: 5'1"   Weight: 140 lbs.
Last Seen: Friday, April 2, 2004, 3:00 p.m. –
in the area of West 105th and Lorain Ave.

Any information, please contact law enforcement
at: 1-888-660-5437 (KIDS)

Georgina "Gina" DeJesus Task Force
P.O. Box 94211, Cleveland, OH 44101

ABOVE: Castro regularly used his Luger revolver to terrify his three prisoners, playing games of Russian Roulette with them. **RIGHT:** The only bathroom at 2207 Seymour Avenue which Castro rarely let his prisoners use. *(Both photos Courtesy The Cuyahoga County District Attorney's Office)*

LEFT: Seymour Avenue, Cleveland, where Ariel Castro kept three women imprisoned for a decade without any of his neighbors suspecting a thing. *(Courtesy John Glatt).* **ABOVE:** The filthy mattress which Michelle Knight and Gina DeJesus shared was infested with bed bugs. *(Courtesy The Cuyahoga County District Attorney's Office)*

ABOVE LEFT: The heavy curtain at the top of the stairs which Castro hung up to hide the bedrooms where he held his prisoners. **ABOVE RIGHT:** The stairs leading down to the basement at 2207 Seymour Avenue. *(Both photos Courtesy The Cuyahoga County District Attorney's Office)*

The McDonald's where Ariel Castro was arrested with his brother Onil. *(Courtesy John Glatt)*

Ariel Castro's mug shot after his arrest. *(Courtesy Cleveland Police)*

ABOVE LEFT: Amanda Berry on the day she escaped.   **ABOVE:** The day after her escape, Amanda was interviewed by Cleveland detectives.   **LEFT:** Gina DeJesus just hours after she escaped from 2207 Seymour Avenue. *(All three photos Courtesy The Cuyahoga County District Attorney's Office)*

RIGHT: Police mug shots of the three Castro brothers. Left to right: Onil, Ariel, and Pedro. *(Courtesy Cleveland Police)*

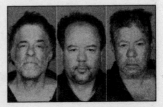

A scale model of 2207 Seymour Avenue, which was displayed in the courtroom at Ariel Castro's sentencing. *(Courtesy The Cuyahoga County District Attorney's Office)*

Michelle Knight bravely confronted her abductor at his sentencing, telling him he would "face hell for eternity." *(Courtesy the court video pool)*

Ariel Castro was sentenced to life without parole plus one thousand years for his horrendous crimes. *(Courtesy The Ohio Department of Corrections)*

The site where 2207 Seymour Avenue once stood after it was razed to the ground. *(Courtesy John Glatt)*

officer knocked on the front door several times before walking round to the side of the house. When no one answered the door, the officers left.

Soon afterward, another neighbor, Juan Perez, was in his basement with his sister, when they heard screaming coming from Ariel Castro's basement and called the police.

"It was the kind of scream that made you uncomfortable," said Perez, who had known Ariel Castro since he was a small boy. "It gave us goose bumps and went on for ten seconds. I had my sister called the police."

Perez, twenty-seven, who lived two doors away, thought the Castro house was vacant, as the windows were boarded up and he rarely saw Castro there.

Once again, Cleveland police came to 2207 Seymour Avenue and knocked on the front door, and then left when no one answered.

21

"DID THEY EVER FIND YOUR COUSIN YET?"

Amanda Berry's daughter, Jocelyn, grew into a pretty four-year-old, who was pampered by everybody in the house. Most afternoons Ariel Castro took her out to play in a local park, telling everyone that it was his girlfriend's baby. He also, reportedly, often took her over to her grandmother's house.

When he visited his cousin Nelson Martinez in nearby Parma, Ohio, he brought along Jocelyn, introducing her as his granddaughter.

"She looked healthy and happy," said Martinez, "and looked as though she liked being with her 'granddaddy.' She had on clean clothes and seemed alert and talked like a normal little girl."

He even took his little daughter to some of his shows, so she could watch him perform.

"He had the nerve to introduce Jocelyn to his band," said Michelle. "That was another stupid move."

During the day, when he was out driving his school bus, Amanda homeschooled her daughter, teaching her how to read and write. She turned their bedroom into a nursery, putting up their paintings on the wall, as she instilled strict values and a religious faith in her daughter.

When Castro came home from work, Michelle would hear him unlock Amanda's door and take Jocelyn downstairs to play. They would spend hours watching cartoons together, with Castro laughing and chuckling.

"My greatest fear," wrote Michelle in her autobiography, "was that after she got older, he would start to mess with her the same way he did with the rest of us."

Little Jocelyn grew up in a dark prison without any sunlight and no medical or dental treatment. One night the little girl woke up from a bad dream screaming. Alarmed his neighbors would hear, Castro ran up the stairs into the white bedroom and ordered Amanda to "shut her up!"

Amanda tried to calm her down by rocking her gently and rubbing her back, but Jocelyn wouldn't stop crying. Then her father put his hand over her face, ordering her to be quiet.

Over the years all three women adapted to their dire situation, learning to keep Ariel Castro happy in order to survive. The seasons changed, with the women sweltering without air-conditioning in the unbearably hot summers, or freezing without any heat in the savage winters.

He strictly enforced his ban of using real names in the house, robbing his hostages of their identity. He also ordered Michelle never to call Jocelyn by her real name.

"I called her Pretty," she said. "That's all I was allowed."

They all tried to get on with each other as best as possible. Michelle and Gina were like sisters, while Amanda devoted herself to Jocelyn and protected her from her father.

"It's mind-boggling what was going on inside that house

between them," said attorney Craig Weintraub, who would later read all the women's personal journals, detailing their innermost thoughts. "They grew accustomed to this life-style, and after a time you lose your identity and who you were when you first got into that house."

April 21, 2011 marked eight years since Amanda Berry had first been tricked into 2207 Seymour Avenue. And yet again Ariel Castro ensured that Amanda, who turned twenty-five the next day, watched the television coverage of the annual vigil in her honor.

"It's eight years ago tonight," said WEWS-TV anchor-woman Danita Harris, "that Amanda Berry disappeared on her way home from work. And tonight people gathered at the spot where she was last seen. Our John Kosich was there and joins us live tonight. John, have there been any new developments in the last year?"

"No, sadly, Danita, there has not been," replied Kosich, standing among a small crowd outside the Burger King, "and that is the tough part for the family that Amanda has left. Each April twenty-first at six P.M., those who knew Amanda Berry gather to remember. It was eight years ago tonight at this time she left work here at this Burger King on West One Hundred and Tenth and Lorain. She was headed to home less than half a mile away. She was on the phone with her sister, Beth, at the time when she said her ride was here. It's a conversation Beth plays over each day in her head."

"My one question is," said Beth Serrano, "why didn't I ask who was giving you the ride?"

Kosich said that after Gina DeJesus had disappeared almost exactly a year later, the girls' two families had united in their search to find their daughters. But as each year passed, fewer and fewer people came to the girls' vigils.

"This'll probably be the last one," said Nancy Ruiz. "But I will always appreciate [the] support."

A few weeks later, Ariel Castro bought an old washer-dryer from Tito DeJesus, who was moving. Castro had seen him clearing out junk in his garage and offered to buy some appliances.

"He wanted all that stuff," recalled DeJesus. "I'm like, 'Dude, you barely have room for the washer and dryer.'"

Then DeJesus helped Castro load the stuff in his Jeep Cherokee, accompanying him to 2207 Seymour Avenue, where they put everything in the driveway.

"I thought we were going to take it to the basement," said DeJesus. "And he told me, 'Just leave the washer and dryer in the driveway, and you can help me put the small stuff in the living room.'"

DeJesus helped him carry it into the house, but Castro wouldn't let him go any farther than the living room.

"I hadn't been inside his house for a long time," said DeJesus, "but it looked normal for a musician's home. He had all his instruments, like his bass and bass amplifier, as well as a couple of conga drums."

Then Castro offered him a Corona beer, saying he wanted to show him his new Fender bass.

"So I stayed and it was odd," recalled DeJesus. "He actually wanted me to hang out with him."

While they were drinking beer and playing along with some Latin music videos on *YouTube*, Castro had a question.

"And out of the blue he said, 'Hey, man, did they ever find your cousin Gina yet?'" said Tito. "I'm like, 'I'm not sure we're related but they haven't found her yet, man.' He says, 'I pray to God that they find her.'"

*   *   *

That summer, Ariel Castro's grandmother, Hercilia Carabello, died in Reading, Pennsylvania. Lillian Rodriguez had moved there a few months earlier to take care of her mother. The whole Castro family attended the funeral with the exception of Ariel, who had been so close to her growing up.

"They were surprised that he didn't go to his grandmother's funeral," said Aurora Marti. "He always said he wanted to see his grandmother, but he never went."

Soon afterward, Ariel Castro, Jr., quit his job at the Fort Wayne *Journal Gazette* and moved to Columbus, Ohio, to work for a bank. He had recently gotten divorced and wanted to start a new life. On his way he stopped off in Cleveland to visit his father, who was as reluctant as ever about allowing him inside the house.

"I would always enter through the back door," he said. "That's where my father would flag me in."

He then brought his son into the kitchen, where they talked for about twenty minutes, before he ushered him out again.

In November, Elsie Cintron was walking home late one night when she saw a little girl staring out of an attic window at 2207 Seymour Avenue. When she got home she told her brother Israel Lugo about the strange little girl in their neighbor's window.

"She was shaken up," he recalled. "She told me, 'I believe I saw a little girl in . . . Ariel's house.'"

Lugo told her that Castro lived alone, but his sister asked him to go and check it out anyway.

"So I go over," said Lugo, "and there's plywood on the windows and bags all over the place, so you really can't see in or out of the house."

Then he called the police and reported his sister seeing the mysterious little girl at the Castro house.

"The cops came maybe half an hour later," recalled Lugo. "They pounded on the door for maybe five or six minutes and there was no answer."

After shining a flashlight into the driveway for a few seconds, they got into their patrol car and drove off.

"They didn't take it seriously," said Elsie Cintron.

A few weeks later, Lugo's niece, Nina Samoylicz, saw a naked girl wearing a dog collar in Ariel Castro's backyard.

"She was walking around naked," said Nina. "We thought it was funny at first but then it was weird, so we called the cops. They thought we were joking, they didn't believe us."

Soon afterward, some residents in a retirement home on Scranton Street, which overlooked Seymour Avenue, saw three naked girls in Castro's backyard.

"They were naked on all fours with a leash and collar on them," said Lugo, "and they were being abused."

Concerned, the ladies called Cleveland police to report it, waiting on Seymour Avenue for the cops to arrive. But they never did.

The next day, Ariel Castro erected an eight-foot fence with chicken wire and blue tarpaulin. Then he let the trees and bushes become overgrown, so no one could see into his backyard anymore.

On February 14, 2012, the Cleveland School District discovered that Ariel Castro drove off his bus route every day to go grocery shopping at a Marc's superstore. He was spotted parking his school bus outside the store at 3:10 P.M., and then going inside. Twenty-five minutes later he came out, carrying three large shopping bags full of food.

Castro then faced a disciplinary hearing, at which he readily admitted the offense.

"[He] blamed it on a route change," wrote his boss, Ann

Carlson, "as he normally stops at the Marc's store at West 154th Street and Putitas Ave."

When asked, in front of six union representatives, if he regularly stopped off at Marc's on his bus, he answered, "Yes." At that point one of the union representatives told him to stop talking.

"This is Mr. Castro's third demonstration of lack of judgment," wrote Carlson. "He has previously been suspended sixty days for leaving a child on a bus and sixty days for making an illegal U-turn in rush hour traffic with a busload of students."

Castro was then suspended for another sixty days without pay and made to sign a "last chance agreement," stating that he would be fired if he committed another offense.

22

TERMINATED

In March 2012, Ohio Governor John Kasich signed an executive order creating the Ohio Human Trafficking Task Force, in response to the growing epidemic of missing persons in the state. Governor Kasich charged it with eradicating the sex-slave trade in Ohio, which enslaves approximately one thousand Ohioans annually.

"It's almost too horrific to imagine," said the governor, "but the fact is that human trafficking is real and is happening across Ohio. It's a modern day slave trade and we need your help to stop it."

A couple of weeks later, at a vigil to commemorate the eighth anniversary of Gina DeJesus's disappearance, Nancy Ruiz announced that she believed her daughter, who would now be twenty-two, had been snatched by human traffickers.

"I always said it from the beginning," she told a TV reporter. "She was sold to the highest bidder."

After all the publicity surrounding Governor Kasich's new executive order, more than forty people turned out for

Gina's vigil, including several FBI investigators who had been working on her case for years. Also in attendance was Ariel Castro, who handed out fliers and led the chants of "Stop human trafficking!" and "We want Gina!"

"He led the prayer at the vigils," said his neighbor Lupe Collins. "He was the first one there to tell everybody to hold hands."

The FBI and Cleveland police said they were still actively looking for Gina.

"We are following every lead that possibly comes our way," FBI Agent Vickie Anderson told WKYC-TV. "We continue to work this case with the Cleveland police and any . . . tip regarding Gina we follow it through, whether it's in our state or out of state."

Nancy Ruiz said that she felt renewed hope after Jaycee Dugard was found, and was certain Gina was still alive.

"I think if she would have passed on," said Nancy, "I would have felt it. I would be feeling empty, lonely, but I'm not."

Three weeks later, Nancy Ruiz held hands with Beth Serrano at a vigil to commemorate the ninth anniversary of Amanda Berry's disappearance.

"Today is Amanda Berry. Nine years!" said Ruiz. "I've suffered eight, they suffer nine. And it should be enough!"

A tearful Beth Serrano told a TV reporter how time had stood still for her since Amanda, who would be twenty-six the next day, had gone.

"There's days where it feels like it's so fresh," she sobbed; "because there's no new leads, it feels like day one. But it feels like so long because . . . I just miss her so much."

Then as the television cameras rolled, the crowd began marching the half mile to Amanda's house, chanting her name.

"We want her to know we're never going to stop looking for her," said Amanda's friend Victoria Dickens. "Where's Amanda at right now? She's not at peace. Her family's not at peace. And we just want her to come home. It's been way too long."

And just three miles away, Amanda Berry was watching the coverage of her vigil with Ariel Castro, who had brought in a birthday cake to celebrate.

Four days later, on Wednesday, April 25, Nilda Figueroa died of brain cancer at the age of forty-eight. And her relatives had no doubts as to who was responsible.

"All my family blames [Ariel] for my sister's death," said Elida Carabello. "He put her six feet under."

In the weeks before she succumbed to the brain cancer, Nilda was partially paralyzed, and couldn't even stand without falling down. Her tragic life was commemorated in a brief obituary in the Cleveland *Plain Dealer.*

GRIMILDA FIGUEROA
(July 30, 1963–April 25, 2012)
GRIMILDA FIGUEROA, 48, loving mother, grandmother, daughter, sister, aunt. She also leaves behind many other relatives and friends.

The following Sunday, a viewing was held for friends and family at the Walter Martens & Sons Funeral Home, followed by a wake. Ariel Castro and one of his brothers turned up, to the horror of Nilda's family, and proceeded to drink heavily and make jokes.

Castro also attended her funeral on Monday at the Interment Riverside Cemetery.

"I saw him," said Elida, "at my sister's funeral. He's disgusting to me. The way he treated my sister."

At her funeral, Nilda's favorite song, "My Heart Will

Go On," by Celine Dion, was played at the graveside, and Ariel, Jr., wrote a moving epitaph in the funeral home's guestbook.

"Dear Mom," it read, "You are gone too soon. But your suffering is over."

Soon afterward, a gregarious African American named Charles Ramsey moved to Seymour Avenue, two doors away from Ariel Castro. The two soon became friends and the forty-three-year-old dishwasher would often see Castro going in and out of the house. At night they would hang out together.

But Castro could also be abrasive with other Seymour Avenue neighbors, whom he did not approve of. Storm Pusztay, who lived a few houses away, said he was having a cookout on his porch in late April, when his dog started growling.

"Then I look up and it's Ariel," recalled Pusztay. "He looked down on me and I said, 'Can I help you?' He goes, 'You can't have that fire there like that, man.'"

Then Pusztay realized that his neighbor had been spying on him from his roof before coming down to confront him.

"The creepiness," said Pusztay. "I don't know how long he was up there watching me."

At the end of June, Cuyahoga County Prosecutor Bill Mason received a letter from Robert Wolford, an inmate at the Southern Ohio Correctional Facility serving a twenty-six-year sentence for involuntary manslaughter and felonious assault. Wolford, twenty-five, claimed he had murdered Amanda Berry with another man, and buried her remains.

After checking out the tip, Mason got a search warrant

and ordered digging to start on a vacant lot at West Thirtieth Street and Wade Avenue.

"I had a good feeling," he told reporters before the digging began. "Thought it was the real deal."

On Wednesday, July 18, Cuyahoga County sheriff's deputies drove Wolford to the site. Then, in shackles and handcuffs, the orange-jumpsuited prisoner walked around the lot for several hours, pointing out specific spots of interest.

At seven the next morning, several dozen FBI agents and Cleveland police officers arrived with shovels and dirt sifters, to begin digging up a sixty-by-eight-foot area. A cadaver dog and a backhoe arrived a few hours later.

At around 6:00 P.M. the digging stopped for the day with nothing being found.

"That's a waste of money," Pedro Castro told a Fox-8 news reporter, as he walked by.

During the day, Amanda Berry's worried family gathered at Beth Serrano's house to await the outcome.

"I don't want her to be gone," said Amanda's aunt Theresa Miller, "but we do want closure."

On Friday morning, the digging continued with a bigger backhoe, as a crowd gathered on Wade Avenue to watch. Daniel Marti was there and ran into his old friend Ariel Castro.

"Castro was around there helping the cops put that crime ribbon around," said Marti. "And he was saying, 'They're not going to find Amanda there.'"

At around 2:30 P.M., police finally called off the search, without any trace of Amanda Berry being found.

Cleveland Police First District Commander Thomas McCartney voiced his frustration.

"We had our hopes up," he told reporters. "Everyone had their hopes up, but the other side of the coin is, we still hope for the family. Maybe somewhere a girl is still alive."

After the search was called off, Beth Serrano handed reporters waiting outside her house a handwritten statement.

> *I want to say thank you to the FBI and the police for their help and support. I'm happy they didn't find my sister there, because my faith and hope is that she's coming home. This time is emotional for me and it's hard for me to keep speaking of this at the moment, but I want to say thank you to everyone. It's been 9 long years and I'm just wishing someone would say something and bring my sister home.*
>
> *Thank you*
> *Beth Serrano.*

In January 2013, Robert Wolford was sentenced to an additional four and a half years in prison, after admitting making up the entire story, just to get out of state prison for a couple of days. The total cost of the two-day dig was $150,000.

That long hot summer of 2012, Michelle and Gina started getting bitten by bedbugs. Ariel Castro had originally found their filthy mattress in an alley, and over the years it had become heavily stained with semen and blood. When Gina first woke up itching and covered in tiny red dots, they had thought it was chickenpox. Then, Michelle saw a bedbug crawling on the mattress and realized what was going on. Castro's first reaction when Michelle showed him a bug was to close the door to Amanda and Jocelyn's bedroom, so they would not get infested too.

He then brought in a plastic sheet and placed it over the mattress, which did nothing to stop the bedbugs, which were now attacking Michelle. The two women spent the sweltering summer locked in the pink bedroom, sweating on the plastic sheet and being eaten alive by bedbugs.

In September, Michelle became pregnant for the fifth time since she had been taken. And soon afterward, Castro took Jocelyn to a carnival, returning with hot dogs smothered in mustard. Michelle was highly allergic to mustard, and as a little girl her mother had rushed her to the emergency room after she ate some deviled eggs. Doctors had warned that mustard could kill her.

Castro was well aware of this, as Michelle would never eat McDonald's burgers, if he hadn't asked them to hold the mustard. When she refused the hot dog, because of the mustard, he threw it on her mattress, took out his gun and threatened to shoot her if she didn't eat it.

So she wiped off some of the mustard with her T-shirt and ate the hot dog. Immediately her face swelled up and she couldn't breathe. Castro told her to get over it, as he walked out of the bedroom, locking the door behind him.

That night Michelle writhed on the bed in agony and thought she was going to die. Her entire body turned bright red and her tongue and throat went numb. Several days later, Castro brought in a bottle of cough syrup for her to take. And for the next four days and nights Michelle was in such terrible pain, she couldn't even move off the mattress.

"I told Gina, 'Just kill me,'" she recalled. "'Just put the pillow over my head and kill me. Let me go.'"

But Gina refused, saying that she must stay alive for her son, Joey. All through her sickness, Gina nursed her night and day, urging her to stay strong and fight.

At 9:30 A.M. on Thursday, September 20, Ariel Castro parked his school bus 978 outside Scranton School and went home. School principal Troy Beadling became concerned when he noticed the yellow bus parked outside his school, as it was blocking the emergency lane used by the fire department. After making repeated appeals to the driver on the school's public address system, as well as checking all the restrooms, he went inside the bus, which was empty. Then he called the Ridge Road Bus Depot to report the abandoned bus.

Four hours after leaving it abandoned, Ariel Castro returned and drove it away for his afternoon route.

He was ordered to appear at a disciplinary hearing on October 4. Now facing termination for his fourth serious offense, Castro handwrote a rambling, almost incoherent letter of explanation, which he presented at the hearing.

> I went to Scranton School after McKinley 9:30 A.M. to get a schedule of pre-school kids days off. Teachers were not available. I left my bus parked in front of the school and walked home two blocks away.
>
> I returned a while later got on bus and went to 49th punched clock to do P.M. Route Lincoln West. My midday was canceled for that day is reason for leaving bus there. Bus was secured and off.
>
> I went home to rest. I've been helping Depot with many routes that needed coverage. I felt tired that day, Scranton is my school; so I didn't think anything wrong with parking there. I do apologize.
>
> Thanks Kindly, A. Castro.

In an official memo, Castro's boss, Cleveland Metropolitan School District Transportation Director Ann Carlson, said that his excuse of not realizing his route had been cancelled was unacceptable.

"Notice was made over the radio," she wrote, "and posted within the depot several days before September

20th. He did not notify the depot nor dispatch that he was leaving the unit unattended. This is Mr. Castro's fourth demonstration of lack of judgment. I am recommending his termination."

On November 6, Ariel Castro was officially fired by the Cleveland Metropolitan School District after nearly twenty-two years of service.

Later, Ariel Castro would claim he had deliberately gotten himself terminated, as he could no longer handle the pressures of a full-time job and his demanding home life.

"I started slacking off," he explained, "trying to get fired because I knew it was just too much. This job is too stressful and coming home to my situation. And I just couldn't juggle both of them."

After losing his job, Ariel Castro sunk into a depression and became even more violent. He stopped rising early for his morning route, and his hostages soon noticed that he no longer wore his bus driver's uniform.

Finally Amanda asked him if he had lost his job, and Castro admitted he'd been fired.

"Now he was at home all the time," said Michelle, "he assaulted me at all hours of the day and night."

He also started taking Jocelyn out with him more, shopping and on trips to the bank.

One morning his brother Pedro saw him at McDonald's eating breakfast with the pretty little girl, and asked who she was. Castro replied that she was the daughter of a girlfriend. When Pedro asked where her mother was, he replied she was grocery shopping.

"So I left it at that," said Pedro, "because he's with this little girl and they're going to have breakfast."

Three weeks later, Pedro saw his brother's red truck parked outside Burger King and went inside to see him.

"Again he's with this little girl," said Pedro Castro, "and

then I questioned him, 'Where's the mother?' 'Oh, she had to do something.' So I just let it go. I believed it."

Over the next few months Ariel Castro was often seen driving Jocelyn to nearby Roberto Clementi Park to play with her pet Chihuahua, named Dina.

"I saw Castro with that little girl . . . at least twice a week," said neighbor Moses Cintron. "They pulled up in his red pickup truck, and he helped her out because it was so high. She got friendly with my dogs. She used to come and pet them."

Jovita Marti said she frequently saw her neighbor with the little girl, whom she presumed was his granddaughter.

"He'd have a little Chihuahua in the back of his red truck," she recalled, "and he's with the little girl in the front. They went to the park and he always took her to the U.S. Bank on Clark Street and West Twenty-fifth."

There were even rumors that one of Ariel Castro's family was giving the little girl regular lessons. Later, Ariel Castro would tell detectives that Jocelyn had started asking him why he was locking Amanda, Michelle and Gina in their rooms whenever he went out. And she was begging him not to lock them in anymore.

In late November, Grupo Kanon fired him from the band. After fifteen years of putting up with his arrogant behavior and lateness, they had had enough and found a new bassist. Bandleader Ivan Ruiz said the tardy bassist always refused to conform to his strict dress code for the band.

"[I] would tell all the musicians the attire for the gig that night," said Ruiz, "and he always had to put on different clothing."

Whenever Ruiz called him out on it, the bassist would get angry.

"He would not like what I would say . . . and he always gave me excuses," said Ruiz, "and I'd tell him, 'I'm sorry,

I'm the director of the band and you have to do what I tell you.' "

On Christmas Day, Jocelyn celebrated her sixth birthday, and her father threw her a party. He bought festive balloons, streamers and a big banner reading HAPPY BIRTHDAY, and had Amanda and Gina decorate the living room with them, deliberately leaving Michelle, who was now three months pregnant, up in the pink bedroom.

Then he put on a salsa CD and brought Michelle downstairs, instructing her not to join in the festivities, as she was not part of them. Castro then produced a video camera and filmed Jocelyn cutting her birthday cake with Amanda, as everyone sang "Happy Birthday" to her. But he was careful not to film anyone but Amanda and Jocelyn.

"Jocelyn looked up at her mother with a huge smile on her face," said Michelle. "We clapped. As horrible as I felt inside and out, it was nice to see her happy."

After the party finished, Castro sent Amanda, Jocelyn and Gina back to their rooms. Then he pointed at the stairs to the basement and ordered Michelle to go down. At the top, he suddenly pushed her full force down the concrete stairs, and she landed on her stomach on the side of a bookcase.

Castro then came in the basement, shouting that he was going to "fix" her once and for all, so she could never have another child. Then he kicked her in the stomach with his heavy boot as hard as he could, as Michelle begged him not to kill another baby. This only seemed to energize Castro, as he kicked her again and again in the stomach. Finally, he hit the side of her head with his open hand and went back upstairs, leaving her on the filthy concrete floor in agony.

When Michelle screamed in pain, he turned up the salsa

music and came back into the basement, threatening to kill her if she didn't stop screaming. He then dragged her back up two flights of stairs and into her room.

Four days later, Michelle started to bleed and Castro brought her into the bathroom.

"You'd better hope that baby is dead!" he told her, as he left, slamming the door. She then pulled down her pants and sat on the toilet seat, and as her body went into convulsions she heard her fetus splash into the water.

With Castro outside screaming at her to hurry up, a tearful Michelle picked her dead baby out of the toilet and apologized to it. He burst in and slapped her in the face, making her drop her fetus.

"It's your fault!" he screamed at her. "You aborted my baby! I should go and get my gun and blow your head off right now."

He then went down to the kitchen for a garbage bag and dropped the fetus into it, and threw it in his backyard trash can.

A few minutes later he brought Michelle back to her room, where a terrified Gina was waiting. Then he threw some white paper napkins on the mattress, ordering Michelle to clean herself off.

23

"MIRACLES REALLY DO HAPPEN"

On February 18, 2013, Ariel Castro signed up for Facebook and started immersing himself in social media. On his new profile page, he posted an old photograph of himself with a full beard and leather hat, taken at least twenty years earlier. He listed the barest details for his profile, merely saying he lived in Cleveland, Ohio, studied at Lincoln West High School and was a member of Grupo Fuego.

As he had alienated so many musicians and now rarely got work, he began searching for new musical contacts in the Cleveland Latin music scene.

"When he started on Facebook he friended me," said Tito DeJesus. "He had never used a computer before and then he started texting. When he saw on Facebook that I was playing in a few bands, he said, 'Hey man, if you ever need me on the strings.'"

So Tito invited Castro over to his new apartment to listen to some CDs and go over some musical charts.

"He brought a twelve-pack of Corona," recalled Tito. "So we sat drinking beer and going over songs."

Once again Castro asked Tito if they had ever found his cousin Gina. When he said they had not, Castro said he prayed to God that they would.

"That was the last time I ever saw him," said DeJesus.

On Friday, February 28, Castro told his fifty new Facebook friends that he was feeling full of optimism, as winter was almost over.

"This morning," he wrote, "I woke up to the sound of a churping [sic] cardinal. Yes! Come on spring."

The next day, his brother Pedro celebrated his fifty-fourth birthday, and the following Tuesday, Castro wrote: "It was a good weekend. Pedro gained yet another year. Bless my bro."

On March 9, he greeted his Facebook friends, posting, "Good day everyone, and blessings."

Four days later, Castro texted bandleader Ivan Ruiz, asking for work. In the four months since Grupo Kanon had sacked him he had rarely played onstage.

"He really wanted to come back with the band," said Ruiz. "I told him, 'We'll keep you in mind.' But I knew I was never going to call him again. Musically he was awesome . . . but his actions and stuff."

That week, his oldest daughter Angie Gregg visited from Fort Wayne, and he showed her a photograph of Jocelyn on his cell phone.

"Isn't this a cute little girl," he told her.

"She's cute," agreed Angie. "Who is that?"

Castro said it was his girlfriend's child, explaining he was not the father.

But Angie was struck by an uncanny resemblance to her sister Emily.

"Dad, that girl looks a lot like Emily," she told him. "She has the exact same nose as Emily."

Becoming visibly uncomfortable, he then turned off the phone and changed the subject.

"I figured at the most he had an illegitimate child out there," said Angie, "and I would find out eventually."

One chilly afternoon in mid-March, Ariel Castro brought Michelle Knight into his backyard. He told her to wait outside his van, soon returning with a large shovel and gloves. Then he announced he was landscaping a garden and handed her the shovel to start digging a hole. The ground was still frozen and Michelle had a hard job getting the shovel even to pierce the soil. Then Castro started digging alongside her with a spade, saying the hole must be deep. And for the rest of the afternoon they dug, with Castro continually saying the hole was not deep enough.

Suddenly, Michelle realized that they were not excavating a new garden, but digging a grave for someone, possibly her. After three hours of heavy digging, Castro announced they were finished for the day and would carry on tomorrow. But he never did ask her to finish digging the hole.

On April 2, the ninth anniversary of Gina DeJesus going missing, her family held a fund-raiser to keep her in the public eye. Once again Ariel Castro attended, playing music with a pickup salsa band, and asking Nancy Ruiz how she was doing.

At the rally, Nancy vowed never to give up searching for Gina.

"I mean, this is nine years," she said. "Nine years there hasn't been nothing. I mean, there's no body—that's letting me know that she's still here and we need to bring her home."

The next night, Felix and Nancy were the guests of honor at a Cleveland Cavaliers game, where Gina's photograph and missing-person's poster were displayed on the Jumbotron at halftime.

Two days later, Castro texted his daughter Angie some

photos from his cell phone of a dog seated on a Porta-Potty. A few months earlier he had sent her a video of a dog in labor. Angie believed that they had been taken in the basement at 2207 Seymour Avenue, and wondered why her father would need a portable potty.

On April 11, Arlene Castro gave birth to a baby boy in Fort Wayne, Indiana. After hearing the news, her proud father announced his new grandson to his friends on Facebook.

"Congrats to my Rosie Arlene," he wrote. "Wishing you a fast recovery. She gave birth to a wonderful baby boy. That makes me Gramps for the fifth time, (2boys 1girl 2boys) Love you guys!"

On April 21, Ariel Castro celebrated the tenth anniversary of Amanda Berry's abduction with birthday cake. And as she watched TV coverage of her tenth vigil, once again Castro mingled with the crowd gathered outside the Burger King on West 110th and Lorain Avenue.

"It is an emotional landmark anniversary for one of Cleveland's most notorious missing-persons cases," said a Fox-8 news anchor. "It was ten years ago today that then sixteen-year-old Amanda Berry disappeared on her way home from work . . . and was headed home for her own birthday party. She never made it."

The camera then zoomed in on a crowd of supporters with large posters reading, A DECADE LOST, AMANDA BERRY, WE MISS YOU AND LOVE YOU, MANDY, and WE WILL ALWAYS HAVE FAITH.

The next morning, Castro posted a cryptic message to his Facebook friends:

A REAL WOMAN WILL NOT USE THEIR CHILD AS A WEAPON TO HURT THE FATHER WHEN THE

RELATIONSHIP BREAKS DOWN. DO NOT LOSE SITE [*SIC*]
OF THE FACT THAT IT IS THE CHILD THAT SUFFERS.

"True that," commented Castro on his posting, which
was liked by two of his Facebook friends.

The last week of April, Ariel Castro, Jr., arrived at 2207
Seymour Avenue to visit his father. The thirty-one-year-
old banker was in Cleveland for the weekend and his dad
had asked him to stop by his house before he went back to
Columbus.

"When I pulled up," said Ariel, Jr., "he poked his head
out from the back of the house and waved me to the backyard."

As he was not invited inside the house, they spoke in
the yard. During the conversation, Castro suddenly asked
his son if he thought Amanda Berry would ever be found.
When Ariel, Jr., replied that she was probably dead after
so many years missing, his father replied, "Really? You
think so?"

On Thursday afternoon, May 2, Ricky Sanchez came over
to 2207 Seymour Avenue, after Ariel Castro expressed interest in a bass guitar he was selling.

"We [had] become friends on Facebook," said Sanchez,
"and he saw a bass guitar that I had for sale and [wanted]
me to come and show it to him."

The musician, who had been visiting Castro's house for
many years, was one of the few people he ever allowed
inside.

"I'd been there about forty-five minutes," Sanchez recalled, "when a little girl walked into the room from the
kitchen at the back of the house. I was a regular visitor in
that house and I'd never seen her before."

Then a grinning Castro asked if he had ever met his granddaughter before, telling the little girl to say hello.

"I said hi to her but she never said hi to me," said Sanchez.

Then Castro took the girl gently by the hand and led her out of the living room. Sanchez thought it "strange," as he knew all Castro's kids and grandkids, and had never seen the little girl before. Castro came back into the room, and soon afterward Sanchez heard a loud banging sound coming from upstairs.

"It was a low-pitched *thump-thump*," said Sanchez. "I couldn't tell where it was coming from in that old house."

When he asked what it was, Castro said he had some dogs on the second floor, and then turned up the radio.

After Ricky Sanchez left, Ariel Castro posted a photograph of the new bass guitar he had bought on Facebook, with the comment, "I know 'quality' when I see it, very nice."

And a few hours later, he posted another, more cryptic message: "Miracles really do happen. God is good :)"

At around 1:00 P.M. on Sunday, May 5, Ariel Castro took Jocelyn to Roberto Clementi Park in his red pickup truck as usual. His neighbor Israel Lugo, who was there playing with his daughter, watched him pull up.

"He had a little kid with him," said Lugo, "a beautiful little girl. Ariel was acting all happy families. He got out of the truck and went to the corner bakery and got the girl a pastry."

Then Castro brought Jocelyn into the park to play with Lugo's small daughter.

"We were sitting there talking as we watched the kids playing," Lugo recalled, "and I asked him, 'Whose kid is this, Ariel?' He told me, 'It's my girlfriend's daughter's kid.' It's like they were a family."

The two little girls played together for about an hour, before Ariel Castro fetched Jocelyn, helped her into his red truck and drove off.

After leaving the park, Castro drove Jocelyn back to 2207 Seymour Avenue. Then around 5:30 P.M. his brothers Pedro and Onil arrived and waited in front of the house.

"Ariel came out to speak to them at one point," said neighbor Ailsa Laboy, "and then went back in the house."

Soon afterward, Angie Castro arrived and went in to have dinner with her father.

THREE

FREEDOM

24

DELIVERANCE FROM EVIL

Just after 4:00 P.M. on Monday, May 6, Ariel Castro poked his head into Michelle and Gina's bedroom, announcing he was going to his mother's house to collect dinner. Soon afterward, little Jocelyn started running up and down the stairs, yelling, "Daddy's gone to Grandma's house! Daddy's gone to Grandma's house!"

She then ran into her mother's room, saying, "Daddy told me to come up here and stay."

Amanda's initial reaction was to lie still and not do anything, in case it was another one of his traps to see if she would try to escape. But eventually she peeked outside and saw Castro's blue sports convertible had gone.

Her bedroom door was not locked, as it usually was, so she opened it and went downstairs. Then she tried the front door, which to her amazement was unlocked. Taking a big breath, she opened the door, but the three-panel screen door in front of it was chain-locked.

Amanda peered through the thick glass, and saw Aurora Marti and her two neighbors sitting on the porch of the house straight opposite. That's when she started pounding on the glass with her fists as hard as she could, to get their attention.

"I kept hitting the glass," she later told police, "but the glass was so thick it wouldn't break."

Then she screamed, "Help me! I'm Amanda Berry! Help me! I'm Amanda Berry!" as she stuck her hand through the narrow opening between the door and the frame, and started waving frantically. Eventually, she saw them stand up and come down off the porch, and start walking toward her.

As they approached, a man told her to break the glass on the screen door. She tried to hit it again and again, but it wouldn't break.

At that point, another man eating a hamburger approached from the driveway, to see what was happening. He told her to kick out the bottom panel as it was the thinnest one, and he kicked it too from the outside.

After a few hefty kicks from both of them the frame started to bend, and Amanda managed to push the rest of it out with her hands. Then she crawled out, reaching back in to bring out Jocelyn.

Terrified Ariel Castro would return, Amanda scooped up Jocelyn, who was screaming for her "daddy," and ran across the street to Altagracia Tejeda's house, begging for a phone. Altagracia handed her the landline phone and Amanda dialed 911.

"Help me, I'm Amanda Berry," she yelled.

"Do you need police, fire or ambulance?" replied the 911 operator.

"I need police."

"What's going on there?" asked the operator.

"I've been kidnapped. I've been missing ten years. I'm here. I'm free now."

Then Amanda implored the dispatcher to send help immediately, before "he" could get back.

"Who's the guy who went out?" asked the operator casually.

"His name is Ariel Castro."

"How old is he?"

"He's like fifty-two. I'm Amanda Berry. I've been on the news for the last ten years!"

"And you said . . . what was his name again?" said the 911 operator.

"Ariel Castro."

"And is he white, black or Hispanic?"

"Hispanic," replied Amanda.

"What's he wearing?"

"I don't know because he's not here right now," cried Amanda hysterically.

"Okay, the police are on their way. Talk to them when they get there," said the 911 operator, who then hung up.

A few feet away, Charles Ramsey had also called 911 and was speaking to another dispatcher on his cell phone.

"Hey, check this out," he said. "I just came from McDonald's, right? I'm on my porch, eating my food, right? This broad is tryin' to break out of the fuckin' house next to me. She's like, 'This motherfucker done kidnapped me and my daughter and we been in this bitch.' She said her name was Linda Berry or some shit. I don't know who the fuck that is. I just moved here, bro."

"Can you ask her if she needs an ambulance?" asked the startled dispatcher.

"She need everything. She's in a panic, bro," yelled Ramsey. "I think she been kidnapped so, you know, put yourself in her shoes."

At 5:54 P.M., Cleveland police officers Anthony Espada and Michael Tracy drew up outside 2207 Seymour Avenue, where a small crowd was already gathering. Two minutes earlier they had received a call to investigate a woman claiming to be Amanda Berry. After so many false alarms over the last decade, the two officers were wary.

"We pull up," said Officer Espada. "We see a crowd on the porch . . . and this girl raising her hand, holding a child. I'm looking at my partner. 'Is it her?' He's like, 'I can't tell.'"

As Officer Tracy parked outside the house, the female ran over holding a screaming little girl.

"Before I could even stop the car," said Tracy, "she was there at the window. And I . . . recognized her as Amanda Berry. I look at my partner and it was like something out of the movies, when you look at each other in disbelief. [We] can't believe it's her right there."

Then Amanda pointed across the road to 2207 Seymour Avenue, saying Ariel Castro had imprisoned her there for ten years.

"We figured he might still be in the house," said Espada. "My partner immediately asked her, 'Is there anyone else inside?' And she said, 'Yes, Gina DeJesus and [Michelle Knight].' And it was just like another bombshell with overwhelming force just hitting me."

Then, after radioing the Second District Station that they had found Amanda Berry, and Gina DeJesus and another girl might still be inside the house, the two officers dashed across Seymour Avenue.

At 5:57 P.M., police officer Barbara Johnson arrived at Seymour Avenue to assist them. She had been writing a report at the station when the call came in about a possible Amanda Berry distress call.

"I was hoping it was true," she said. "I wanted to be there if that was the case."

Officer Johnson jumped into her patrol car, turned on her flashing lights and siren and raced through the West

Side. She pulled up outside 2210 Seymour Avenue, just in time to see Officers Espada and Tracy running across the street.

"I followed them over to the house," said Johnson. "Officer Espada advised me that Amanda Berry was across the street and she'd escaped . . . and there were others in the house."

Unsure if Amanda's kidnappers were in the house, the officers drew their firearms and proceeded cautiously. Officer Tracy then crawled through the broken bottom panel of the storm door, but was unable to open it as it was still chained shut. Then Officer Vasile Nan crawled in after him and they kicked the storm door open.

After Ariel Castro had left for his mother's house, Michelle and Gina had turned on the radio, flipping through the stations for music to dance to. Then they heard Jocelyn run into Amanda's room next door, yelling that her daddy had gone to Grandma's house, followed by the sound of footsteps going downstairs.

Michelle assumed that Castro had summoned Jocelyn and Amanda downstairs, so the three of them could spend a few hours together in the living room, as they often did.

"The next thing I know I hear pounding," Michelle would later tell Dr. Phil. "So I [tell] Gina, 'Turn down the radio. Something's going on downstairs.'"

They turned down the radio and there was a few seconds of silence, before an even louder pounding on the front door.

"I was like, 'Well, something's going on,'" said Michelle. "We're scared. We're terrified. We thought somebody was breaking in because it was a bad neighborhood."

Suddenly, there was a loud explosive noise. Michelle whispered, "Hide," and they hid behind the dresser.

* * *

After entering 2207 Seymour Avenue, Officers Tracy and Nan went into the basement with their guns drawn, while Espada and Johnson went up to the second floor. Although it was bright sunshine outside, the house was pitch black. Officer Johnson turned on a flashlight attached to her drawn weapon, to see where they were going.

"I had to climb over . . . furniture to get up the steps," she recalled. "As we got to the top of the steps, there was a big heavy curtain and . . . Officer Espada pushed it over to the side."

Then Espada yelled, "Cleveland police! Cleveland police!" as he held the curtain open for Johnson to come through.

"I took a quick look to the right and he went to the left," she said. "I saw a room with kids' toys [but] I didn't see anybody inside."

Then Officer Johnson yelled out, "Police!"

Inside the pink bedroom, Michelle and Gina huddled together behind the dresser, as they heard footsteps coming up the stairs. The two women were trembling, thinking robbers were about to burst in and kill them.

Michelle then heard a woman's voice shouting, "Police!" but was suspicious, telling Gina anyone could say that. But then they heard the sound of a police walkie-talkie.

Tiptoeing to the door, Michelle looked out. At first all that she could see in the dark was a blue sleeve, so she went back inside. She whispered to Gina, who followed her through the connecting door to Amanda and Jocelyn's bedroom, where they hid behind a TV cabinet.

Seconds later, the door opened and Michelle saw Officers Johnson and Espada come in with their guns drawn, their silver police badges gleaming in the flashlight.

"Is anyone in here?" asked Espada, and Michelle came out running and jumped into his arms.

As officers searched 2207 Seymour Avenue, Amanda Berry and Jocelyn waited in the back of an EMS wagon. Inside, Amanda warned police officers Harrigan and Daugenti that Ariel Castro was probably close by, and would be driving a 1993 blue Mazda Miata.

At 5:55 P.M. an APB went out to pick up Castro immediately. Several minutes later police officers Brill and Hageman spotted his distinctive sports car a few blocks away, heading north on West Thirty-third Street. They followed it for a couple of minutes, before it pulled into the McDonald's parking lot on Clark Avenue.

At 6:04 P.M. the officers called for reinforcements and walked over to the car, asking Ariel Castro, who was driving, for his ID. When his younger brother, Onil, asked if they wanted to see his too, the officers went for their weapons.

The Castro brothers were then separated, read their rights and handcuffed. Then they were taken to police headquarters. When they arrived, Ariel Castro looked unfazed and didn't say a word, but his visibly nervous younger brother was most talkative.

"If there is something going on," Onil told the officers, "you have to talk to Pedro about it. He's at our mom's house on Hyde."

Onil explained their older brother had passed out drunk in the backyard of their mother's house after lunch. Then Ariel gave the officers her address, asking them to make sure the two dogs in the back of his car were taken care of.

A few minutes later, two Cleveland police officers arrived at Lillian Rodriguez's home at 3617 Hyde Avenue, where they found Pedro Castro lying unconscious in the backyard, naked to the waist. He was patted down and handcuffed, before being driven to the Cleveland Police Second District, where his two brothers were being photographed, fingerprinted and processed.

After putting on orange jail scrubs, the three Castro brothers were then taken to Cleveland City Jail, with blankets over their heads, to be booked.

After Michelle Knight threw herself into Officer Anthony Espada's arms, she refused to let go.

"She just kept repeating, 'You saved us! You saved us!'" said Officer Johnson. "I told her, 'It's okay, honey, you're safe. She then . . . jumped in my arms, as I'm trying to reholster my weapon."

Then, as Officer Tracy joined them, Espada asked Michelle if there was anyone else inside the house, and she said there was. The two officers then gently tried to coax Gina out.

"And it seemed like an eternity," said Johnson, "but all of a sudden you see another face peeping around the corner of the doorway. Officer Esapada asked her, 'What's your name?' and she said, 'Georgina DeJesus.'"

It took Johnson a few seconds to recognize the emaciated cropped-haired girl that emerged from the shadows, bearing little resemblance to all the MISSING posters she had seen over the last ten years.

"She was a lot thinner," said Johnson, "and pale compared to the pictures. She had real short hair and was real thin and pale. But you could see the resemblance."

But the sight of Michelle, now thirty-two, who had never had a MISSING poster, was even more startling.

"I thought she was a little girl," recalled Johnson, "until I put her down and got a good look at her, and realized she was a grown woman. She was very, very scared."

Then Michelle started hyperventilating and struggling for breath, and Johnson radioed for an ambulance.

As Michelle Knight and Gina DeJesus finally came out of 2207 Seymour Avenue with blankets over their heads, half a dozen police squad cars converged on it from all over the West Side. They were taken straight to the ambulance, where Amanda and her daughter were waiting.

For the next twenty minutes, the three women tearfully poured out their stories in the back of the ambulance to the astonished police officers.

"They all started telling us how Ariel Castro was able to get them into his vehicle," wrote Officer Johnson in her police report. "All three women victims stated that Ariel chained them up in the basement, but eventually he let them free from the chains, and let them live upstairs on the second floor."

Michelle told the officers that Castro had made her pregnant at least five times during her incarceration, making her abort each time.

"She stated that he starved her for at least 2 weeks," wrote Johnson, "then he repeatedly punched her in the stomach until she miscarried."

Amanda was then asked about her daughter, Jocelyn.

"Amanda stated that she had the baby in the house," read Johnson's report. "They put a black plastic pool under her while she was delivering, so the mess was easier to clean up. Michelle delivered the baby [and] Ariel told her that if the baby died that he'd kill her; Michelle stated that Jocelyn, victim #4, stopped breathing at one point, but she breathed into her mouth and 'breathed for her,' to keep her alive."

Amanda said that Ariel Castro was Jocelyn's father, and the six-year-old had never seen a doctor or gone to a hospital, and neither had they since being abducted.

"Gina stated that Ariel had sex with her," read the police report, "but she do [sic] not think she was ever pregnant; she said she 'fainted' once, but [do] not think she was pregnant."

All three women said that Castro would keep the doors locked and not let them out, except occasionally into the backyard, when they had to wear wigs and sunglasses and keep their heads down.

"Amanda stated that Ariel would sometimes take Jocelyn out with him," wrote Officer Johnson, "[but] Jocelyn did not know Michelle or Gina's real names in case she said their names in public."

Then Officer Johnson accompanied the four hostages in the ambulance to MetroHealth Hospital to be examined by doctors and be reunited with their families.

As the three women were telling their stories in the ambulance, FBI Special Agent Andrew Burke of the Violent Crimes Task Force arrived. He immediately began coordinating the investigation, soon to become one of the biggest Cleveland had ever seen. The multiagency task force comprised investigators from the FBI, the Cuyahoga County Sheriff's Office, the Cleveland Police Department, as well as the local parole and housing authorities. The task force would work together over the next several months to investigate how Ariel Castro could possibly have snatched three women off the streets of Cleveland in broad daylight, keeping them in his private prison for so long.

Agent Burke arrived to find officers securing 2207 Seymour Avenue with yellow crime tape, having closed off the street several blocks on either side of Castro's house. First he was taken to the ambulance, parked in front of 2207 Seymour Avenue.

"I'll never forget it," he recalled, "They opened the door and inside the ambulance [I immediately recognized] Gina

DeJesus and Amanda Berry. I did not have the familiarity with Michelle Knight, but I also noticed her as well as Amanda Berry's daughter."

After assuring the women they were in safe hands, Burke left to start setting up a chain of command and brief his team. He ordered search warrants for Ariel Castro's home, vehicles, telephones and DNA to be executed immediately. Then he drafted in the FBI's Evidence Response Team, who would be responsible for searching 2207 Seymour Avenue and gathering evidence.

He also ordered the Cleveland Sex Crimes/Child Abuse Unit to begin the delicate process of interviewing and medically testing the four victims, as well as informing their families they had been found and orchestrate the reunions.

"[We wanted] to return them to their loved ones in a safe manner," explained Agent Burke. "[They needed] things as simple as clothing and shoes. We had to provide them with somewhere to stay."

The experienced FBI agent knew that once the story broke, there would be an avalanche of media interest, and the women would need protection.

"So our attention was focused primarily on their safety and security at that point," he said.

At around 6:30 P.M., the four victims arrived at Metro-Health Medical Center, less than a mile away from 2207 Seymour Avenue. They were rushed into the emergency room, to be examined by Dr. Gerald Maloney, the emergency physician on duty. It was the first time any of them had received any medical treatment since they had been taken.

"All three appeared emotionally distraught," said Dr. Maloney, "but glad that they were free. They were cheerful [but] emotionally fragile at the time they arrived."

Amanda, Michelle and Gina told the doctor how they'd been held against their will, and raped repeatedly over the long years of their imprisonment.

"Miss Knight in particular related that she'd been pregnant," said the doctor, "and had been subject to both deprivation of food and physical assault to try and induce miscarriage."

They all told the doctor they'd been physically assaulted by Ariel Castro, but Michelle, who weighed just eighty-four pounds and suffered from malnutrition, was in far worse medical condition than the others.

"Michelle had several bruises and appeared somewhat emaciated," said Dr. Maloney. "[She] was very upset and actually preferred not to have a male physician or nurse in the room. After the initial evaluation, she had the rest of her care done by female nurses and a female resident physician."

All the victims underwent rape-kit examination by a sexual assault nurse examiner, with the exception of Jocelyn. Then doctors took buccal swabs from Amanda and Jocelyn, so their DNA could be tested against Ariel Castro's to prove he was the father.

"They related information regarding the sexual assaults to us," said Dr. Maloney," and also to the sexual assault nurse examiner. All three of them were raped vaginally . . . multiple repeated times. Again it was all against their will and they suffered physical harm while they were raped."

While they were being examined and photographed, a nurse gave Michelle a Nutribar, which she ate ravenously. Then she nervously asked for another one, and the nurse told her she could have as many as she wanted.

"And she grabbed the nurse's arm and hugged her," said Cuyahoga County Prosecutor Timothy McGinty, who was there, "and said, 'Thank you. Thank you. Thank you.' It just showed what she's been through. I said, 'My God, this girl has been starved [and] she's that grateful for such a small item.' "

Doctors found that Michelle's jaw was badly injured, after being punched countless times by Castro, including once with a barbell. She had also suffered nerve damage in both arms from his beatings, and had a life-threatening bacterial infection, from eleven years of rotten food and starvation.

Her first meal in the hospital was a Steak 'n Shake cheeseburger and fries and a cheesecake Blizzard, which she later described as "going to heaven."

That night at MetroHealth Medical Center, Officer Barbara Johnson remained with them all the time. She accompanied them to the restroom and waited outside, so they were never alone and always had someone with them.

During the hours she spent with them that night, she watched their reactions to finally being free.

"Amanda had [Jocelyn] so she seemed to be a little more grounded," said Johnson, "as far as trying to protect her daughter and making it seem like everything was okay . . . [although] you know it . . . wasn't. That was all she thought about. Michelle was still very frightened. She just held herself close.

"Gina was just confused by the whole thing, but a lot of the nurses and hospital staff would come up and just give her a big hug, and say, 'We've been praying for you, honey.' And she just stood there with her arms at her side looking around."

Around 7:00 P.M., Nancy Ruiz heard a rumor that her daughter Gina had been found alive in Ariel Castro's house, along with Amanda Berry and Michelle Knight. She fell to the ground shouting, *"Matalo,"* meaning "kill him," and rushed straight over to Seymour Avenue.

When Ed Tomba, Cleveland deputy chief of Homeland

Security and Special Operations, arrived, Nancy ran up to him asking if it was true.

"It was a mob scene," said Tomba, who had worked on Amanda's and Gina's missing-persons cases since the beginning. "Gina's mom was screaming, 'Is it true? Is it true?' I said, 'I don't know, Nancy. Come on.' And I took her up to the house."

Then an FBI agent showed Nancy a photograph of one of the girls who had been rescued, and she identified her as Gina.

One block away, Cesi Castro had been working in his Caribe bodega when he saw all the police cars and ambulances outside his nephew's house, and came over to investigate.

"I thought somebody had got killed over there or something," he said. "So I ran over there and I saw a cop going into the door and said, 'Hey, that's my nephew's house! Is he there?'"

After finding out what had happened, Cesi began calling around the Castro family to tell them three girls had been found in Ariel's house, and he and his brothers had been arrested. On hearing the news, Angie Gregg, who had dined there the night before, immediately went round to her grandmother's house, where Detective Todd Staimpel was interviewing Lillian Rodriguez, who was in shock after Pedro's arrest.

Angie told the detective that she visited her father's house on average six or seven times a year, usually accompanied by her husband, Sam, and their two young sons. She said he always insisted she called ahead, and would make them wait outside for several minutes, until he appeared. Angie told the detective he kept a "barricade-style board" on the back door and always kept the back fence chained.

"He told Angie he was very cautious of burglars and

wanted his privacy," Detective Staimpel later wrote in his police report. "She described a sound bar receiver which was hooked up to the television. It had a 'repeat' mode and blasted away during the entire visits. She commented on the volume, at first, but then accepted that her father just liked keeping the music very loud."

Angie said her father always kept the doors to the basement and bedrooms upstairs locked, and only allowed visitors into the downstairs living area. The only time she had ever been in the basement was when she was a little girl and had picked the lock and sneaked downstairs.

"She remembered a male mannequin and a porch type, two-seat swing," he wrote. "She re-locked the basement door and her father never knew she's been in the basement."

Angie described her father as "violent and intimidating," saying her mother had left him because of his physical abuse.

She also described how he had recently shown her a photo of a cute girl on his cell phone, saying it was the granddaughter of a friend. She had asked if it were her sister, as she bore such a close resemblance to Emily Castro.

At the end of the interview, Angie said that although at the time she had never questioned all the locks and loud music in the house, now it made sense.

"If my father was responsible for these crimes," she said, "he must have led a double life."

25

"DEAD GIVEAWAY"

At 7:02 Monday night—less than ninety minutes after Amanda Berry's escape—the Cleveland *Plain Dealer's* Web site broke the story to the world.

"It had come across on the police scanners," said *Plain Dealer* reporter Leila Atassi, "that they had found Gina DeJesus and Amanda Berry and that this could be real. [They] were both very highly publicized missing-persons cases, widely accepted to have been abductions."

When reporters saw that there was a third woman rescued, everyone in the newsroom wondered who she was.

"Who is Michelle Knight?" said Atassi. "That was the question we asked out loud. The first thing I did was [go] to the Cleveland police's Web site of missing people . . . and Michelle Knight wasn't even on the list."

Then she sat down at her computer to write the first story on the dramatic escape.

BERRY, DEJESUS, KNIGHT FOUND ALIVE, POLICE SOURCE CONFIRMS, was the headline.

"We've confirmed it's them," she quoted an unnamed Cleveland detective as saying. "They are alive and safe."

It had the barest facts, only describing how Amanda had "frantically told a dispatcher that she was alive and free after being kidnapped 10 years ago and held captive in a house on Seymour Avenue." Police had arrested three brothers, ages fifty, fifty-two and fifty-four, but had not released their names yet.

Atassi's story was immediately picked up by the wire services, and within hours would be making front-page headlines around the world.

The mayor of Cleveland, Frank Jackson, first learned they had been found after receiving a text from a city official.

"Alive?" he replied.

After receiving confirmation that they were, Mayor Jackson issued a press release.

"I am thankful that Amanda Berry, Gina DeJesus and Michelle Knight have been found alive," it read. "We have many unanswered questions regarding this case, and the investigation will be ongoing. Again, I am thankful that these three young ladies are found and alive."

Across town, the FBI brought Gina's parents and elder brother, Ricardo, to the MetroHealth Medical Center for an emotional reunion. When they walked into a conference room and saw Gina for the first time in nine years, they rushed into each other's arms.

"We just grabbed each other and held on," said Nancy. "There was no words. It was just hugging and kissing and crying."

Ricardo DeJesus said Gina was noticeably thinner, but appeared in good health.

"I was very excited," he said. "It was nine years. Nine

long years and I was just happy to be able to sit there and hug her and say, 'Yep, you're finally home.'"

Amanda was also reunited with her sister, Beth Serrano, at the hospital, where they were photographed by nurses posing with a smiling Jocelyn.

But no one came to see Michelle Knight that night, and a victim's advocate was summoned to the hospital to look after her.

By now, Detective Andrew Harasimchuk, of the Cleveland Divisional Police Sex Crimes/Child Abuse Unit, had been appointed the lead investigator in the case. He was briefed by Special Agent Burke and Deputy Tomba at 2207 Seymour Avenue, before heading to the MetroHealth Medical Center to interview the victims. There he was met by Detectives Laura Parker and Cynthia Adkins, who would conduct the highly sensitive interviews. After having all three women identify Ariel Castro from a photograph, the initial interviews began.

"They were very brief," recalled Detective Harasimchuk. "It was a very chaotic excitement at the time at the hospital."

While the three detectives interviewed the three women, hospital staff and close friends and family were constantly coming in and out.

Amanda told them how she had been walking home from work in her Burger King uniform on April 21, 2003, when she passed a van. Inside she saw a girl that she thought she recognized and a male driver. A few minutes later, she was talking to her sister, Beth, on her cell phone, when the van pulled up beside her. Then the driver asked if she needed a ride home.

Amanda told her sister she would call back, and spoke to the man driving the van. He introduced himself as Ariel Castro, asking if she knew his son, who used to work at Burger King, and his daughter Angie. Amanda recognized their names and she walked around the van, as Castro opened the front door for her.

Once inside, she realized that they were alone, and the girl she had seen was no longer there. When Amanda asked where she was, Castro said Angie was back at his house.

Then Castro had driven past her street without stopping, but Amanda was not nervous, as she'd seen the girl with him earlier.

"When they got to the house on Seymour," Detective Parker wrote in her police report, "he pulled into the back of the driveway and went into the house by the back door, leading into the kitchen."

He told Amanda that Angie was taking a bath, and started showing her around the house. She followed him upstairs, going past a closed door with a hole where the handle had been removed. Amanda looked through and saw a woman inside, whom she would soon learn was Michelle Knight. When she asked Castro who it was, he said it was his roommate.

"Once they were upstairs in what was his bedroom," Harasimchuk later testified, "Amanda Berry told Ariel Castro to please take her home or she would call the police. She attempted to run out of the room and became disorientated and ran into a closet.

"It was at this time that Ariel Castro first sexually assaulted her. He then used duct tape to tie her wrists and her legs. He put duct tape on her mouth and a motorcycle helmet on her head. He then carried her down to the basement where he physically restrained her with a chain. He left her overnight alone in the dark basement."

Amanda then described giving birth to Jocelyn in the basement, assisted by Michelle Knight.

Next the detectives interviewed Gina DeJesus, who

recounted her abduction. She was walking home from school with her best friend Arlene "Rosie" Castro, when they had telephoned her mother for permission for Gina to come over and play. Arlene's mother had said no, as she was grounded.

"After that DeJesus and Rosie went in separate directions," wrote Detective Harasimchuk in his report. "Rosie's father, Ariel Castro, drove down the street and asked if DeJesus had seen his daughter. DeJesus stated that she had just seen her and then Castro asked if she would help him out."

After Gina was inside his Jeep Cherokee, Castro informed her he had to stop off at his house to get some money.

"Once at Castro's house, 2207 Seymour," wrote Harasimchuk, "he asked if she could help him pick up a speaker. [They] went into the bathroom and [he] was looking at himself in the mirror. Castro then asked her to show him her privates. DeJesus states she got uncomfortable and wanted to leave. Castro said she could leave but would have to go out of a different door than she came in."

Castro had tricked her down into his basement and attacked her. After chaining her to a pole and handcuffing her wrists with plastic ties, he raped her for the first time.

Finally, Michelle Knight told detectives how she got lost on August 22, 2002, on her way to meet a social worker about her son, Joey. She had been in a Family Dollar store asking directions when Ariel Castro had suddenly appeared and offered to drive her. She told detectives that she had only accepted his help because she knew his daughter Emily.

He then drove her to 2207 Seymour Avenue, where she had remained until a couple of hours earlier.

"All the victims said that they were repeatedly sexually assaulted by Ariel Castro," Harasimchuk later testified, "either vaginally, orally or anally. [They] all described a pattern of being repeatedly sexually, physically and emotionally assaulted by Ariel Castro, during the entire time that they were held captive."

As the news that Amanda Berry and Gina DeJesus had been found spread around Cleveland like wildfire, hundreds of people gathered on the streets of the West Side to celebrate, with passing drivers honking their horns in support. Many more gathered outside the MetroHealth Center, awaiting word on the rescued women's conditions.

All the local TV affiliates, as well as national cable stations, went live, preempting regular programming that night. And scores of newspapers from all over the world dispatched reporters out to Cleveland on the first available flights.

By 8:00 P.M., a small encampment of TV news crews had moved into Seymour Avenue, where they would remain for the next several weeks. And reporters scurried around interviewing anybody that lived on Seymour Avenue and had ever seen Ariel Castro.

But the big scoop was WEWS-TV reporter's John Kosich's first interview with Amanda Berry's rescuer Charles Ramsey, who was already being hailed a hero.

Kosich began by asking Ramsey to walk him through what had happened.

An animated Ramsey responded that he heard screaming. "I'm eating my McDonald's. I come outside and see this girl going nuts, trying to get out of the house. So I go on the porch . . . and she says, " 'Help me get out! I've been here a long time.' "

Ramsey said he had initially thought it was a domestic dispute, as he tried to open the screen door, which was locked, with only enough room to get a hand through.

"So we kick the bottom," he said, "and she comes out

with a little girl and she says, 'Call nine-one-one. My name is Amanda Berry.'"

At first the name didn't register, but when he finally spoke to the emergency dispatcher he realized exactly who she was.

"I thought the girl was dead," he told Kosich.

Ramsey said he had then watched the police go into the house, coming out a few minutes later with Gina DeJesus and Michelle Knight.

Then Kosich asked about his neighbor Ariel Castro.

"You got some pretty big testicles to pull this off, bro," replied Ramsey, without missing a beat. "Because we see this dude every day. I mean every day . . . I barbecue with this dude. We eat ribs and whatnot and listen to salsa music."

Kosich asked about the girls' reactions to being outside the house in the sunlight.

"Bro," replied Ramsey, "I knew something was wrong when a little, pretty white girl ran into a black man's arms. Something is wrong here. Dead giveaway. Dead giveaway."

And within minutes that interview had gone viral, turning Charles Ramsey into a media sensation.

Soon after 8:00 P.M. the Cleveland Police Department released mug shots of the three Castro brothers, along with audio of Amanda Berry's dramatic 911 call. It would be played countless times over the next few weeks, becoming synonymous with the story.

When her brother called to say their cousin Amanda Berry had been found, Tasheena Mitchell had not dared believe it. There had been so many hoaxes and false alarms in the past. But as soon as she turned on her TV and saw it was true, Tasheena, and another cousin Destiny Berry, had driven straight to the MetroHealth Center to see Amanda.

"I'm just so excited," Destiny told WKYC-News. "I think about her every day. I've prayed about her every night. We're just so close but so far away, because they won't let us in."

Destiny said the three of them had grown up together, and were all best friends before she disappeared.

"We were so close," said Destiny. "Inseparable, and when she came up missing it killed us. All the hoaxes and games and the rumors that went on during the years. That's another thing."

Destiny said the biggest tragedy of all was Louwana Miller dying without knowing her daughter was alive.

"She left without knowing," said Destiny. "And now she's coming home, her mother's not even here to see that."

At around 9:00 P.M., Dr. Gerald Maloney, who had admitted the four victims in the emergency room, gave an impromptu press conference outside MetroHealth Medical Center.

"We're assessing their needs," he told reporters and the large cheering crowd. "The appropriate specialists are evaluating them now. This isn't the ending we usually get to these stories."

Later that night MetroHealth Medical Center released an official statement.

"The women have had a preliminary physical examination and are in fair condition," it stated. "They have been reunited with their families. MetroHealth joins our community in grateful appreciation for their safe return."

After finishing work that night at his bank in Columbus, Ohio, Ariel Castro, Jr., had dined with his best friend, Trevor. He had inadvertently turned off his cell phone ringer, and on checking it after the meal, there was a stream of messages from friends and family members. They all said that Amanda Berry, Gina DeJesus and another girl, whose name he didn't recognize, had been found alive in a house on Seymour Avenue. And a man in his fifties driving a blue car had been arrested.

On hearing the news, Castro was delighted that the girls had been found safe, especially Gina, whom his sister Arlene had been the last to see.

He immediately called Arlene, asking if she had heard the great news. She said that she had and was going straight out to celebrate.

"My sister was so excited," Castro said later. "She had worried so much about Gina all those years. She had felt so much guilt that she was with her just before she went missing."

It was only when he called his aunt Elida Carabello that he sensed something was terribly wrong. Elida said she suspected his father had been arrested, as he perfectly fitted the description of a fifty-two-year-old man who drove a blue car and lived on Seymour Avenue. Ariel, Jr., told her that she must be mistaken, as he would never do anything like this.

Then when he turned on the television and heard Amanda's 911 call, mentioning his father by name, he knew his aunt was right.

"When I heard Amanda Berry . . . say his name," said Ariel, Jr., "I knew he was guilty. I mean, who would come up with a name like Ariel Castro or invent that kind of story?"

Lillian Roldan had been eating dinner with her new husband and their two-year-old daughter when a friend called her cell phone, asking if she'd heard that Amanda Berry, Gina DeJesus and another girl had been found alive, and who had been arrested. When Lillian said she hadn't, her friend said it was her ex-boyfriend.

"I said, 'What do you mean, "my ex-boyfriend"?' " said

Lillian. " 'You mean Ariel Castro?' And I'm saying, 'No! No! No!' "

Then Lillian turned on the television to see Ariel Castro's mug shot, and knew it was true.

"Oh my God," Lillian tearfully recalled, "I felt everything. Upset. Really mad. Angry. Sad. Why did he do it? How he did it? I don't know."

Jovita Marti, whose mother had helped Amanda Berry escape, went round to Lillian's house that night to comfort her.

"She was crying a lot when she found out," said Jovita. "I said, 'Girl, you're lucky that you're not with them.' "

At eleven Monday night, Amanda called her father, Johnny Berry, and grandmother Fern Gentry in Tennessee, to tell them she was safe.

"She said, 'Hi, Daddy, I'm still alive,' " said her father, who is terminally ill with pulmonary disease. " 'I love you, I love you, I love you.' We were both crying . . . it was the happiest day of my life."

Then, in an emotional telephone call, broadcast live on WEWS-TV, Gentry had a tearful reunion with her granddaughter.

"How are you?" asked Fern.

"I'm fine," replied Amanda.

"I'm glad to have you back. I thought you were gone."

"No, I'm here," said Amanda, her voice welling up with tears.

"And we're happy down here for you," said her grandmother. "The little girl is your baby?"

"Yes," replied Amanda, "she is my daughter, born on Christmas."

"We have to get together soon."

"I know it," said Amanda.

Gina DeJesus also spoke to relatives via speakerphone

from the MetroHealth Medical Center. She requested they not ask about her captivity, but volunteered how Ariel Castro liked to celebrate their "abduction day," as if it were their new birthday.

Now living in Naples, Florida, Barbara Knight was watching the evening news when she first learned Michelle had been found alive. She spent the rest of the evening trying to call her daughter at the MetroHealth Medical Center, but Michelle refused to take her calls.

Late Monday night, Cuyahoga County Prosecutor Timothy McGinty, who would prosecute the case, joined dozens of Cleveland police officers and FBI agents at 2207 Seymour Avenue, as they began searching the house. Across town at Cleveland City Jail, the three Castro brothers were put on suicide watch. At one point Ariel Castro was escorted past his brother Onil's cell.

"Onil," he said, "you're never going to see me again. I love you, bro."

26

"THE NIGHTMARE
IS OVER"

Early Tuesday morning, Amanda Berry and Gina DeJesus
were discharged from MetroHealth Medical Center and
taken to a hotel at a secret location in Cleveland. The FBI
had arranged twenty-four-hour security, to protect them
from the media. Michelle Knight, who was still in a serious condition, remained in the hospital undergoing
treatment.

The Cleveland abductions were now making front-page
headlines all over the world: HORROR HOUSE: 3 WOMEN
MISSING FOR A DECADE RESCUED IN OHIO, trumpeted the
New York Post; US WOMEN ABDUCTED TEN YEARS AGO
FOUND ALIVE, read the *Daily Telegraph*; and *The Guard-
ian* proclaimed: CLEVELAND POLICE CRITICIZED AS CITY
ASKS: WHY WERE WOMEN NOT FOUND SOONER.

Much of the TV and newspaper coverage that morning
featured dramatic interviews with various neighbors, who
reported seeing: naked women on leashes crawling on
their hands and knees in the back garden; suspicious

screams coming from the house; and a woman clutching an infant and pounding on the window for help.

They spoke of calling Cleveland police on numerous occasions, who had come to 2207 Seymour Avenue and then left again after not getting an answer.

Comparisons were already being made to the Anthony Sowell serial killings two years earlier, where Cleveland police had been accused of not taking the missing-persons reports of the eleven female victims' families seriously enough.

At 9:00 A.M. the Cleveland Department of Public Safety held a press conference to update the media, and try to head off the mounting criticism.

"Now this morning we're happy to announce," Mayor Frank Jackson told the hundreds of reporters gathered at city hall, "that Amanda Berry, Gina DeJesus and Michelle Knight have been found and are alive. We're happy that they have returned to us, but their absence . . . has plagued their families, our community and Cleveland police . . . for years."

Mayor Jackson said although three suspects were in custody, there were still many unanswered questions as to why and how it had happened.

Then Special Agent Steve Anthony, who is in charge of the FBI's Cleveland Office, took the microphone.

"The nightmare is over," he declared. "These three young ladies have provided us with the ultimate definition of survival and perseverance. The healing can now begin."

Special Agent Anthony said the FBI and Cleveland police had relentlessly pursued every tip that had come in over the years.

"And the families of these three young ladies never gave up hope," he said, "and neither did law enforcement. As you can imagine, words can't describe the emotions being felt by all. Yes, law enforcement professionals do cry."

Ed Tomba then fielded questions from the press, reminding them that the investigation was ongoing and he must be sensitive to the victims. One TV reporter asked if this was an isolated incident or part of a larger human-trafficking operation.

"It possibly could be something that is outside of Cleveland," replied Tomba, "but as of right now we have no indication that it's bigger than our neighborhood here."

Associated Press reporter Tom Sherman asked if the three girls had been held as sex slaves during their imprisonment.

"You know, Tom," he said, "that hasn't been determined yet. We were very, very careful with the interview process last night. Today when we have our expert come in from the FBI, they're going to do a little more in-depth interviews. And I'm sure that as time goes by, there'll be more information that will be provided from these young ladies as to exactly what took place."

Then a cable TV news reporter asked why Cleveland police had not been more aggressive with Ariel Castro, especially after the 2004 incident of the boy being left on his school bus.

"If that questioning was done," said the reporter, "these ladies may have been out. Why wasn't this guy questioned more aggressively about this and will this change your protocol for looking for missing people?"

Tomba explained that Castro had been interviewed "extensively" about the boy left on his bus, and was not a suspect in any other complaint.

"Our policies are solid," he said. "I can tell you as part of being [in] this division for the last twenty-eight years, and being very, very involved in this over the last ten years, that the amount of effort, the amount of leads, the amount of work hours and dedication that went into this—I've never seen it before. Over the last ten years every single lead was followed up no matter how small."

Tomba reminded them how Cleveland police and the FBI had "dug up a couple of backyards," re-canvassed the neighborhood and organized vigils.

"So our goal was to get them back safely," he said. "The real hero is Amanda. I mean, she's the one that got this ball rolling . . . we're just following her lead. Without her none of us would be here today."

Later that day, Cleveland City Hall released a statement denying all allegations of sightings of suspicious behavior at Ariel Castro's house, supposedly reported to the police.

"Media reports of multiple calls to the Cleveland police reporting suspicious activity and the mistreatment of women at 2207 Seymour are false," it stated.

A few hours later, Ariel Castro was transported from Cleveland City Jail to police headquarters, for the first of two interviews he would give. Deputy Sheriff David Jacobs of the Cuyahoga County Sheriff's Office was in charge of his interrogation, mapping out a careful approach before meeting Castro in an interview room in the Sex Crimes Unit, where it would be videotaped.

"My strategy," he would later explain, "was to be non-confrontational. To obtain information from Mr. Castro that would meet the elements of the crimes that we thought he may be charged with in the near future."

After reading Castro his Miranda rights, Jacobs began questioning him about each of the women in the order he had taken them, and was surprised at his candor and eagerness to talk.

"His answers were very succinct," said Jacobs. "When I asked him a question, he answered the question. Typically, in my experience in interviews, when you ask somebody an incriminating question, you may not get the answer. I felt that Ariel Castro . . . answered those questions."

Referring to himself several times as a "sexual predator," Castro spoke in chilling detail about the circumstances of his three abductions, saying that he had later had "extensive conversations" about them with each of his victims.

"He used the word 'abduct,'" said Jacobs. "I asked him, 'What do you consider [is] a sexual predator?' And he said, 'Somebody that continually repeats offenses.'"

Castro told the deputy sheriff that he had acted alone, and his two brothers, Pedro and Onil, had no idea what he had done.

"I'm the criminal," he declared, "and I knew what I did was wrong."

Castro admitted abducting the women purely to satisfy his sexual needs. He admitted being particularly callous when he had taken Gina DeJesus, after going to Wilbur Wright Middle School to see his daughter Arlene, and then seeing her walking with Gina. He watched them separate on Lorain Avenue, and then go off in opposite directions before he pounced.

"I did a cold-blooded thing to my daughter that day," Castro said. "I drove past my daughter to get to Gina."

He told Jacobs he feared being caught after Gina's abduction, as he knew there were surveillance cameras outside the school.

Ariel Castro also readily admitted using Amanda's cell phone to call her mother, a week after taking her.

"I think I said something," he told Jacobs, "that I have her daughter and that she's okay and that she's my wife now—something like that."

He told Jacobs that he and Michelle Knight had

"consensual sex," from her 2002 abduction until a week before his arrest. He claimed she had only told him of one pregnancy, when the two of them had "devised a plan" for her to go on a tea diet for several days, as well as "knee bends and jumping jacks," so she would miscarry.

At one point in the interrogation, Castro said he realized he was in big trouble.

"I know I am going away for a long time," he said.

After a short break for lunch and a trip to the restroom, Ariel Castro was brought back to the interview room. During the next session, he told Jacobs that he wanted all his money and property to be divided among his victims, who he identified through photographs.

He also expressed surprise that he had not been caught earlier. Asked why, he mentioned an incident soon after he had abducted Michelle Knight, when Lillian Roldan had noticed a television on in a room where he was holding her.

"She seen that I had a TV on in the upstairs room," said Castro. "And she says, 'What is that? You have a TV on up there.' And my heart started beating, and I was like, 'Okay, she's probably catching on to something.'"

Later, when asked about the television incident, Roldan had no memory of it.

He was also questioned about his 2004 confession letter, which had been found by detectives the previous night near the kitchen counter sink. He admitted writing the letter, saying he had done so in the event something happened to him, so people could see he had been a victim too.

Castro also told Jacobs that he was now contemplating suicide, as he knew they were going to throw the book at him.

"I just want to crash through the window," he said.

*   *   *

As Ariel Castro was being led through the underground car park at the Justice Center in shackles for the drive back to Cleveland City Jail, WOIO-TV news reporter Ed Gallek found himself face-to-face with him.

"I was checking some police records," recalled Gallek, "and all of a sudden investigators started walking this guy down to another room. Here's this guy, the house of horrors, the man everybody is talking about right there in front of my eyes."

With his cameraman filming, Gallek started firing questions at Castro, who attempted to hide his face with his shackled hands.

"How could you do this?" he shouted. "What would you say to these women?"

Ariel Castro didn't say a word as detectives helped him into a police car to return to jail.

Three miles away at 2207 Seymour Avenue, the FBI's Evidence Recovery Response Team spent the day photographing every inch of the house, inside and out. Several dozen amplifiers and assorted musical instruments were seized, and Ariel Castro's large collection of cars and motorcycles towed away for forensic examination.

Cadaver dogs were led around the basement, searching for signs of other victims. Investigators had found the REST IN PEACE sign along with a woman's name scrawled on the wall, after Michelle Knight had told them that Castro had mentioned another girl, who may have been down there earlier. There was also much speculation that the search might produce some leads for the still-missing Ashley Summers and other missing Cleveland girls. But nothing tying Castro to any other cases would ever be found, and he vehemently denied taking any other girls.

When Special Agent Andrew Burke arrived at midday, more than three hundred pieces of evidence, including yards of rusty chains, ropes and bondage materials, had been removed in black plastic bags for forensic testing.

The FBI's lead evidence technician, Special Agent Chris Garnett, met Burke at the front door, where a Puerto Rican flag still flapped listlessly in the wind. Then, after donning white hazmat suits, Garnett took him on a tour of the house. First he pointed out specific locations where Ariel Castro had installed physical restraints, as well as showing Burke how Castro had carefully fortified certain areas, cunningly concealing the existence of additional rooms used to imprison the women.

Entering through the front door, Special Agent Burke saw a series of alarm clocks wired together, stretching the entire length of the first floor, to create a sophisticated alarm system. Both the front and back doors would set off alarms if opened.

Then, walking into the kitchen, Special Agent Burke observed how Castro had blocked it off from the rest of the living area, so visitors could not see beyond it.

"There was a kind of a heavy curtain or maybe even a bedspread," said Burke, "that separated the kitchen from the rest of the living area."

Attached to the kitchen was the only bathroom in the house. And next door was a dining room that Castro had converted into his bedroom, with a queen-size mattress.

Coming out of the bedroom, Special Agent Burke saw a porch swing positioned at the base of the staircase to the second floor, effectively obstructing access to the second floor.

Special Agent Burke walked up the first set of stairs to a landing, where there was another flight at a ninety-degree angle leading to the second floor. At the top of the stairs, Castro had hung a large brown curtain, totally concealing the second-floor landing.

They then went into the front bedroom, where Amanda

and Jocelyn had spent most of their time. The white room measured eleven and a half feet by eleven and half feet, and the walls were crudely decorated with various pictures of animals and cartoon characters, with a row of stuffed animals lying neatly on the bed. To one side was a blackboard, which Amanda was using to teach her daughter how to read and write.

Special Agent Burke then closely studied the bedroom door, observing how it had been modified to keep Amanda locked inside.

"There's a handle on the outside that's been screwed in," explained Burke. "It functions to . . . hold the door closed as there's no doorknob attached either to the inside or the outside."

As Castro had boarded up all the windows from the inside with heavy closet doors, he had cut a hole in the bottom panel of the door to ventilate the bedroom. He had also rigged an eyebolt lock, so the door could be locked from the outside.

Lying off Amanda and Jocelyn's room was an even smaller bedroom with pink walls, measuring just seven feet two inches by eleven and a half feet, where Michelle Knight and Gina DeJesus lived. A rusty chain attached to several locks lay on the floor by a filthy mattress next to a commode. Several of Michelle's paintings, including one saying, LOVE, hung on the wall over an old radio and a doll. The room was also boarded up from the inside, and the only ventilation was a small cutout in the ceiling for a box fan in the attic.

Then the two FBI agents went down into the basement and saw the white support pole in the middle, to which all the girls had been chained at one time or another. At the far end of the basement was a washing machine, containing thousands of dollars in small bills, which Ariel Castro would throw at his victims after raping them.

* * *

On Tuesday afternoon, Deputy Sheriff Jacobs interviewed Onil Castro at police headquarters. As he was being escorted out of the Central Processing Unit, his brother Ariel yelled out, "It's all my fault. He doesn't know anything about it."

In the Sex Crimes/Child Abuse Unit, Onil was read his Miranda rights and taken into an interview room where Jacobs was waiting. He still had no idea why he had been arrested.

At the beginning of the interview, Jacobs asked about Ariel Castro. Onil said his brother had lived on Seymour Avenue for about twenty years, and had recently been fired from his job. He lived alone, but had a girlfriend with a daughter. Onil said he had not been inside his brother's house for five years, and upstairs for at least seven. He remembered how Ariel used to drive around town with a mannequin in the passenger seat, wearing a wig.

Then Jacobs started showing him photographs of Amanda Berry, Gina DeJesus and Michelle Knight, asking if he had ever seen them before. When Onil said he had not, Jacobs told him they were photos of three girls who had been found in his brother's house.

"And my heart fell," said Onil. "I just dropped, not physically, but I hit the ground after he said that."

Onil Castro then strenuously denied knowing anything about the women being in his brother's house, or how they had gotten there.

Later that day, Deputy Sheriff Jacobs interviewed Ariel Castro's mother, who provided background information about the family. Lillian Rodriguez said that Ariel had never lived with Onil or Pedro, and avoided his elder brother because of his drinking problem. The Castro matriarch said it had been years since she had been inside

2207 Seymour Avenue, and denied ever meeting her grand-daughter Jocelyn.

It was late afternoon when two Cleveland police officers arrived at Lillian Roldan's house to bring her to the Justice Center for questioning.

"They asked me, 'Do you know why?'" said Lillian. "And I said, 'I know it has to do with Ariel Castro.' So I went downtown with my husband and my daughter, and they interrogated me for two hours."

During the interview, Lillian was asked if Ariel Castro had ever mistreated her during their three-and-a-half-year relationship.

"And I said, 'No, there's nothing bad about him,'" said Lillian. "'I have nothing bad to say about him, because there isn't.'"

She was also asked if she knew that Michelle Knight and Amanda Berry had been in the house, when she had stayed over.

"So I said, 'I'm aware because they said it on TV, not because I knew about it,'" she recalled. "Because if I would have known something, I would never leave those girls there. I have a daughter of two years old and I would never do that to anyone."

Less than a mile away, at the Cleveland FBI Office at 1501 Lakeside Avenue, Amanda Berry, Gina DeJesus and Michelle Knight were photographed and interviewed in far greater detail than they had been the night before. The interviews were conducted by the FBI Child/Adolescent Forensic Interviewer Catherine Connell, with Cleveland Detective Karl Lessmann observing.

Once again the three victims recounted how Ariel Castro had tricked them into his house. They all went into harrowing detail about all the beatings, rapes and mental abuse, which were then broken down into various time periods to allow prosecutors to frame charges against Castro.

Michelle Knight was also closely questioned about her five pregnancies, and how Ariel Castro had forced her miscarriages.

Later, back at the MetroHealth Medical Center, Michelle's brother Freddie Knight came to visit her.

"She was as white as a ghost," said Freddie, who was now thirty-two. "But she told me, 'Come over here and give me a hug. It's been ages.' She was happy to see me. It was emotional."

That night, Barbara Knight flew to Cleveland from Naples, Florida, complaining to reporters that she still had not spoken to her daughter.

On Tuesday afternoon, Officer Larry Guerra was escorting a prisoner through the Cleveland Central Prison Unit, when he heard a familiar voice.

"Hey, Chiqui, what's happening?" asked Ariel Castro.

Guerra turned around to see Castro, whom he had grown up with, smiling at him in a holding cell.

"I really fucked up now," Castro told him in Spanish, "but I'm a victim too."

Explaining he was now a policeman, Guerra asked how he could possibly be a victim. Castro replied he had been molested as a child.

"Yeah, but you know Felix [DeJesus]," Guerra told him. "You know the family."

"I've known the family my whole life," replied Castro, "but I didn't force her into the car."

"Yeah," said Guerra, "but it's been ten years, how can you watch this on the news every anniversary?"

Castro said he understood what he was saying, and then asked how his daughter, Jocelyn, was doing.

"Yeah, that's your daughter out of consequences?" asked Guerra.

"I didn't rape her," Castro declared, "she did it willingly."

Then the officer asked what part his two brothers had played in all this.

"Nothing," Castro replied. "They knew nothing about this. This was my secret."

"How did you keep it a secret for ten years?"

"It was hard, but it was my secret and I'm glad it's over. Now I can die in prison. But I'm a victim too."

"Okay, I'll see you later," said Guerra, who continued on to the booking area with his prisoner.

Immediately afterward, he informed his superior about his strange conversation with Ariel Castro, and wrote out a report.

At ten on Tuesday night, Anderson Cooper presented his entire *Anderson Cooper 360°* show from outside 2207 Seymour Avenue.

"First, we're live from Cleveland, Ohio, with many new developments here," said Cooper. "Three women who were missing for about a decade are finally free, after allegedly being held captive at a home across the street from where I'm standing. It's that white house with the lights still on, on the porch."

Then the CNN host interviewed Charles Ramsey, who had just been saluted by McDonald's for the part he'd played in Amanda Berry's escape. A few days later, the company would award him complimentary burgers for a year, for all his free advertising.

That afternoon, Angel Cordero and Aurora Marti had challenged Ramsey's version of what had happened on local TV news, claiming Angel was the real hero. But as he could not speak English, reporters had interviewed Ramsey instead. After hearing their accusations, Ramsey went on the offensive.

"So yesterday," asked Cooper, "What happened?"

"I'm going to tell it all," declared Ramsey. "Heard that girl scream and saw him run across the street and I went outside. And Amanda say, 'I'm stuck in here. Help me get out.'"

"So [Angel Cordero] don't know English that well or panicked. He just looked at me and was like, 'It's a girl.' And that's all he did. So I come with my half-eaten Big Mac and I looked and I say, 'What's up?' And she's like, 'I have been trapped in here and he won't let me out, me and my baby. I said, 'Well, you ain't going to talk no more. Come on.'

"I'm trying to get the door open and can't because he's torture-chambered it some kind of way and locked it up, right? So I did what I had to do and kicked the bottom of the door. She grabs her baby, which threw me off. All right, so fine. I got some girl and her kid."

Then Cooper asked if he felt like a hero, as a lot of people were now calling him.

"No, no, no," Ramsey replied. "Bro, I'm a Christian, and American, and I'm just like you. We bleed the same blood, put our pants on the same way."

Cooper said many people might have ignored Amanda's screams and kept walking down the street, but he had not.

"You have to have some cojones, bro," Ramsey told him. "That's all it's about. It's about cojones on this planet."

Cooper then asked if the FBI had mentioned a reward, as there was a $25,000 one out there.

"I will tell you what you do," said Ramsey. "Give it to them. You know, I got a job, anyway. Just went and picked up [my] paycheck. What that address say?"

Then Ramsey thrust his paycheck into Anderson Cooper's hand.

"I don't have my glasses," said the anchor, fast losing control of the interview. "I'm as blind as a bat."

"That's sad," said Ramsey, taking back his paycheck. "Twenty-two-zero-three Seymour. Where were them girls living? Right next door to this paycheck. So yes, take that reward and give it to that little girl."

Four hundred miles away, at the Ritz Carlton Hotel in Washington, D.C., Jaycee Lee Dugard was being honored at the National Center for Missing and Exploited Children's annual Hope Awards. During her speech she alluded to the three women in Cleveland, who had been rescued the previous day.

"What an amazing time to be talking about hope, with everything that's happening," said Jaycee, who had been imprisoned as a sex slave for eighteen years in Antioch, California. "These individuals need the opportunity to heal and connect back into the world. This isn't who they are, it's only what happened to them. The human spirit is incredibly resilient. More than ever this affirms we should never give up hope."

That night Ariel Castro went to sleep on suicide watch in administrative segregation to protect him from the other inmates. A judge had also extended the period that the three Castro brothers could be held without being charged from the normal thirty-six hours to forty-eight, to give investigators more time to prepare a case.

But incredibly Ariel Castro seemed unfazed by everything that was going on and slept like a baby.

27

MOTHER'S DAY

On Wednesday morning, First Lady Michelle Obama spoke about the dramatic rescue of the three missing Cleveland women, and how moved she had been by it.

"My heart just . . . swells up with relief," she said on NBC's *Today* show, "because just imagine first losing a child and not knowing whether they're alive or dead or in harm's way. And to be holding out hope for a decade and to finally have those prayers answered is just probably the best Mother's Day gift . . . that these families will receive."

All three network morning shows were reporting live from outside 2207 Seymour Avenue. It would soon become a must-see tourist destination. Finally, a faded black-and-white photograph of Michelle Knight as a high school freshman had emerged, giving the media a face to put to the name.

On the *Today* show, Cleveland Police Chief Michael McGrath described all three women's physical condition as "very good, considering the circumstances.

"We have confirmation that they were bound, and there were chains and ropes in the home."

He said the three suspects were talking to police and that the victims were still being interviewed.

Then Barbara Knight, whom NBC had flown in from Naples, Florida, the previous night, was interviewed by Savannah Guthrie, outside the house where her daughter had been imprisoned for eleven years. She admitted having "a complicated and sometimes troubled relationship" with her daughter, whom she had still not spoken to since the escape.

Guthrie asked if she thought Michelle wanted to see her.

"Well, the way I understood it by certain people," said Knight, "they told me that maybe she didn't want nothing to do with me. But still in my heart I thought, 'No,' because I know my Michelle."

Knight said that after Michelle had disappeared in 2002, she had filed a missing-persons report, and then waited to hear something.

"They just told me," she said, "if she breaks the law or [if they] spot her they'll let me know, but nothing happened. Well, because she was twenty, they figured that she had just left because of the upset of the baby and everything."

Then Guthrie asked what she would say to Michelle if she did get to see her.

"That I love you and I missed you all this time," she replied, "and hopefully whatever happened between us, if something did, I hope it heals, because I really want to take her back to Florida with me. I don't want to leave her in Cleveland."

Savannah Guthrie then interviewed Julio "Cesi" Castro and his daughter Maria Montes by a police barricade outside the house.

"Mr. Castro," asked Guthrie, "did you have any inkling that these nephews could be involved?" asked Guthrie.

"Nothing whatsoever," replied Cesi, who was smartly dressed in a suit and tie, adding that he had not seen Ariel for six years.

"Maria," asked Guthrie, as the three Castro brothers' mug shots came on screen, "what do you know about these men?"

"Ariel [is a] beloved cousin," she replied. "This is an incredible thing to believe, but one of the things I want to say, Savannah, on behalf of the Castro family—you know we are elated obviously that these girls have been found and that they are alive. And our hearts are full of joy for this reason. At the same time this family is suffering a great sadness to know that these girls have suffered at the hands of family members of ours."

Then on behalf of the Castro family, Montes apologized to Amanda Berry, Gina DeJesus and Michelle Knight for everything they had gone through.

"And we want them to know," she said, "that if they ever need anything . . . we are here for them. We certainly hope that an entire family is not judged over the actions of one person."

Guthrie then asked if in hindsight they had seen anything suspicious over the years.

"No, absolutely not," said Montes. "[If] anyone had ever told my father, who lives in this neighborhood, that they thought anything suspicious was going on with his nephew or that house, no one in this entire family would have kept anything secret or protected them."

Cesi was then asked how close his family was to Gina's family.

"We grew up together," said Cesi, "especially the Ruizes. Gina's grandfather moved to Florida years ago, but we're still in touch. He was one of the first persons I called, to inform him that his granddaughter had been found and how happy I was."

Then Guthrie asked about reports now surfacing that Nilda Figueroa had filed charges against Ariel Castro for his violence.

"No idea," replied Montes. "Obviously this is a story that is unfolding with the investigation. We as a family are just as shocked and stunned and we're hearing all of these things for the first time as well. There has been a distance with these cousins for some time, and it's shocking and very hurtful and very shameful to hear all of this at this point."

At 9:00 A.M. on Wednesday, Ariel Castro was back in the interview room at the Sex Crimes/Child Abuse Unit for his second interview. Once again he seemed keen to talk, answering every question, however difficult, that Deputy Sheriff Jacobs posed. First he was also shown an explicit "sexual image" that the FBI had found in his cell phone, which he admitted was his.

Jacobs also asked about the Luger gun police had found in his house, and Castro said it had been part of his father's gun collection, which he had inherited.

"I showed the gun to the girls as a form of control," he told the deputy sheriff.

Then Jacobs asked him about his victims' claims that he had used the gun to play a Russian roulette–type game of trust, removing the bullets without them knowing.

"His response was that he didn't recall," said Jacobs, "but if the girls said it, then it probably happened."

Castro was also asked if he had ever tried to abduct any other girls, and he said no.

At 11:31 A.M., after ten hours of interviews, Jacobs gave Ariel Castro a last opportunity to show some remorse for what he had done.

"I had explained to him that I wanted the statement to be in his words," said Jacobs, "and if there was something that he wanted to put in the statement to include an apology, I would accommodate that."

There was no response.

Then Ariel Castro signed a three-page written statement, summarizing what he had confessed to over the last two days. He also signed photographs of the three women, admitting they had been his victims.

Finally, at the end of the interview, Jacobs asked if he wanted to say anything to the families of his victims. Again, there was no response.

As Ariel Castro was signing his confession, Amanda Berry returned home in triumph, for the first time in ten years. Around a hundred friends and neighbors had gathered outside her sister Beth Serrano's house on West 111th Street, where a huge banner reading, WELCOME HOME AMANDA! hung over the front door. Yellow ribbons adorned the trees outside, and on the porch lay flowers, party balloons and stuffed animals, left by well-wishers. A small army of TV cameras were positioned across from the house, and scores of reporters mingled with the crowd in the festival atmosphere.

At 11:35 A.M., a motorcade, escorted by a line of police motorcycles, drew up outside to the cheers of the crowd. Behind them was a black minivan, containing Amanda and Jocelyn. When it came to a stop outside the house, the rear door opened. Then, Amanda pulled a blanket over Jocelyn's head to protect her from cameras, and they hurried into the house through a back door, without a word to reporters.

A few minutes later, a red-eyed Beth Serrano came outside to read out a statement, as a dazed-looking Amanda looked out of a window.

"I just want to say we are so happy to have Amanda and her daughter home," said Beth, overcome by emotion. "I want to thank the public and the media for the support and encouragement over the years. But at this time our family would request privacy, so my sister and niece and I can have time to recover. Please respect our privacy until we are ready to make our statements. And thank you."

FBI Special Agent Vicki Anderson, who had worked on the case for years, was overcome by emotion as she brought Amanda and Jocelyn home.

"There were tears of joy," said Anderson. "I think everybody's eyes were misty . . . [Amanda] was hugging everyone and she was a little quiet. She was just overwhelmed."

Three hours later, Gina DeJesus came home too. Just before 3:00 P.M., an SUV pulled up outside her parents' bungalow on West Seventy-first Street, as a huge crowd applauded. Then Gina, wearing a bright yellow hooded shirt, was escorted past a line of balloons, stuffed toys and banners into the house by half a dozen Guardian Angels. Gina then gave a thumbs-up to the large crowd, who were chanting, "Gina! Gina!" Her jubilant father pumped the air with his fist and hugged a police officer.

A *Fox News* helicopter hovered overhead, shooting Gina's arrival, which was broadcast live. A few minutes later Gina's smiling parents came out to the porch, joining Cleveland Police Commander Keith Sulzer for an impromptu press conference.

"I'm Gina's father," said an emotional Felix DeJesus, to a burst of applause. "I am the one that kept this family together. I'm the one that had the hardest role, to fight to see this day, because I knew my daughter was out there alive."

Then Felix thanked the Cleveland police, the FBI and everybody involved with Gina's, Amanda's and Michelle's cases.

"These people were by my side every day and every night and every hour," he said. "I don't know how they did it but they did."

He then urged the community to be more alert, so no more girls like Gina would go missing.

"Too many kids these days come up missing," he said, "and we always ask the question, 'How come I didn't see what happened to that kid?' Why? Because we chose not to. Get up early in the morning. Go out walking with your dog. Do something while these kids are going to school. Because I thought that this problem that has happened to me, and this joyous day that I got my daughter back, would never happen to my family. But it came knocking on that door."

Then an ecstatic Nancy Ruiz addressed the cheering crowd. She first thanked Charles Ramsey for helping Amanda Berry to escape, and not ignoring her pleas for help.

"These three women are at home," she declared. "I want everybody to know that the three of them are doing great. Yes, I do thank the Lord for miracles. I want to thank everyone that believed, even when I said she was alive. I still want to thank . . . even the ones that doubted the most, because they're the ones that made me stronger."

While Gina's and Amanda's families celebrated their homecomings, Barbara Knight arrived at MetroHealth Medical Center with flowers for Michelle. She reportedly had a brief meeting with her daughter, before tempers flared and Michelle asked her to leave.

At 5:06 Wednesday afternoon, the City of Cleveland Chief Prosecutor Victor Perez held a press conference to announce that he had just signed criminal complaints charging Ariel Castro with four counts of kidnapping and three

counts of rape. No charges would be filed against Onil and
Pedro, as there was no evidence of their involvement.

"The defendant will be arraigned tomorrow morning in
Cleveland Municipal Court," Perez told reporters, "and his
case will be transferred over to the Cuyahoga County Court
of Common Pleas."

He said the case, to be prosecuted by the Cuyahoga
County Prosecutor's Office, would soon go before a grand
jury. He expected Ariel Castro would be indicted on these
seven charges as well as additional ones.

Then the prosecutor, who was born and raised in Puerto
Rico, appealed for Cleveland's Latin community not to be
judged by this horrific case.

"I want everyone to know," he said, "that the acts of the
defendant in this criminal case are not a reflection of
the rest of the Puerto Rican community here or in Puerto
Rico."

Then Ed Tomba took reporters' questions, and was
asked if Castro had drugged the women to stop them escaping.

"If they were drugged," said Tomba, "that's yet to be
determined. The only opportunity . . . to escape was the
other day when Amanda escaped. They don't believe that
they've been outside of the home for the last ten years re-
spectively."

Then a reporter wanted to know the little girl's relationship with Ariel Castro.

"That is Amanda's daughter," said Tomba, "and as far
as the relationship [with the defendant], that hasn't been
determined. There's going to be a paternity test taken.
There was a search warrant executed on the suspect to
obtain his DNA."

A TV reporter then asked if Charles Ramsey would be
receiving any reward money.

"We are actually discussing that," said the deputy chief, "but Mr. Ramsey does deserve something [and] a lot of credit. He is the true key to this case."

Then *Channel 8 News* reporter Bill Sheil asked about Fernando Colon's claims that he had told the FBI to investigate Ariel Castro after Gina DeJesus's disappearance in 2004.

"We have obviously heard that same statement," said FBI Special Agent Steve Anthony, "and with due diligence we have scrubbed our entire investigative file, and have no reason to believe that [Colon] made the comments that he's purporting to the media."

On May 8, two days after the girls' escape, somebody leaked the official Cleveland police incident report to WKYC-TV investigative reporter Tom Meyer, who broke the story on that evening's six o'clock newscast. It revealed how Michelle Knight had delivered Amanda Berry's baby, as she lay in a plastic baby pool in the basement to contain "the mess." When the baby stopped breathing Castro threatened to kill Michelle, as she breathed into the baby's mouth and saved her life.

The sensational report, which would make headlines all over the world the next morning, also revealed that Michelle had been pregnant at least five times during her captivity, with Castro forcing her to abort each time.

"She stated that he starved her for at least two weeks," it read, "then he repeatedly punched her in the stomach until she miscarried."

Late that night, WOIO-TV news reporter Scott Taylor was leaked Ariel Castro's 2004 four-page confession, which had been found in his kitchen. And over the next hour he began tweeting choice parts of it to his Twitter followers.

At 11:08, Taylor tweeted: "Castro writes 'They are here

against their will because they made a mistake of getting in a car with a total stranger.'"

One minute later, he tweeted: "Castro continues 'I don't know why I kept looking for another. I already had 2 in my possession.'"

At 11:10 came another: "Castro writes about wanting to kill himself and 'give all the money I saved to my victims.'"

And his last tweet at 11:58 read, "Castro writes he was surprised how young Gina DeJesus really is cause he thought she was a lot older."

That night was Gina DeJesus's first at home in nine years, but she was too traumatized to sleep in her bedroom upstairs, as it reminded her of the room she had been imprisoned in.

"She says, "'Mom, I don't want to stay in a room,'" said Nancy Ruiz. "So I said, 'You don't have to anymore.'"

So instead, she slept on an inflatable mattress in the living room, with all her family.

28

"THIS CHILD KIDNAPPER OPERATED A TORTURE CHAMBER"

On Thursday morning, the three Castro brothers were led into a Cleveland municipal courtroom. With his hands cuffed and chin buried in his dark blue jail jumpsuit, Ariel Castro stood by his two brothers with his eyes tightly shut, avoiding the row of photographers and TV cameras at the back of the courtroom.

After Pedro Castro pleaded no contest to an old open-container charge, and unspecified minor offenses against Onil were dismissed, Judge Lauren Moore freed both men on time served.

Then public defender Kathleen DeMetz, who had spent thirty minutes with Ariel Castro earlier, told Judge Moore that she was waiving examination on each case.

Cuyahoga County Assistant Prosecutor Brian Murphy told the judge that Ariel Castro was charged with three separate charges of kidnapping and rape, and a fourth charge of kidnapping.

"These charges against Mr. Castro," said Murphy, "are based on premeditated, deliberate and depraved decisions to snatch three young ladies from Cleveland's West Side streets, to be used in whatever self-gratifying, self-serving way he sought fit."

The prosecutor said Amanda Berry and Michelle Knight had "endured this horrifying ordeal" for more than a decade, and Gina DeJesus slightly less.

"The ordeal grew to eventually include a little girl," he said, "believed to have been born to one of the women while in captivity."

He told the judge that during their imprisonment, all the women had suffered "repeated beatings," as well as being "bound and restrained and sexually assaulted." They never left Castro's property the entire time.

"Then just as suddenly, unexpectedly and, quite frankly, inexplicably as they disappeared," said Murphy, "they re-emerged, thankfully, miraculously three days ago at the home of Mr. Castro.

"Today the situation's turned, Your Honor. Mr. Castro stands before you captive, in captivity, a prisoner. The women are free to resume their lives that were interrupted . . . with the promise and hope that justice will be served."

The prosecutor asked for bail to be set at five million dollars, to "protect the victims and the community that Mr. Castro manipulated and deceived."

Judge Moore then set a $2 million bond on each of the charges, totaling $8 million, ordering the defendant to have no contact with his victims.

Then Ariel Castro was led out of the courtroom in shackles, showing absolutely no reaction.

Outside the court, Cuyahoga County Prosecutor Timothy McGinty, who had now been assigned the case, addressed the media.

"This child kidnapper," he declared, "operated a torture chamber and private prison in the heart of our city. The horrific brutality and torture that the victims endured for a decade is beyond comprehension."

He told reporters that he might seek the death penalty, relating to Michelle Knight's alleged miscarriages she suffered at Castro's hands.

"I fully intend to seek charges," he said, "on each and every act of sexual violence, rape, each day of kidnapping, every felonious assault, all these attempted murders, and each act of aggravated murder he committed by terminating pregnancies, that the offender perpetuated against the hostages during this decade-long ordeal."

McGinty asked the media to respect the victims' privacy, while his office prepared the criminal case against Ariel Castro.

"These victims have gone through something few of us will ever understand," he said. "They need a chance to heal before we seek more evidence from them. The women (and Amanda's daughter) were courageous victims to outlast their tormentor."

After leaving the courtroom, Ariel Castro was transferred to the Cuyahoga County Jail, where he was placed in isolation, remaining on suicide watch. Every ten minutes, guards checked his nine-by-nine-foot cell, containing a metal bed with a plastic-covered thin mattress, a mat, a metal sink and a safety mirror. Unlike his prisoners at 2207 Seymour Avenue, Castro had a window to look out of.

The first couple of hours after arriving he lay on the mat, but then at 11:30 A.M., he got up and started walking around his cell naked.

At 1:38 P.M., three detectives arrived to see Castro in his cell. They took a DNA swab, bringing it straight to the Ohio Bureau of Criminal Investigation (BCI) for testing.

Then, Dr. Leslie Koblentz, a prison psychiatrist, arrived to interview Castro for half an hour. After he left, Castro started prowling around his cell naked.

* * *

Earlier that morning, an emotional Arlene Castro appeared on *Good Morning America* to apologize to Gina DeJesus. Anchor George Stephanopoulos asked for her reaction, as the last person to see Gina, when she learned her father was responsible.

"I would have to say I'm really disappointed," Arlene replied, "embarrassed, mainly devastated about this whole situation."

Arlene said she hadn't spoken to her dad for a couple of weeks and had never been very close to him.

"Every time we would talk it would just be a short conversation," she said. "Just a 'Hello, how are you doing? And let me know if you need anything.' And that was it. Every time."

"And did you ever meet the little girl?" asked Stephanopoulos.

"No," she said. "I have never met her before."

"Did you ever witness violence in the home?"

"Oh no. Never. Never," replied Arlene.

Then Stephanopoulos asked if there was anything she wanted to say to Gina and her family.

"I am absolutely so, so sorry," sobbed Arlene. "I really want to see you, Gina. and I want you to meet my kids. I'm so sorry for everything."

A few hours later on CNN, Ariel Castro's oldest daughter, Angie Gregg, also apologized to her father's victims, saying his actions were "sickening" but his family should not be stigmatized.

"We don't have monster in our blood," she said. "My father's actions are . . . definitely not a reflection of myself or my children."

Angie said she never wanted to see her father again and had cut him out of her life.

"I would like to ask him," she said, "When did you

think that this was going to be over? How did you think it was going to end? You're fifty-two years old, did you think you could carry on this charade forever? What did you think was going to happen? And eventually you would have been caught, and then what of these girls? What of your family? You didn't care?"

Arlene finally reached out to Amanda Berry and her daughter, Jocelyn, whose DNA was now being analyzed to see if they were half sisters.

"I would love to see the little girl, Jocelyn," she said, "but I don't want to pressure them at all. And that's maybe further down the road and maybe it will be a possibility. I would really love that but right now these girls need to heal."

That same day, reporters staking out Lillian Rodriguez's home surrounded her when she emerged from the house.

"I am a mother in a lot of pain," she told them in Spanish. "My son is sick and I have nothing to do with what my son did."

Then she got in a car and was driven away.

Cleveland City Councilman Brian Cummins, who represents Ward 14, which includes Seymour Avenue, had been briefed on the case from the beginning. He would play a crucial role in helping the large Hispanic neighborhood come to terms with what had happened under their very eyes. And several Seymour Avenue residents had guilty consciences because they had not asked more questions over the years.

"How possibly could this happen?" asked Cummins. "So, I think we must not try to be too judgmental on the official bodies, the FBI, the police. Everybody wishes we could have ended this sooner and there's a lot of self-doubt, questioning."

Over the next few months, Cummins and several other council members met regularly to discuss ways of helping the victims financially.

The FBI had arranged for local attorney Kathy Joseph to examine Michelle Knight's legal issues, including her custody rights with her son, Joey, who was now a teenager and had been adopted soon after she disappeared.

At their first meeting at the MetroHealth Medical Center, Michelle complained she couldn't get in touch with Gina. And on Thursday morning, Joseph reached out to Councilman Cummins.

"Kathy said, 'I want to get Michelle an iPhone,'" recalled Cummins. "I said, 'What else?' and this is really touching. Kathy says, 'Well, she really wants something that represents Puerto Rico, like a T-shirt, a flag or a poster, because she attaches that to Gina.'"

So Cummins called one of his main contacts in the local Puerto Rican community, asking if he could help.

"So within days somebody had brought three iPhones," said Cummins, "and we were able to get the phone to Michelle so she could talk to Gina."

Ironically, a few days later, the FBI would order the girls not to communicate with each other until after the trial, so as not to jeopardize the criminal case now being built against Castro.

On Thursday morning, Councilman Matt Zone, who represented Ward 15, visited the DeJesus home to see if there was anything he could do for Gina.

"Gina was smiling from ear to ear," said Zone, who had become close friends with Felix and Nancy over the years. "It was a special moment. I was very choked up."

On his way out, Councilman Zone told reporters that Gina wanted to get her hair done, buy makeup, and see a dentist.

Another visitor that day was Pastor Angel Arroya, a close family friend and one of the DeJesus family's staunchest supporters at the annual vigils.

"[Gina's] asking for ice cream and chicken sandwiches," he said, "and she's just very happy to be back home and surrounded by her relatives."

During her nine years of captivity, Gina had forgotten how to speak Spanish, and kept asking her family and friends to speak only English.

On Thursday afternoon, Gina and her mother went out into the backyard for about an hour and a half, until a TV news helicopter came and hovered overhead.

Gina's cousin Sylvia Colon said that all the media attention was making Gina and her family feel trapped.

"It comes down to freedom," said Colon. "And I think she came out of one prison and, to some degree, she's in another prison."

On Thursday night, more than 150 people honored Michelle Knight at a rally in an open field on Seymour Avenue. The bells at the Immanuel Evangelical Lutheran Church rang out, as the crowd formed a circle, releasing eighty balloons into the night sky.

Community activist Judy Martin said the neighborhood wanted to honor Michelle, who had never had a vigil held for her while she was missing.

"We want her to know that we care about her and are thinking about her," said Martin. "If we had known, we would have been there to help her too."

Meanwhile, Michelle remained in the MetroHealth Medical Center, reportedly undergoing facial reconstruction surgery. Her room was full of flowers, cards, gifts and balloons from strangers who wanted to show their love.

"People who didn't even know me," she said, "were showing me more love than I had ever felt in my entire life."

* * *

On Friday morning, Ohio Attorney General Mike DeWine confirmed that Ariel Castro had fathered Amanda Berry's six-year-old daughter, Jocelyn. He said the DNA test had been fast-tracked, with Ohio BCI forensic scientists working through the night. The normal turnaround for a DNA result is three weeks. Castro's DNA was also compared against samples taken from other crime scenes in Ohio, but so far there were no matches.

That morning, Cleveland City Council members Brian Cummins, Matt Zone and Dona Brady announced they were setting up the Cleveland Courage Fund, to help the victims financially. So much money was now pouring into the Cleveland Police Department from people moved by the women's story that an organization was needed to ensure it all went to them. It was agreed that everyone would work pro bono, and the fund would be set up as a tax-free, nonprofit organization.

The idea of giving Michelle Knight a new identity was also discussed, so she could totally break free from her past and start a new life.

"Like in a witness protection program," Councilman Cummins explained. "I think it's such a fluid situation with their counseling and their mental issues, that it's literally day-by-day."

Amanda and Gina's families had also hired the Cleveland-based Jones Day law firm to represent the victims and become their main point of contact.

"We knew we were going to be deluged," said Cummins. "We [soon] discussed book and movie deals with attorneys . . . we were talking about the fund and raising money for them and making sure we somehow cared about their future."

It was also announced that the three women would all be represented by the Cleveland public relations firm

Hennes Paynter Communications, which specializes in crisis management.

"We were floored to get the call," said the firm's co-owner Bruce Hennes, "and when we were asked to do this pro bono the answer was, immediately, of course. We're honored to be able to help them."

On Friday afternoon, Michelle Knight was released from the MetroHealth Medical Center and quietly moved into a hospice facility, as there was nowhere else for her to go.

"I felt really alone," said Michelle. "That nobody really understood."

On her release, the hospital issued a statement: "Michelle Knight is in good spirits and would like the community to know that she is extremely grateful for the outpouring of flowers and gifts. She is especially thankful for the Cleveland Courage Fund. She asks that everyone please continue to respect her privacy at this time."

That night, Nancy Ruiz told *ABC News* that she had forgiven Ariel Castro for what he had done to Gina. Only four days after wanting to kill him, she said she had found compassion for him.

"I would hug him and say I did not hate him," she said. "I forgave him many years ago. I said it, 'I forgive whoever done it. Just let her go.'"

On Saturday morning, workmen erected a ten-foot-high metal fence around 2207 Seymour Avenue, to protect the still-active crime scene. After several arson threats, Ariel Castro's house was now under around-the-clock surveillance. An abandoned house next door, which had been searched Thursday, was also boarded up and closed off.

The big question was what should be done with the now

notorious "horror house," which was in foreclosure for over $2,501 in unpaid taxes.

"It's a decision for neighbors and also for the women," explained Councilman Cummins. "The issue is how do we respect the wishes of the survivors in this case, and it's too premature to know what their wishes would be."

Two years earlier, the East Side house where convicted Cleveland serial killer Anthony Sowell had murdered eleven women had been torn down after his trial. Many believed this should set a precedent for 2207 Seymour Avenue to be demolished.

"We can't take it down until it's cleared for evidentiary purposes," explained Cummins. "I don't want to make a decision without [the survivors' input]."

On Saturday, Amanda's grandfather Troy Berry and three of her cousins arrived in Cleveland, after driving from Elizabethton, Tennessee. Her father, Johnny Berry, was too sick to travel, and Amanda planned to visit him and her grandmother Fern Gentry as soon as possible.

The seventy-three-year-old family patriarch said he was looking forward to meeting his great-granddaughter Jocelyn for the first time, as well as keeping a promise he had once made to Amanda. When she was a child, Troy had promised to give Amanda his 1986 Chevrolet Monte Carlo once she was old enough to drive. And during their phone call after her escape on Monday, Amanda had asked if he still had the car. Troy said he did and it was waiting for her.

"When she went missing," Berry said, "I could never bring myself to get rid of the Chevy. Every time I looked at it, I imagined her smiling . . . and I prayed to God that she'd come back to us."

That afternoon, Barbara Knight hired Cleveland attorney Jay Milano to assert her rights to see her daughter. She was angry at not being informed Michelle had left the hospital, and that no one would tell her where she was.

"Barbara Knight is a mother whose daughter has lived through hell," Milano said. "It was hell for her too. She came up to be with her daughter, to hug her, to help her heal. She's been stonewalled down the line. It's abhorrent."

MetroHealth Medical Center pointed out that Michelle Knight was an adult, quite capable of making her own decisions. They were merely protecting her rights.

"I'm not saying that Michelle is legally incompetent," said Milano. "That's baloney. But nothing she says is reliable. Anyone that damaged doesn't have a handle on what they need."

The attorney denied that Barbara and Michelle had a "strained relationship," saying that they had always got on.

"Ten years of hell have passed," he said. "Family is important to the healing process."

That night, *Saturday Night Live* featured comedian Bobby Moynihan portraying Ariel Castro in a skit, lampooning the lack of media coverage of the recent Benghazi hearings, which had been overshadowed by the Cleveland abductions story and Jodi Arias's murder conviction.

In the skit Arias was first called to testify before a panel by Republican committee chairman Darrell Issa, played by Bill Hader, who is then challenged by a Democratic representative played by Kenan Thompson, calling it a cheap ploy to get ratings.

"What next," asked Thompson, "the guy from Cleveland who kept those women in his basement?"

Then *SNL* star Bobby Moynihan, playing Ariel Castro, is seen slumped in a chair, dressed in an orange jumpsuit and looking creepy.

"Does this mean I don't get to testify?" Castro asked the panel.

29

"THE MONSTER'S
A GONER"

Sunday was Mother's Day and at 10:00 A.M., Jones Day attorney James Wooley held a brief press conference. After appealing to the media to leave them alone, he read out statements from each of the three victims, thanking everyone for their support.

"Thank you so much for everything you're doing and continue to do," read Amanda Berry's statement. "I'm so happy to be home with my family."

Gina DeJesus's statement read: "I'm so happy to be home. I thank everybody for your prayers. I just want time now to be with my family."

"Thank you to everyone for your support and good wishes," read Michelle Knight's statement. "I'm healthy, happy and safe and will reach out to family, friends and supporters in good time."

After reading the statement, Wooley said none of the women would be doing any media interviews during the criminal investigation into Ariel Castro.

"Respect this most basic request," he said, "give them

time, space and privacy so they can get stronger. There may be a time at some point they will want to tell their story, but that will not be until they tell us they're ready and criminal proceedings are over."

Besides Wooley, attorneys Kathy Joseph, Heather Kimmel, and Henry Hilow, were also representing the survivors on a pro bono basis.

A few hours later, at a secret location outside Cleveland, Pedro and Onil Castro gave an exclusive interview to CNN reporter Martin Savidge. They were now well groomed and wearing smart shirts and ties, looking nothing like their grungy, unshaven mug shots taken almost a week earlier.

"You all went to your mom's for dinner?" asked Savidge at the beginning of the seventeen-minute interview.

"Yeah," replied Onil, "we went to Mom's for dinner."

Onil said the first sign of trouble came when police pulled over his brother Ariel's sports car in the McDonald's parking lot.

"I'm wondering why he's pulling [in]," said Onil, "we just ate."

When Onil asked if he needed the bathroom, Ariel replied that the police were right behind them and he didn't know why. Within seconds two officers were standing on either side of the car, asking for Ariel's ID. Then Onil had reached for his own ID, and one of them went for his weapon.

"And I said, 'I haven't done anything, what's going on here?'" said Onil. "He says, 'All I can tell you is that you are in for some serious allegations.'"

Soon afterward, police had arrested Pedro, who was passed out at his mother's house.

"I was sleeping," he told Savidge, "and I don't remember the police in my room. And I was thinking because I had an open container . . . they were taking me in because of that."

The Castro brothers had spent the next two days in jail, without knowing why they had been arrested. Pedro had finally asked a prison officer to find out.

"So she comes back [with] a piece of paper written down whatever I was in for," said Pedro. "I didn't have my reading glasses. I looked and said, 'Oh, open containers?' She said, 'No, read it again.' And I said, 'Oh, kidnapping. What's this kidnapping?'"

In jail they were kept in separate cells, but Pedro and Onil did see Ariel as he was escorted past their cells by guards to use the toilet.

Pedro said that Ariel had only said the word "peace" to him, while Onil said he had told him he loved him, but they were never going to see each other again.

They said they only discovered what Ariel had done after investigators told them the three missing women had been found in his house. Onil described that moment as "heart-dropping," saying he could not believe it.

"You had been to the house?" asked Savidge.

"Yes," replied Pedro.

"How often?"

"I didn't go to his house very much," said Pedro, "but when I did he wouldn't let me in past the kitchen. I would sit down . . . in the kitchen because he had alcohol. He would take me in the kitchen, give me a shot."

Pedro said when he had once asked Ariel why he had blocked off his house with heavy curtains, he said it was to keep the kitchen warm and save on his gas bill. Pedro said the radio or the television would always be turned up high, so it was impossible to hear anything else.

"Did you in any way know, help, assist your brother in the horrible things he's accused of doing?" asked Savidge.

"Absolutely not," replied Onil. "No idea that this horrific crime was going on."

"No," Pedro agreed.

"You know [there are] people who say you had to know?" observed Savidge.

"For those people out there, I'm going to tell you something," said Pedro angrily. "I had nothing to do with this and I don't know how my brother got away with it for so many years."

"He fooled you?" asked Savidge.

"He fooled me," Pedro agreed, "because I used to go there . . . to work on cars, clean the yard, help him out and stuff. But I never went beyond the kitchen."

Then Savidge asked how they felt about Ariel, now they knew what he had done.

"A monster," Onil replied. "I hope he rots in that jail. I want him to suffer to the last extent. I don't care if we even feed him, for what he has done to my life and my family's."

"I feel the same way," said Pedro.

"To the both of you now," asked Savidge, "he no longer exists?"

"Yeah," replied Onil. "The monster's a goner. I'm glad that he left the door unlocked. Maybe he did it on purpose . . . and wanted to get caught. Maybe [his] time was up. But if he did it that way he shouldn't have went to Mamma's house and picked me up and put me in a car, if he knows that was going to happen."

Finally, Savidge asked the brothers what they would have done, if they had known Ariel had three kidnapped women and a child under his roof.

"I would call the cops because that ain't right," said Pedro. "If I knew I would have reported it, brother or no brother."

*   *   *

Gina DeJesus celebrated Mother's Day with her family for the first time in nine years. After having her hair done in a local beauty salon, Gina came home to her favorite home-cooked meal of corn beef empanadas and potato balls (ground beef and potatoes rolled into balls and fried).

"It was the best Mother's Day I could ever have," said a beaming Nancy Ruiz. "I still feel it is a dream."

Felix was so delighted to have his family together again, he was already planning the next celebration.

"We want to have a block party and close the streets down," he told a reporter. "That's the best Mother's Day present any mother can have."

As part of her healing process, Gina had now adopted Lola, one of the three dogs living at 2207 Seymour Avenue. Gina had bonded with the small terrier mix while she was a prisoner and wanted to keep her.

After the escape, Ariel Castro's dogs, a Chihuahua named Dina, a shih tzu called Drake, and Lola, had been housed by an animal rescue group. Now Lola would move in with Gina, while the two other dogs would be put up for adoption.

Amanda Berry celebrated Mother's Day with her visiting family from Elizabethton, who had decided to stay an extra day in Cleveland. But it was a bittersweet occasion without her late mother there.

Troy Berry said he had really bonded with his new great-granddaughter, Jocelyn.

"She jumped on my lap and said, 'Papaw, give me a hug,'" he told a TV reporter. "She's so smart. [Amanda] said she taught her a lot at home when [Castro] wasn't around."

Berry said the family took photographs of the reunion but were told by the FBI not to have them developed until after the trial.

On Monday morning, Amanda visited her mother's

grave. It was a moving occasion as Amanda was finally reunited with her beloved mother, who had died seven years earlier of what many believed to have been a broken heart.

"[Amanda] went to the cemetery this morning," her uncle Curtis Berry told the New York *Daily News.*

He also revealed that Amanda was now considering moving to Elizabethton, Tennessee, with Jocelyn, to get away from Cleveland.

"She has more kin here than anywhere else," he said. "This is her home."

As Amanda Berry visited her mother's grave, private investigator Chris Giannini interviewed Emily Castro at the Rockville Correctional Facility in Rockville, Indiana, where she was serving twenty-five years for attempting to kill her infant daughter. Giannini, who audio-recorded the interview, was seeking evidence to appeal Fernando Colon's 2005 conviction for sexually molesting Emily and her younger sister, Arlene.

He first asked Emily what she now thought of her father.

"He's a monster," she replied, "and then actually seeing the guy that hugged us and smiled with us and took us to eat and cared about us supposedly, is the guy who's in handcuffs."

A tearful Emily, now twenty-five, said she now felt her father had used her in the kidnappings of Amanda Berry and Gina DeJesus, both of whom she knew from school. Giannani asked if she was aware that Gina and Amanda were saying that she was in the car just before they were abducted.

"It hurts so bad," said Emily. "I'm just saying that, that I feel used. I feel like I'm nothing to him, do you know what I mean? I feel nothing anymore."

Emily said it bothered her that her father hunted for victims in the streets around Wilbur Wright Middle School, which she and her sisters attended.

"He would come to his own kids' neighborhood," she told Giannini. "He didn't consider anything about us being his kids. He didn't consider that he's not only [kidnapping children] but he's hurting us."

During the interview, Emily said her father was often violent when she was growing up and savagely beat her late mother. Once she had jumped on her father's back, and tried to stab him with a pencil, when he attacked her mother after her brain surgery.

She said that her father had never abused her or her sisters and was overprotective, insisting they always wear shorts under their skirts, T-shirts over their bathing suits and even shower with their underwear on.

She said she rarely visited 2207 Seymour Avenue after her parents broke up, and when she did, was never allowed past the kitchen.

"I'm thinking of the dates, to where he would actually have [the girls]," said Emily. "The upstairs was blocked off with a big bass speaker."

She had last spoken to her father three days before he was arrested, and now felt betrayed by him as she and her sisters had all known Amanda and Gina.

"I've seen Gina a couple of times," she said, "and then it couldn't be coincidence. And so I had to bury my dad as being a good person completely."

Finally, when Giannini asked if she had been coerced by her father to testify that Fernando Colon had sexually abused her, she refused to change her story.

"She's standing by her father," said Giannini, "so you get this conflict in her head of, 'My dad's a bad man but my dad told me to say these things.'"

30

"THE BEST DEFENSE
WE CAN"

On Tuesday at noon, Cleveland police removed the barriers outside 2207 Seymour Avenue, allowing pedestrians and drivers their first glimpse of the "horror house." Seymour Avenue would become a ghoulish sight-seeing destination, and from now on, to the annoyance of neighbors, hundreds of people would arrive daily to stare at it and pose for photographs outside.

"I just came to see it with my own eyes," said Stan Miller, who lived on the other side of Cleveland, "but the next time I come, I'll probably bring my cell phone, take a picture."

Armed police still guarded the house around the clock to prevent curiosity seekers coming in, as it was still a crime scene.

"It's like a movie . . . over there," said neighbor Arivar Santiago. "A lot of people are going to come from other states to take a picture of the house."

Late Tuesday afternoon, Ariel Castro met with his new criminal attorneys, Craig Weintraub and Jaye Schlachet for the first time. The two prominent Cleveland lawyers, with more than sixty years' legal experience between them, had been contacted by Castro's uncle Cesi two days after his arrest.

"Both my partner and I have had high-profile cases in our careers," said Weintraub, "and when the call came in we both had to decide the advantages and disadvantages of getting involved in this . . . extremely high profile case. And we had to talk to our families, because we knew that there's the potential to be scorned as the attorney for someone . . . accused of committing such heinous crimes."

Since his transfer to Cuyahoga County Jail, Castro's behavior had become increasingly bizarre. He spent most of his time lying on his mat, either sleeping or staring at the empty bunk overhead. Occasionally he would walk around his tiny cell naked, even though he had complained it was too cold. Several times he was seen by guards drinking Kool-Aid and staring at himself in the mirror.

As he was still on suicide watch, every ten minutes a guard looked through his cell door window, to make sure he was okay. He did not have a radio or television in the cell or access to newspapers or magazines.

On Sunday morning, Castro had refused to take a shower, complaining of a headache. Later, he had attempted to floss his teeth using the loose strings from his mat. A sergeant had reprimanded him, before trimming the mat to stop him from doing it again.

During Tuesday's three-hour meeting with his two attorneys, Castro insisted on being naked. And whenever tough questions came up, he would order Weintraub to turn off the air conditioner. From the beginning he appeared to enjoy toying with his two defenders.

As he had already confessed to detectives without a lawyer present, the main issue for the defense was whether

Castro would face the death penalty, as fetus murder is classed as aggravated homicide under Ohio law.

"The majority of the charges were indefensible," Weintraub said later. "We knew he would spend the rest of his life in prison, so it would just be keeping him off death row."

When Weintraub and Schlachet left Cuyahoga County Jail, they were besieged by media representatives with interview requests for Ariel Castro.

"There were television producers from the major networks waiting for us," said Weintraub. "We spoke to them and took their business cards, and said maybe we'll be in touch."

The next morning, the two attorneys told a TV reporter that their client would plead not guilty to all the charges if a grand jury indicted him. Weintraub said Ariel Castro had been "demonized" by the world's press before anyone knew the whole story.

"The initial portrayal by the media has been one of a 'monster,'" said Weintraub, "and that's not the impression I got when I talked to him for three hours."

Asked how the three women ended up in 2207 Seymour Avenue, Weintraub was evasive.

"That fact will be disclosed as the case progresses," he said. "I am aware of how he came into contact with them."

Jaye Schlachet vowed that he and his partner would mount the "best defense" possible.

"I know the media wants to jump to conclusions," he said, "and all the people in the community want to say terrible things about the person who's accused. We're not even at the beginning of the process. If this was a marathon race, we're not even at the starting line yet."

Weintraub also said that Castro loved his daughter Jocelyn, and was determined to remain in her life.

"I can tell you that Mr. Castro is extremely committed to the well-being and positive future for his daughter, who he loves dearly," said Weintraub. "And if people find that to be a disconnect from what he's alleged to have done, then the people will just have to deal with it."

The next day, the three first responders to 2207 Seymour Avenue spoke publicly about it for the first time at a special ceremony at the Cleveland Police Patrolmen's Association headquarters. Police officer Barbara Johnson said that after getting the initial call that Amanda Berry had been found, she prayed it was not another hoax. She became emotional as she described going upstairs and Michelle Knight running into her arms.

"Michelle hugged me first," said Johnson, "then clutched me and said, 'Don't let me go!' You can't really describe how I felt . . . it rips the heart out of my chest."

Following the rescue, Johnson spent the next six hours with the victims at MetroHealth Medical Center, comforting them. She said no amount of police training could have prepared her for this, and she can't get it out of her mind.

Officer Anthony Espada said he too was haunted by that day.

"I've broken down [crying] a few times . . . in private since then," he said. "Those three girls are my heroes . . . after what [they] went through in that house all those years."

On Friday afternoon, as the Cleveland Courage Fund hit the $500,000 mark, Ariel Castro's mother, Lillian Rodriguez, and sister Marisol Alicea Castro visited Inmate C29. Later that day two reporters arrived from New York but were turned away.

"Ariel Castro was emphatic that he did not want to meet with any news person," wrote one of his guards in a report.

Cuyahoga County Jail logs also showed that Castro periodically cleaned his cell, and thanked the guards who bought him breakfast. Every morning he was allowed out into the pod for twenty minutes under close supervision, while his cell was searched. Then he would be returned to his cell and locked up for the rest of the day.

Soon after his arrest, the Castro family met to discuss how to proceed.

"We had a family meeting," said Maria Montes, "and talked about it. We've all tried to remain vigilant of the fact that he does still have a mother . . . and siblings who at one point loved him and were fooled. Obviously this has to be hurting them."

At the meeting, it was decided that Ariel Castro, Jr.,—who was now using his middle name Anthony—would be the Castro family spokesman. From now on all media requests would officially go through him, although his uncle Cesi Castro would give the occasional interview.

The Cleveland abductions was now a huge story worldwide, and hundreds of media requests were pouring into Hennes Paynter Communications, all vying for interviews with the victims.

"They're looking for the 'get' right now," explained founder Bruce Hennes. "There's a worldwide scramble. They want the picture, the interview. This is *the* hottest news."

Hennes said that so far no one at his PR company had spoken to the three women, and everything was being handled by their attorneys at Jones Day. The main priority was not to compromise the criminal case against Ariel Castro.

"That's why the women are not speaking publicly," he

explained. "At this point, our only role is to compile a list of media people who are interested in interviewing them. At the appropriate time the women will make their own decisions about whom they want to talk to and when."

On Tuesday, May 21—two weeks after their escape—the Cleveland Courage Fund had raised more than $650,000, from more than five thousand donors. To mark the occasion, Hennes Paynter Communications released a special message from the three women to all their supporters.

AMANDA, GINA & MICHELLE OFFER
THANKS TO COMMUNITY

We are the attorneys who have come together to help Amanda Berry, Gina DeJesus and Michelle Knight. These three brave women have asked us to give this message to everyone who has expressed concern and support. Amanda, Gina and Michelle want you to know they are doing well. They are happy and safe and continue to heal, a process that requires time and privacy.

Since we first spoke publicly on their behalf, it has been wonderful to see that their plea for privacy has been answered and respected. The media has disappeared from their front lawns and their neighborhoods are no longer experiencing traffic jams from news vehicles and curious onlookers. You have no idea how much this means to them and has helped in their recovery process.

Their first public message included a simple, heartfelt thanks to well-wishers and supporters for "Everything you are doing." That "everything" now includes perhaps the greatest gift of all—the space and time to reconnect with their families and recover and rebuild their lives. And so they say again, "Thank you. Thank you so much!"

We continue to receive numerous generous offers to support Amanda, Gina and Michelle and their families. The outpouring of public support has been nothing short of remarkable.

To have complete strangers offer loving support in the form of money, goods and services, reaching out to help like a family member, is appreciated in ways that are impossible to put into words. Amanda, Gina and Michelle, who have asked for nothing, are frankly over-whelmed by it all.

You have touched their hearts in ways they will never forget. So again, they collectively say "Thank You. Thank you so much."

We understand some people may be confused about the best way to help. We are in direct, private and on-going conversations with Amanda, Gina and Michelle about many matters, including your generosity.

While they appreciate the generous offers of goods and services, for now, they are trying to assess what they need today and for years to come. That's why do-nations to the Cleveland Courage Funds are so wel-come.

We are confident the Cleveland Courage Funds are the legitimate, appropriate and most effective vehicles for this effort. In fact, donations to the Cleveland Cour-age Funds are already being distributed to the four sur-vivors consistent with the concepts behind the trusts that are being set up. And as soon as the trusts are in place, one hundred percent of all donations to the Cleveland Courage Funds will go into those trusts.

Cleveland is known for its generosity. Amanda, Gina, Michelle and Amanda's daughter are indeed grateful for that generosity, as are we.

Charles Ramsey was now making the most of his fifteen minutes of fame. Rap superstar Snoop Dogg played his now infamous profanity-filled cell phone call to the police dispatcher on his GGN news network, before inviting him into the studio for an interview.

"You're a real hero," said the rapper. "You're somebody that I want to meet. You're a great guy and you should be commended. There should be more people like you in the world, and hopefully we'll be able to rid the world of fucking peasants that's knocking up girls like that. We love you, Mr. Ramsey."

A local restaurant chain also offered him free hamburgers for life, and Hodge's restaurant, where he still washed dishes, launched a special Charles Ramsey–inspired hamburger and T-shirt in his honor.

A Taiwanese online gaming company released a video game called *Charles Ramsey's Burger Bash*. To the sound track of Ramsey's infamous WEWS-TV interview, players hurl cheeseburgers at dozens of little Ariel Castro avatars, poking their heads out of a house closely resembling 2207 Seymour Avenue. One of the Castro avatars strums a bass guitar, while another is on a motorcycle.

Furious, Ramsey's newly appointed attorney issued a statement on his behalf, saying he did not endorse the game, "Ramsey Burgers" or "burgers for life."

"I want everyone to know that I have nothing to do with this trash," read his statement.

But Ramsey did sign a book deal with a Cleveland publisher to write his autobiography, as well as inking a $10,000 contract to go on the celebrity speaking circuit.

But to top it all, the Eric C. Conn law firm in Stanville, Kentucky, announced plans to commission a statue of Charles Ramsey, which would be donated to a Cleveland museum.

"I can't think of a better way to commend my friend

Charles," said Conn, "than having a statue made in his honor."

But less than two months later, Ramsey would tell the *MailOnline* that fame had ruined his life and he was broke.

"I'm broke, bro, and that's the truth," he said. "I don't have an address, I don't live anywhere."

On Friday, May 24, the Ohio BCI started testing the several hundred pieces of evidence recovered from 2207 Seymour Avenue. These included various chains, padlocks and other restraints, as well as Castro's .357 Luger service revolver, which he used to play Russian roulette with his terrified victims.

BCI forensic scientist Joshua Barr examined the powerful weapon and successfully test-fired it in his laboratory.

"I determined that it was operable," said Barr. "It could expel a projectile."

He also measured and weighed the various lengths of rusty chains that Castro had used to restrain his three captives.

"There was a huge amount of evidence," explained Barr. "Some of the chains had smaller chains attached to them by padlocks."

The total length of chains scattered all over Castro's house measured 99 feet, 3 inches and weighed 92.29 pounds.

Compared with his victims, Ariel Castro was living in five-star luxury. He had now requested to be taken off suicide watch and his jailhouse logs, still updated every ten minutes, show he was most concerned with cleanliness and hygiene. He regularly showered and brushed his teeth, even asking for disinfectant and a brush to clean out his cell and toilet facilities.

When he wasn't sleeping or having one of his three regular meals, Castro liked to snack, using his commissary money to purchase peanut butter crackers and Snickers bars. Under Cuyahoga County Jail rules inmates can spend up to $30 a week—taken from any money they had at the time of their arrest—to buy various items on sale at the commissary.

He constantly complained to his guards that his cell was too cold, but rarely bothered to put on any clothes.

"It's not the Ritz-Carlton," said his attorney Craig Weintraub. "It's been difficult."

At the beginning of June, Ariel Castro was taken off suicide watch and moved to another part of the jail. In his new cell, he was provided with a television with a remote control and now spent most of his time watching movies. As he was no longer considered a suicide risk, Inmate C29 was put on the "razor list," but declined the privilege as he was now growing a full beard.

31
INDICTED!

Late Friday afternoon, June 7, a month and a day after his arrest, a Cuyahoga County grand jury returned an unprecedented 329-count indictment against Ariel Castro. The indictments only covered the period from August 2002, when the first victim, Michelle Knight, was abducted, until February 2007. Prosecutor Tim McGinty promised there would be more to follow.

"Today's indictment represents a first major step in the criminal justice process," said McGinty. "Our investigation continues and we will present our findings to the grand jury."

The 142-page indictment accused Ariel Castro of two counts of aggravated murder, for causing the unlawful termination of a pregnancy. He was also indicted on 139 counts of rape, 177 counts of kidnapping, seven counts of gross sexual imposition, three counts of felonious assault and a single count of possessing criminal tools.

After the remaining indictments came down, the County Prosecutor's Capital Review Committee would meet to decide whether to attach a death penalty specification to it.

After the grand jury indictments, the three victims' lawyers released a statement expressing their satisfaction.

"We have a great legal system," read the statement, "plus confidence and faith in the prosecutor's office and its decisions. Now, we stand back and let the judicial process unfold."

On Saturday morning, Ariel Castro's attorneys announced he would plead not guilty to each and every charge, warning prosecutors not to use the death penalty as a bargaining chip.

"The indictment is being reviewed," Jaye Schlachet told the Reuters news agency, "and a 'not guilty' plea will be entered at the scheduled arraignment."

Schlachet said the death penalty was inappropriate for Castro's case, noting there was no physical evidence or medical records relating to the miscarriages.

"It would be unprecedented to pursue the death penalty for an alleged death of a fetus," he said, "without the death of the mother. We remain hopeful that the prosecutor's office and the public understand and agree that a death penalty should never be used as leverage to attempt to obtain a plea bargain."

At 1:45 P.M. on Wednesday, June 12, a handcuffed and shackled Ariel Castro was led into the Cuyahoga Common Pleas Court for his arraignment. It had been moved to Judge Deena Calabrese's twenty-second-floor courtroom, to accommodate all the media.

Just before walking in through the courtroom doors, Castro, handcuffed, shackled and dressed in a bright orange prison jumpsuit, had a smirk on his face. Then as soon as the courtroom opened, he lowered his head and shut his eyes, as bailiffs escorted him to the defense table.

Throughout the one-minute hearing he kept his head bowed, staring at the floor, as a line of news photographers and TV camera crews filmed him from the public gallery.

"Good morning," said Judge Calabrese. "I have a very hefty indictment in front of me."

The defense then waived the reading of the 329-count indictment, telling the judge that their client was pleading not guilty to everything. After entering the plea, Judge Calabrese announced that Judge Michael Russo had been assigned to the case, with the first pretrial hearing scheduled for June 19.

Then the judge continued Castro's $8 million bond and dismissed the court.

Outside the courtroom, Craig Weintraub acknowledged that some of the kidnapping charges "cannot be disputed." He told reporters that Castro's not guilty plea would force prosecutors to decide if it was worth pursuing the death penalty, thereby compelling the three victims to testify at a high-profile trial.

"We are very sensitive to the emotional strain and impact that a trial would have on the women, their families and this community," said Weintraub. "Mr. Castro currently faces hundreds of years in prison . . . and it is our hope that we can continue to work toward a resolution, to avoid having an unnecessary trial about aggravated murder and the death penalty."

When asked if the defense would accept a plea deal to avoid going to trial if prosecutors agreed to drop the murder charges, Weintraub was evasive.

"We're not answering any questions at this time," he snapped. "The statement speaks for itself."

After the arraignment, attorney Jim Wooley issued another statement on behalf of the victims.

"We understand the legal process needs to run its course," it read. "We are hopeful for a just and prompt resolution. We have great faith in the prosecutor's office and the court."

The next day, Amanda Berry and Jocelyn made the eight-hour drive to Elizabethton, Tennessee, for a five-day reunion with her father over the Father's Day weekend. A few weeks earlier, Johnny Berry had sold his exclusive story to the *National Enquirer*. And a photographer was at his house to take the first photographs of Amanda, which would be on the front page of the next edition.

"When Amanda came through my front door it was like a miracle," said Berry. "She started crying and ran up to me and we hugged for the first time in ten years."

Then Amanda gave her father a silver ring with the word DAD engraved on it, as a Father's Day gift.

During the visit, Berry got to know his new granddaughter, who soon became the apple of his eye.

"She gave me a hug," he said, "and I instantly knew deep in my heart that she's a Berry. She has her mom's beauty, strength and intelligence. I said to her, 'Hi, Jocelyn, I'm your grandpa Johnny, and I love you.'"

On Father's Day, Amanda and Jocelyn attended a barbecue at a local campsite, so they could meet the rest of the Berry family. Amanda told them how she was busy getting her life back on track, and had almost completed her and Jocelyn's medical and dental checkups.

"[She's] thinking about putting Jocelyn into school next year," said her father. "Amanda is going to finish up her high school education and wants to eventually go to junior college."

But he also revealed that Amanda was suffering from post-traumatic stress disorder.

"She's having nightmares every night," he told the

Enquirer, "waking up screaming and crying, terrified that Castro is coming after her, or that she's still a prisoner. She told me she's afraid her freedom is a dream and she's going to wake up to the horror of finding out she's still a prisoner."

Back in Cleveland, Ariel Castro wrote several Father's Day letters to his children from his jail cell, which were never delivered.

"I still can't believe what I did," he wrote, "to put me in the situation that I'm in now."

At 9:00 A.M. on Wednesday, June 19, Ariel Castro was back in Cuyahoga County Common Pleas Court for his first pretrial hearing. He was led into the courtroom in leg irons and handcuffs, wearing his bright orange jail garb. Once again he kept his head down and his eyes clenched shut for the entire hearing.

Later, Prosecutor Tim McGinty would accuse Castro of putting on an act to gain sympathy.

"Don't be fooled by this head-down, woe-to-me demeanor he has displayed since his arrest," said the prosecutor. "He's a manipulator. He has no remorse."

As Judge Michael Russo entered the courtroom, Castro, who was sitting at the defense table between his two attorneys, refused to look at him.

"Mr. Castro, you are here for a first pretrial [hearing] in your matter," said the judge. "Are you aware of that, sir?"

"Yes," answered Castro, without looking up.

"Okay," Judge Russo continued, "you are here with your attorneys, Mr. Schlachet and Mr. Weintraub. Have you been working with them over the past couple of weeks?"

"Yes," Castro replied.

Then the judge asked the prosecution about the transfer of discovery to the defense. Prosecutor Tim McGinty said his office had now handed over all the defendant's interrogation videos, and was soon going to make the victims' journals available. He said the BCI were still analyzing DNA and other forensic evidence, which would be completed sometime in July.

"What is the status of any additional charges that might be presented to the grand jury?" asked Judge Russo.

"We are presenting additional evidence to the grand jury next week and the week after," said the prosecutor. "We expect that we are going to request further indictments to cover the additional period."

McGinty added that the defense wanted to visit 2207 Seymour Avenue, and he had no objections.

Then Judge Russo set a tentative trial date for August 5, saying he wanted a "speedy trial." But he promised to give the defense more time if needed. Then he set another hearing for the following Wednesday, by which time the defense would have received more discovery materials and have a better idea of how to proceed.

"Mr. Castro," said the judge, "do you have any questions for the court?"

"No," said Castro, who was then led out by a bailiff to a barrage of clicks from the news cameras in the public gallery.

After the hearing, Craig Weintraub told reporters the defense was now focusing on whether the prosecution had enough evidence for an aggravated murder conviction, for forcing a miscarriage.

"That's the most important aspect of the case to us," he explained. "But as of right now, we haven't received any of the evidence that would support an aggravated murder conviction."

He also repeated that his client did not want his victims to have to go through all the stress of a public trial.

"It is not our intent to have to do that," he said.

That same day, as the Cleveland Courage Fund approached the $1 million mark, Cleveland Democratic Representative John Barnes introduced a bill that would provide Amanda, Gina and Michelle with $25,000 for every year of their "involuntary servitude," as well as college tuition and medical assistance.

The bill, which had the support of both sides in the Ohio House of Representatives, would require a federal waiver to make the women eligible for a lifetime of government medical assistance.

On Wednesday, June 26, Judge Michael Russo ordered Ariel Castro to undergo a psychiatric competency evaluation, to see if he was fit to stand trial. At the second pretrial hearing, Castro's defense said they had not met with their client since the previous week's hearing, but would soon do so to discuss the nine hundred pieces of discovery they had received the previous evening.

"So, Mr. Castro," said Judge Russo, "are you aware your attorneys have received a number of documents from the state and they will be sharing the information with you?"

"Yes," said Castro, his eyes glued to the floor.

The judge then told him that as the question of his competency to stand trial might be raised at a later stage, he would undergo a full competency evaluation, so there would be no grounds for an appeal.

"I don't know anything about Mr. Castro," said the judge, "and our meetings here in court are very brief, so I am going to refer him for a competency evaluation."

The judge told Castro that he had arranged for the director of the Court Psychiatric Clinic, Dr. Phillip Resnick, to examine him the next day and report back to the court.

"So, Mr. Castro," said Russo, "you are going to be talking with Dr. Resnick. He'll only be assessing your ability to understand these proceedings and to assist your attorneys in your defense. Do you understand that?"

"Yes, I do," Castro replied, without looking up.

Then Prosecutor Tim McGinty stood up and said the defendant was quite competent to stand trial.

"We understand your desire to . . . make sure he is competent," said McGinty. "There's absolutely no doubt from the hours of tape and other evidence that he's entirely competent. Knows exactly what he's doing now and did then. But we understand the court's caution."

After the hearing, the three victims' attorneys issued a joint statement, calling for a quick resolution of the case.

"The longer this process lasts, the more painful it is for them," said Michelle's attorney, Kathy Joseph. "And the more sordid details of this horror that get disclosed in this process, the more painful it is for them."

Amanda and Gina's lawyer, James Wooley, said his clients just wanted it all over and welcomed an early trial.

"Any date set by which this may end," he wrote, "is like light at the end of the tunnel."

The next morning, Ariel Castro was taken to the Cuyahoga County Court Psychiatric Clinic in the Justice Center, for his two-and-a-half-hour competency examination by Dr. Phillip Resnick and Dr. Jason Beaman. He told them about his early childhood in Puerto Rico and how he had been sexually abused by an older boy when he was five. He also claimed that after moving to America, his mother had physically abused him daily. When Dr. Resnick asked him how he felt about that, Castro said he had prayed that she would die.

Then Dr. Resnick asked him about his educational history, and Castro said he was a "satisfactory" student, but was "teased" by the other boys and could not remember why. He admitted to being suspended in junior high for touching a girl's breast, saying his first relationship was in seventh grade and had lasted five months.

He told the doctors that his next girlfriend was Nilda Figueroa, whom he met when he was twenty and she was seventeen. Over their thirteen year relationship they had four children, and Castro claimed the relationship had ended after she was unfaithful.

"He said the relationship was often violent," wrote Dr. Resnick in his report, "and that he was charged with domestic violence twice. He said, 'I hit her because she hit me first.'"

Castro maintained that all the violence had been his reaction to her verbal harassment and being hit first, although he did admit to striking Nilda with a dumbbell, requiring her to have stitches.

"He was eager to tell his story," said Dr. Resnick, "in a self-serving way."

Castro said his next relationship was with Lillian Roldan in 2000, but they did not live together or have children. He had ended the relationship, after abducting Michelle and Amanda because "my life was very stressful at the time."

Castro said he had been fired the previous September by the Cleveland School District after twenty-one years driving a bus, and had been out of work since. He received unemployment, as well as supplementing his income as an "active musician."

Asked about his psychiatric history, Castro said he had experienced his first mental health problem around 1980, when he began getting headaches and feeling disoriented and confused.

"He had these periods of confusion 'off and on,'" wrote Dr. Resnick. "He said that during these periods, he would 'make bad decisions.'"

Castro said he had also suffered bouts of depression since the age of ten, but they never lasted more than a week.

"Mr. Castro told us he has never had suicidal thoughts," wrote Dr. Resnick. "He was on suicide watch when he was first arrested, because 'I knew that this was a way to be separated from the general population.'"

Castro said he knew he was facing more than three hundred counts, including rape and kidnapping, and the prosecutor would soon be filing even more charges and considering the death penalty.

"He said he does not want the death penalty," wrote Dr. Resnick.

At the end of his six-page report, Dr. Resnick wrote that Ariel Castro was competent to stand trial.

"In summary," wrote Dr. Resnick, "it is our opinion, with reasonable medical certainty, that Mr. Castro is capable of understanding the nature and objectives of the proceedings against him and able to assist counsel in his own defense."

On Tuesday, July 2, Amanda Berry, Gina DeJesus and Michelle Knight met for the first time since their escape, in the offices of the Jones Day law firm. With the Cleveland Courage Fund now past the $1 million mark, they had each prepared handwritten notes to thank the nearly ten thousand complete strangers who had given.

After attorney James Wooley first vetted their three statements, one by one Ariel Castro's victims recorded a three-and-a-half-minute video that would be released on *YouTube* a week later.

"First and foremost," said Amanda confidently, looking

straight at the camera, "I want everyone to know how happy I am to be home with my family and my friends. It's been unbelievable. I want to thank everyone who has helped me and my family through this entire ordeal. Everyone who has been there to support us. It's been a blessing to have such an outpouring of love and kindness.

"I'm getting stronger each day and having my privacy has helped immensely. I ask that everyone continues to respect our privacy and give us time to have a normal life."

Then a nervous-looking Gina DeJesus appeared, sporting a chic new hairdo and flanked by her parents.

"I would like to say thank you for your support," she said with a smile.

Felix continued, "I'd like to thank everybody who donated to the Courage Fund for these girls. I'd also like to thank the family, for having so much passions [*sic*] and faith and the strength to go along with us."

Then Gina's mother, Nancy, came on camera.

"I would like personally to thank the Courage Fund, everybody in general, and I'm also saying my community, my neighbors—every single one—they know who they are. Awesome. So people, I'm talking at—not just people but parents in general that have a loved one missing, please do me one big favor—count on your neighbors. Don't be afraid to ask for the help, because help is available."

Last, Michelle came on screen and was totally unrecognizable from the high school pictures that had been so widely circulated after the escape. She looked well groomed and radiated confidence, as she spoke for the first time in public.

"I just want everyone to know I'm doing just fine," she said. "I may have been through hell and back but I am strong enough to walk through hell with a smile on my face and with my head held high and my feet firmly on the ground.

"Walking hand in hand with my best friend, I will not let the situation define who I am. I will define the situation. I don't want to be consumed by hatred, but that being said, we need to take a leap of faith and know that God is in control.

"I am in control of my own destiny with the guidance of God. I have no problems expressing how I feel inside. Be positive. Learn that it's [more] important to give than to receive. Thank you for all your prayers. I'm looking forward to my brand-new life. Thank you."

At 8:45 the next morning, Ariel Castro returned to Judge Michael Russo's courtroom for his competency hearing. This time Castro, who was still shackled with blue wrist restraints, had his eyes open.

"Mr. Castro," began Judge Russo, "recently you took a trip to our court clinic. Do you recall the individuals you met with there?"

"Your Honor," replied Castro. "Two gentlemen."

Then the judge asked the defense if they wanted to call any witnesses to testify about the defendant's competence.

"No, Your Honor," said Jaye Schlachet. "We are prepared to stipulate to Mr. Castro's competency."

Judge Russo then asked the prosecution if they had any witnesses to call.

"No, Your Honor," said Tim McGinty. "We stipulate the conclusion that Mr. Castro is competent to stand trial."

Then the judge ruled that Ariel Castro was competent to stand trial, and able to assist his counsel in his defense.

"Mr. Castro, do you have any questions for the court or your counsel at this time?" asked the judge.

"Yes," replied Castro, looking straight ahead.

"One moment, Your Honor. May I?" said Craig Weintraub, who seemed surprised by his client's answer.

Then Castro, who was allowed jail visits only with his mother and sister, asked if his children could come.

"You'd like your children to be able to visit you in jail?" asked the judge.

"Yes," he replied.

"Obviously, we would object to him having any contact with the minor child in the case," said Assistant Cuyahoga County Prosecutor Blaise Thomas.

"He's aware of the no contact law, Your Honor," said Schlachet.

"I don't think that will be an issue, but we'll address that," said the judge. "Mr. Castro, what's the issue?"

"If you could please reiterate on contact with my child," Castro mumbled.

"Do you want me to readdress the issue of contact with your child?" asked Russo.

"Yes, my six-year-old," said Castro.

"Are you referring to the minor child?" asked the judge.

"Yes, please," replied Castro.

"I won't be allowing that," said the judge, "not during the pendency of this case. I just think that would be inappropriate."

"Thank you, Your Honor," said Schlachet. "He obviously had great concerns in asking you to address it."

Then Judge Russo adjourned the hearing and Castro was once again led out of the courtroom to a salvo of clicking cameras.

On July 4, The DeJesus family invited relatives and friends over to their house for a backyard cookout. Although it was a celebratory occasion, Gina appeared uneasy and mainly kept to herself.

"She didn't want to talk a lot," said an old friend. "You

could tell her nerves are really bad. She just can't look anybody in the eyes for very long."

Forensic psychiatrist Dr. Michael Stone of Columbia University said that Gina, Amanda and Michelle were undoubtedly suffering from post-traumatic stress disorder, as a result of their years of torturous imprisonment.

"They are going to have the full syndrome of nightmares, startled responses and tremendous anxiety," said Dr. Stone. "I mean, that's torture to rape repeatedly. It's like a soldier coming back from Vietnam or Afghanistan, where they've been used to bombs going off. If they hear a noise they can't account for, they become very frightened and they have nightmares."

Most lunchtimes, prosecutor Tim McGinty jogged past 2207 Seymour Avenue on his daily runs from the Justice Center. A passionate marathon runner, with more than 120 marathons under his belt, McGinty liked to strategize his criminal cases during his five-mile runs.

"He runs around Seymour to check the place out," said Councilman Brian Cummins. "He told me he ran that area."

The tall lean Cuyahoga County prosecutor had worked as a probation officer to put himself through law school. After receiving a master's degree from the University of Nevada, Reno, he served ten years as an assistant county prosecutor, being named Ohio Prosecutor of the Year. He then spent ten years as a judge in the Cuyahoga Common Pleas Court, before being elected Cuyahoga County prosecutor in November 2012, on a platform of reducing crime in Cleveland.

Married for thirty-nine years with two grown-up children, McGinty made national headlines in 1994, when he had a very public feud with shock jock Howard Stern. The DJ was broadcasting live from a bar in downtown

Cleveland, when an engineer from a rival radio station cut his cable and stopped the broadcast.

After sentencing the engineer to ten days in jail, Judge McGinty attacked Stern, calling him a "crude and obscene rabble-rouser."

Stern was furious and began a long spat with McGinty, culminating in him endorsing the judge's opponent in the next election. When McGinty won he sent Howard Stern some candy and roses, along with a note of thanks for getting him elected.

At the stroke of midday on Tuesday, July 9, Hennes Paynter Communications released the three women's video statement on *YouTube*. It was the first time the outside world had seen or heard them speak and the effect was stunning.

"The women appear upbeat," said the Cleveland *Plain Dealer*, "and two of them talk about having the strength to move on."

The women's attorneys also issued a statement in the wake of the video.

"[They] wanted to say thank you to people from Cleveland and across the world," said Kathy Joseph. "People are recognizing them as they go about in public; they decided to put voices and faces to their heartfelt messages."

After the video was released, Hennes Paynter Communications was deluged with hundreds of requests for interviews with the three women. Oprah Winfrey, Katie Couric and Dr. Phil all wanted to be the first for an exclusive sit-down interview with the victims. There had also been dozens of proposals for books and movies, with offers of big money.

"For the most part the media has been respectful," said Bruce Hennes, adding that "some of them have been just downright rude."

After the video release, *Plain Dealer* columnist Regina Brett, who had covered the missing girls' story from the beginning, wrote that it had moved her to tears.

"For so long the only glimpse we had of them was from posters," she wrote, "that hung on utility poles begging for their return, posters that faded away as the days turned into a decade.

"I cried watching Amanda speak. She's even more beautiful than her mom described her all those years ago in her living room. If only Louwana had lived to see her daughter free."

32

"HE'S NEVER COMING OUT EXCEPT NAILED IN A BOX"

On Thursday, July 11, the day after Ariel Castro's fifty-third birthday, the Capital Review Committee (CRC) met in the Cuyahoga County Prosecutor's Office to discuss whether or not to seek the death penalty. Before the meeting, Castro's defense team had presented a list of mitigating factors against it.

Craig Weintraub and Jaye Schlachet claimed that there was absolutely no medical or forensic evidence to corroborate Michelle Knight's claims that Castro had forced her to miscarry on multiple occasions. They had also found no cases of any state seeking the death penalty for a fetal homicide in the first trimester.

"Clearly, an indictment for the aggravated murder of a fertilized egg with a death specification is unprecedented," they wrote, "and will be subject to strict scrutiny by all courts through the extensive and very lengthy appellate process."

They also warned that as Michelle Knight's testimony could not be corroborated by the other victims or experts, prosecuting Castro for fetal homicide would prove very expensive with years of appeals lying ahead.

"And [it] will continue to draw significant publicity," they wrote, "to events that do not need further media attention."

The defense also argued that putting Ariel Castro on death row would cost the State of Ohio millions of dollars.

"Ariel Castro is 53-years-old," read the motion, "and the average time on death row is 16.6 years. Clearly, he will be at the end of his natural life expectancy if he is ever executed."

It noted that the health of older inmates in protective custody or isolation declines faster than that of average prisoners.

"It is certainly plausible and likely," the motion continued, "that Mr. Castro may develop physical and cognitive diseases as he ages in prison, including Alzheimer's and dementia."

The defense had also pored through all the hours of the victims' interviews, cherry-picking quotes favorable to their client.

It referred to one interview where Gina had said she hoped Castro would be treated well as a prisoner.

"I asked my mom," it quoted Gina as saying, " 'are they going to be mean to him in prison?' And my mom said, 'That's just the way it is.' I said, 'That's so mean. I don't want that.' "

The defense also warned that if the prosecution went for the death penalty, their client would be forced to take the stand and refute the allegations against him.

"[This] will unfortunately cause these women," read the motion, "to endure agonizing testimony that will be sensationalized across the world."

The two defense attorneys argued that their client's

daughter, Jocelyn, would be irreparably damaged if her father were executed.

"It is apparent in home videos," they wrote, "that Jocelyn loves her father very much. It is probable that she is very confused about the current circumstances and the whereabouts of her father. It is unimaginable how she will try to reconcile her past as she matures and learns about her life. It's unknown whether she will continue to maintain any interest in seeing her father. If he receives a death sentence and is on death row, this may have more of a psychological impact on her than anyone can comprehend."

The next morning, a Cuyahoga County grand jury handed down a superseding 977-count indictment, covering the entire period the three women were held. The new 576-page indictment included 512 counts of kidnapping, 446 counts of rape, seven counts of gross sexual imposition, six counts of felonious assault, three counts of child endangerment and a single count of possessing criminal tools. It also included the two counts of aggravated murder from the original indictment.

After the indictment came down, Prosecutor Tim McGinty told reporters that his office would be meeting again the following week to discuss whether to go for the death penalty.

"Today's indictment moves us closer to resolution of this gruesome case," he said. "Our investigation continues, as does our preparation for trial."

Craig Weintraub and Jaye Schlachet then issued a statement, urging the prosecutor's office to take the death penalty off the table.

"It is our hope," they said, "that we can continue to work toward a resolution of this matter so that the women do not have to endure additional trauma."

* * *

Five days later, on July 17, Ariel Castro was arraigned on the new superseding indictment. Once again he entered the courtroom with his head down and eyes closed, but Judge Pamela Barker, who was sitting in for Judge Michael Russo, immediately ordered him to pay attention, while she read him his rights.

"Mr. Castro," she said sternly, "would you please look at me, sir."

The defendant looked up, opened his eyes slightly and squinted.

"I need to make sure you understand what I'm saying, okay," she told him.

"Ummm," Castro mumbled.

Then, as Judge Barker read out the names of the counsel present, Castro lowered his head again and shut his eyes.

"Again, you *must* look at me, sir," said the judge. "Can you open your eyes, please?"

Jaye Schlachet, who was sitting next to him, whispered something in his ear.

"I'm trying," Castro said.

After Castro had been read his rights, Schlachet told the judge that his client pleaded not guilty to all 977 charges, and waived the right to be read the entire indictment.

As Judge Barker summarized all the counts against him, Castro defiantly kept his eyes shut and head bowed. Then she continued the $8 million bond and ordered the defendant not to have any contact with the victims.

Straight after the arraignment, Tim McGinty messengered a letter to the defense, saying he was now ready to begin "off-the-record" discussions for a plea deal to drop the death penalty.

"We are interested in pursuing this matter," wrote

McGinty, "in formulating an appropriate resolution to the . . . case."

Outlining the State's terms for dropping the death penalty, McGinty said Castro must undergo an FBI polygraph examination, to see if there were any other crimes he had committed.

"The purpose of this polygraph examination," he wrote, "is to provide Ariel Castro the opportunity, in the context of the protection of a potential plea agreement, to divulge truthful information about any other victims and any other crimes."

In return for this, McGinty agreed not to prosecute him for further crimes that could carry the death penalty. He wrote that the State was now considering not pursuing the death penalty, to "provide closure" for the victims and their families.

"I trust that you will find these ground rules fair and reasonable," wrote McGinty at the end. "If your client wishes to engage in a proffer under these ground rules, you and your client both must sign this letter where indicated below."

The following day, Ariel Castro and Jaye Schlachet signed the letter, accepting all the State's demands in return for dropping the death penalty.

On Wednesday, July 24, with his trial just two weeks away, Ariel Castro was back in the courtroom for a brief hearing. Assistant Cuyahoga County Prosecutor Blaise Thomas told Judge Michael Russo that more than four thousand documents had now been turned over to the defense. But Craig Weintraub and Jaye Schlachet complained that the State had been slow, and they were having trouble preparing for the upcoming trial.

Prosecutor Tim McGinty said he was ready for trial, denying he had been tardy with evidence. He said the defense had been given more evidence faster than any case in Cuyahoga County history.

"We've got nearly a thousand counts in a period of ten years of solid crime," said McGinty. "Never stopped, day after day after day."

Then Judge Russo stopped him, saying it was not time for speeches.

"My understanding is that the parties have discussed possible pleas," said the judge, "and that you're working to see if that would be an effective resolution," said the judge. "Is that correct?"

The prosecution and defense both agreed, without elaborating. Then Judge Russo adjourned the hearing.

Two days later, a very different Ariel Castro sat on the defense bench, after a plea deal had been reached. With his head up high and wearing a new pair of glasses, Castro was focused and articulate at the hastily called hearing so Judge Michael Russo could officially approve the plea deal.

Under the deal, which would put him in prison for life without parole, plus a minimum of a thousand years, Ariel Castro had agreed to plead guilty to 937 counts out of the 977-count indictment. These included the two charges of aggravated murder, relating to terminating Michelle Knight's pregnancies.

"Mr. Castro, you've received your glasses now, is it better?" asked Judge Russo at the beginning of the hearing, which was being carried live by *ABC News*, who broke into normal programming for a special report.

"Yes, it is, Your Honor," replied Castro, looking straight at the judge.

"Mr. Castro," said Judge Russo, "my understanding from meeting with your counsel and counsel for the State is that a plea agreement has been reached in this matter.

Are you fully aware of the terms and do you consent to that plea agreement?"

"I am fully aware and I do consent to it," replied Castro.

"You understand by virtue of a plea, you'll not be having a trial?"

"I am aware of that."

Castro then told Judge Russo that he had fully cooperated with the FBI after his arrest.

"I said to Mr. Dave [Jacobs] that I was willing to work with the FBI and I would tell him everything."

Then the judge explained that a prisoner serving life imprisonment without parole will die in prison.

"Do you understand this?" asked the judge.

"Yes, I do, Your Honor," he replied.

"Do you believe for any reason that you'll be released from prison before you die of natural causes?"

"Excuse me?" asked Castro.

"Do you think there is any reason, any hope that you might be getting out of prison before you die?" explained Judge Russo.

"I don't think there's any reason," he answered.

"So finally, sir, again, do you understand, Mr. Castro, that by entering this plea you'll never be released from prison?"

"I do understand that and I stated to Dave . . . at Sex Crimes that I knew I was going to get pretty much the book thrown at me."

Judge Russo then asked if he had any questions.

Castro said he realized he was giving up his rights to a trial, but there were some things he did not "comprehend because of my sexual problems" through the years.

Later in the hearing, Castro said he wanted to put on record that he had been "a victim as a child," and everything had stemmed from that.

"My addiction to pornography and my sexual problem," he told the judge, "has really taken a toll on my mind."

The judge cut him off, saying that he could talk about his problems at sentencing.

Judge Russo then went through the charges with him, but when he came to the count of being a sexually violent predator, a pained expression came over the defendant's face.

"I don't care for the wording," he told the judge, "but I will plead guilty to that."

At the end of the hearing, the judge told Castro that he would also have to sign over the deed to 2207 Seymour Avenue.

"Is that understood?" asked Judge Russo.

"I don't have a problem with that," said Castro.

"In addition to forfeiting the house," the judge continued, "you understand you're forfeiting the twenty-thousand-dollars plus in currency, as well as some other property to the State. Is that clear?"

"I understand," he replied.

Craig Weintraub told the judge that the State had agreed that Castro's personal photographs and clothing would be given to his children.

"I had other items in there," Castro said, "that I would like for them to release to my family. I would just like to state I miss my daughter very much."

Finally, Judge Russo asked the defendant yet again if he agreed to relinquish all his rights under the plea deal.

"You understand you're giving up your right to any future challenges to this," said Russo. "You're giving up your right to appeal the sentence. Is that clear?"

"Yes, it is clear," Castro replied.

At the end of the two-and-a-half-hour hearing, Judge Russo officially accepted the plea bargain, setting sentencing for August 1.

* * *

After the hearing, Craig Weintraub conceded that the evidence against his client had been overwhelming.

"There are no winners," he told reporters, "even though we avoided the death penalty in this case, which was our primary goal. But my client understood that the last thing he wanted to do was re-victimize these women, who he actually had some relationship with despite how it started."

Jaye Schlachet said that Castro would read a statement at his sentencing with "an explanation of how he got to where he is."

Prosecutor Tim McGinty told the press that justice had been done.

"He's never coming out except nailed in a box or in an ash can," he said. "He is not stepping out."

The prosecutor called Ariel Castro "a fraud and a coward," announcing that the $22,268.83 in seized cash would go toward demolishing 2207 Seymour Avenue, along with two houses beside it.

"The house will be torn down," he said. "We do not want it to be a symbol of Cleveland. This man's the worst of the worst."

A statement from the victims expressed relief that there would be no trial.

"Amanda, Gina and Michelle are relieved by today's plea," it read. "They are satisfied by the resolution to the case, and are looking forward to having these legal proceedings draw to a final close in the near future."

That afternoon, Cleveland Police Second District Commander Keith Sulzer and Officer Michael Tracy paid an emotional visit to 2207 Seymour Avenue, marking the end of the case they had worked on for so long.

"I'm just happy for the girls," said Officer Tracy, who

was one of the first responders to the house after Amanda's escape, "so they won't have to relive those horrors again."

Commander Sulzer said the plea deal was the best thing that could have happened for the community.

"And I think we need to get this over with," he told a reporter. "We need to put it to bed and get on with making things better in the city. The girls can put this behind them and move on with their lives, and so can my officers, who have been living this case every day."

A few blocks away, Onil Castro told reporters outside his front gate that he was glad about the plea deal.

"If that's what he's got to do to save his life," said Onil, "then that's good. He didn't kill nobody."

The youngest Castro brother said he did not know why Ariel had done it, but he deserved to spend the rest of his life in jail.

"It's destroyed my life," said Onil. "I'm very sorry for the three girls. I'm glad they got out of that and not a lot of people would. Ariel didn't [kill] anybody but he still didn't do right . . . but I didn't have anything to do with that."

On Saturday night, Amanda Berry made her first public appearance at the Roverfest 2013 concert, starring rap superstar Nelly. During his performance, Nelly suddenly brought Amanda onstage, to thunderous applause by the audience.

"I can't even imagine the type of strength and courage it took to keep going," Nelly told Amanda. "I commend you!"

Amanda, who was wearing a blue T-shirt, jeans and sunglasses, then went backstage with her family.

During his encore, Nelly called Amanda back to the stage, dedicating his triple-platinum hit "Just a Dream" to her. Although Amanda didn't speak, Cleveland radio host Shane "Rover" French told the crowd that she had "some partying" to catch up on, and to help her out. Amanda then raised her arm to acknowledge the crowd, pumping her fist and mouthing the lyrics to the next couple of songs.

On Monday, July 29, Anthony Castro appeared live on the *Today* show, saying he had no plans to visit his father in prison. He told Savannah Guthrie that his father had gotten what he deserved.

"If he really can't control his impulses," said Anthony, "and he really doesn't have any value for human life the way this case has shown, then behind bars is where he belongs for the rest of his life."

Guthrie asked how he felt, knowing his father was capable of such cruelty.

"What's horrifying is," Anthony replied, "I have the same first and last name. I look in the mirror and see the resemblance, and I think about what he did and how horrible it was, and I can't help sometimes just being overcome with it."

Anthony said his father had brutally beaten him and his mother when he was growing up, and he would often cry himself to sleep.

"Your mom would have turned fifty tomorrow," said Guthrie, "in some ways do you think about this as justice for her and what she went through?"

"I do," he replied. "The first morning he wakes up in prison and the sun shines down. That's going to be her justice."

On Monday, a six-foot-high privacy fence went up to screen off Gina DeJesus's backyard. The $4,000 fence was donated by well-wishers to protect the DeJesus family, who had been besieged by ghoulish sightseers seeking a glimpse of Gina.

"It meant a lot to me," Gina told *News 5* reporter Stephanie Ramirez.

Nancy Ruiz said the privacy fence would finally allow them the freedom to go outside and enjoy themselves.

"It's awesome," said Nancy. "You know we don't have to worry about . . . anybody coming in my yard. So this means a lot to us."

Nancy said that Gina was now being homeschooled, and would go to college after she got her high school diploma.

"She's got her future planned," said Nancy. "First thing I want her to do is to enjoy the summer before school starts."

On Tuesday afternoon, as the Cleveland Courage Fund announced it had now raised more than $1.3 million, Amanda Berry and Gina DeJesus arrived at 2207 Seymour Avenue. After going inside for a few minutes to collect Jocelyn's paintings and other personal items, they came out and spoke to neighbors, before being driven away.

That night, Michelle Knight posted a handwritten note on Facebook, thanking Commander Keith Sulzer and his officers, who had collected the thousands of cards and gifts from well-wishers.

"I'm overwhelmed by the amount of thoughts, love and prayers expressed by complete strangers," she wrote. "It's comforting. Life is tough, but I'm tougher. Just when the caterpillar thought the world was over, she became a butterfly. Thanks."

Late Wednesday, July 31, the Cuyahoga County Prosecutor's Office submitted a sentencing memorandum to Judge Russo, throwing new light on the case. It revealed for the first time exactly how Ariel Castro had lured his three victims into 2207 Seymour Avenue, using his daughters as bait. And it gave horrific insight into the terrible conditions they had endured for a decade or more.

"The Defendant preyed on vulnerable young women," read Prosecutor Tim McGinty's memorandum. "He was able to trick them and nullify their defensive instincts until he had them restrained in his house. Once the Defendant had them in his personal prison, he went to great lengths to ensure their captivity."

The prosecutor wrote that Castro had controlled his three prisoners' movements for years, with chains and other physical restraints.

"Every aspect of the victims' physical freedom," he continued, "was dictated by the Defendant. There is only one bathroom in the house, on the first floor. The Defendant would not allow the victims downstairs to use the bathroom. They only had access to plastic toilets in the bedrooms. They were emptied infrequently."

McGinty explained how Castro also exerted his control through the temperature of the house during the steaming hot summers and freezing winters, as well as how much food and drink they were allowed.

"He used the cold of the basement and the heat of the attic as punishment techniques," wrote the prosecutor.

He also tortured them psychologically, making them believe that their very survival depended on him, constantly threatening to kill them with his ever-present Luger.

"Through a program of prolonged physical, sexual and psychological violence," wrote McGinty, "the Defendant was able to keep the victims in a state of powerlessness."

The sentencing memo also revealed the existence of detailed diaries kept by all the women throughout their imprisonment. The diaries had been used by prosecutors to compile many of the 977 counts in the indictment.

"Several diary entries document abuse and life as a captive," wrote McGinty. "The entries speak of forced sexual conduct, of being locked in a dark room, of anticipating the next session of abuse, of the dreams of someday escaping and being reunited with family, of being chained to a wall, of being held like a prisoner of war, of missing the lives they once enjoyed, of emotional abuse, of his threats to kill, of being treated like an animal, of continuous abuse, and of desiring freedom."

33

"THE SCOPE AND MAGNITUDE OF ARIEL CASTRO'S CRIME IS UNPRECEDENTED"

At 9:00 A.M. on Thursday, August 1, Cuyahoga County Common Pleas Courtroom 17C was overflowing with press and spectators for Ariel Castro's sentencing. An exact-scale model of 2207 Seymour Avenue, constructed by the FBI's Quantico laboratory, had been placed at the front of the courtroom. And the big question on everyone's lips was whether any of the victims would address the court.

The entire sentencing would be broadcast live by *Fox News*, MSNBC, CNN and HLN cable networks, as well as all four Cleveland network affiliates.

Now that Castro had pleaded guilty there would not be a trial, but Tim McGinty still planned to present evidence and call witnesses. He was determined to tell the world exactly what had happened inside 2207 Seymour Avenue, so there would be a record of Ariel Castro's evil, in case he ever tried to appeal.

At around nine-fifteen, defense attorneys Craig Weintraub and Jaye Schlachet came into the courtroom, after meeting their client in a holding cell downstairs. Then ten minutes later, a shackled and handcuffed Ariel Castro was led in by two sheriff's deputies. He stared through his glasses at the public gallery and appeared to smile, before sitting down at the defense table between his attorneys. Soon afterward the court rose as Judge Russo entered.

"Well, we're here this morning," said the judge, "for sentencing the case of the State of Ohio versus Ariel Castro. Mr. Castro, did you have the chance to speak to your attorneys since the last Friday you were in court?"

"Yes, I have," replied Castro confidently.

"And have they discussed with you your rights at the sentencing, and the procedures to be followed?"

"Yes, they have."

"Do you understand you have the right to speak, if you wish?"

"Yes, I do," replied Castro.

Then the judge asked the two defense attorneys if they had anything to say on behalf of their client.

"Judge," said Schlachet, "can I just make a quick objection before we start?"

He then objected to the prosecution presenting any witnesses or evidence, apart from the victims or their representatives' impact statements. He accused McGinty of basically wanting to retry the case.

"[It] didn't go to trial for the exact purpose of avoiding a public spectacle," he said, "of everything that's going to happen. And we absolutely, Your Honor, object. Introducing doctor reports or photographs or a model of the house has absolutely nothing to do with what's happened."

Then Craig Weintraub reminded the judge that both sides had agreed not to disclose any graphic details of what had gone on inside the house, to protect the three women.

"This is a unique case," said Weintraub, "and a story

about an incredible survival, as well as a man with significant, undiagnosed mental illness."

Weintraub said his client accepted full responsibility for his conduct, and that his mental illness and childhood sexual abuse could never justify his crimes.

"Mr. Castro pled guilty to over nine hundred counts and does not dispute any of [them]," said Weintraub. "The upcoming presentation that's going to be captured by the media and played all over the world will forever memorialize the facts of the brutality that occurred.

"That is what we wanted to avoid; offering up the details and salacious facts. We wanted to avoid this, however it's the prosecutor's decision to have to show the world these facts."

Judge Russo then asked Castro if he had anything to say in mitigation of his sentence.

"I would like to apologize to the three women," he replied. "Can I do that now . . . or should I do it at the end of the day?"

Judge Russo said he could apologize to them now and also later when he spoke to the court.

Then, addressing the defense objections, Russo said he had already advised the State of what could and what could not be presented.

"I think the State's concern," he said, "is that there would be an adequate record so that any reviewing court . . . would know the foundation [of] why such a sentence might be appropriate. And why it's not symbolic but actually justified."

Prosecutor Tim McGinty then stood up, saying it was necessary to put on record the defendant's "horrendous" offenses.

"Mr. Castro's now an admitted murderer, rapist, serial kidnapper," he told the judge, "and it's only appropriate that we put before this community, this state, this country and the world, what he did for over ten years."

Judge Russo ruled that the presentation could proceed, explaining sentencing hearings were not bound by the rule of evidence, and other relevant information was often introduced.

Assistant County Prosecutor Anna Faraglia then called the State's first witness, Cleveland police officer Barbara Johnson.

"Can you lay out for the court," asked Faraglia, "the conditions that you observed when you went into the house at 2207 Seymour?"

"I remember it was very dark," said Officer Johnson, "because I didn't take my flashlight with me because it was a bright sunny day. But fortunately I had a flashlight on my firearm."

Johnson told the court how she and Officer Anthony Espada encountered obstacles on their way up the stairs, like heavy curtains and furniture. As they reached the top, Espada yelled out, "Cleveland police! Cleveland police!"

"Then you hear some pitter-patter steps," said Johnson, "and I can hear someone running. But it stopped and . . . I kind of shined the flashlight, so whoever it was could see we were the police. We waited for Michelle Knight as she literally launched herself into Officer Espada's arms . . . just choking him and she just kept repeating, 'You saved us! You saved us!' She then came over to me and jumped in my arms. As I'm trying to re-holster my weapon her legs are wrapped around me, so it was kind of hard to get my weapon back in my holster."

Soon afterward, Johnson had seen another face "peeping around the corner of the doorway." When Espada asked her name, she meekly replied, "Georgina DeJesus."

The assistant prosecutor then asked Johnson about the

three women's condition when they were put in an ambulance outside the house.

"All three of them were . . . thin, pale, scared," she testified. "Still kind of reluctant and not really sure what was happening. There was a lot of talking. They were very nervous, saying all kinds of things that happened to them."

"Do you recall," asked Faraglia, "some of the details they were giving you about what happened to them?"

"I didn't ask a lot of questions," she said, "I just let them talk. I do remember at one point looking at Amanda and asking her, 'Well, how about when you had your daughter? Didn't you go to the hospital?' And she said, 'No, I had my daughter here at the house. Michelle delivered her for me.' And I was just dumbfounded. I couldn't believe it."

The next witness was MetroHealth Medical Center ER physician Dr. Gerald Maloney, who was on duty when the three women came in. He told the court that they all appeared "very emotionally distraught," as they spoke about being imprisoned and sexually assaulted in a house for many years.

"Miss Knight in particular related that she's been pregnant," he testified, "and had been subject to both deprivation of food and physical assault to try and induce a miscarriage. All three related various sorts of physical assault as well."

The doctor said Michelle did not want any male nurses or physicians in the room during her examination.

"Without getting into specific detail," asked Faraglia, "were there various documentation given to you, with regards to what sort of sexual assault the women underwent?"

"Yes," he replied, "they related information regarding the sexual assaults to us, and also to the sexual-assault nurse examiner."

"And in a very general description, of what nature would those assaults be?" she asked.

"Forcible rape," he replied. "Multiple repeated times. Again it was against their will and they suffered physical harm while they were raped."

The next witness was Detective Andrew Harasimchuk of the Cleveland Police Department's Sex Crimes Unit, who had interviewed the victims at the MetroHealth Medical Center just hours after their escape. The detective told Assistant Prosecutor Max Martin that it was "very chaotic" at the hospital that night.

One by one, the women had told him how Ariel Castro had lured them back to his house, using his daughters as bait. Once there, Castro had physically attacked them and brought them down to his basement, where he chained them to a pole and put a motorcycle helmet on their heads.

Then Martin asked the detective to outline his investigation into the case.

"I interviewed Ariel Castro," he said. "I visited the crime scene. I read dozens of reports . . . and examined hundreds of photographs. I reviewed hundreds of pieces of physical evidence that were taken from the house. I reviewed written materials kept by the victims during their years of captivity."

"And what did your investigation reveal?" asked the assistant prosecutor.

"After reviewing all that evidence, it was determined that Ariel Castro, and Ariel Castro alone, was the only person involved in this incident."

Harasimchuk said that Castro had imprisoned all three women, restraining them with chains or locking them inside a room, as well as depriving them of food, and bathroom and bathing facilities. He had repeatedly raped them "vaginally, orally or anally," as well as inflicting physical and emotional abuse.

The assistant prosecutor asked how the 977-count indictment against Castro had been arrived at.

"Some of these charges reflect specific instances of assault that were reported to me by the victims," he testified, "or through the investigation of various written materials. The abuse was continuous and without interruption during the time they were held captive."

Then Craig Weintraub stood up to cross-examine the witness, asking what Amanda told detectives about when she discovered she was pregnant with Jocelyn.

"She did inform law enforcement," said the defender, "that despite the circumstances of being kidnapped and held hostage, and any sort of Stockholm syndrome that may have been in effect, she did use the words . . . that it was consensual. Is that correct?"

"That is correct," Harasimchuk replied.

"Thank you," said Weintraub, as he sat down at the defense table, next to a smirking Ariel Castro.

The next witness was Joshua Barr, a forensic scientist with the Ohio BCI. Under Assistant Prosecutor Max Martin's questioning, Barr described examining Castro's .357-caliber Luger revolver and finding it in good working order. He had also examined the rusty chains found in the house, testifying they were almost one hundred feet long and weighed ninety-two pounds.

"Was it also your organization that determined the paternity of the minor child that was found in the house?" asked Martin.

"Yes," said Barr.

"Paternity was established that Ariel Castro was the father of the minor child found in the home?"

"Yes."

FBI Special Agent Andrew Burke then took the stand,

describing how he had coordinated the multiagency investigation at the beginning. He testified how he had organized the victims' medical treatment, as well as arranging for them to be reunited with their families. Over the ensuing weeks, he supervised their ongoing medical and psychological care.

"Based on your knowledge of the course of the investigation," asked Max Martin, "have each of the victims been in need of ongoing medical care, as a result of their captivity, abuse and victimization by Ariel Castro?"

"All of the victims' needs are ongoing," Special Agent Burke replied. "I don't know if anyone could expect anything different, really. They've made dramatic improvements from the time that I've spent with them. They are with the people that love them. They are getting world-class medical, psychological care. But you can't turn off ten years of systematic, sustained psychological, sexual and physical abuse like a light switch."

Then Martin asked about the scale model of the 2207 Seymour Avenue house in the middle of the courtroom.

"That model was created by the FBI's operational project unit in Quantico," he explained. "They took measurements from the house, using . . . a surveyor's measurement tool. And then they constructed this house as a scale model, one inch equaling one foot."

Burke said that each of the model's rooms had been painted in the actual color of each room in the house. And it was used during the victims' questioning, so they could describe exactly what room they were in during each incident they described.

The assistant prosecutor then asked about Burke's first visit to 2207 Seymour Avenue, just hours after the escape.

"Well, it was surreal to me," Burke replied. "I've been involved in the missing-persons investigation for quite some time and it was a difficult experience."

Martin then asked Special Agent Burke to explain how the defendant had transformed his residence into a prison. Then using photographs taken inside the house, which were displayed on a large TV screen at the front of the courtroom, Burke described a crude system of alarms and mirrors Castro had rigged, as well as heavy curtains and other materials to block off certain areas of the house.

Upstairs on the second floor, Burke pointed out how Castro had removed all the inside doorknobs, attaching slide locks on the outside, so he could lock in his prisoners. As Castro had boarded up all the windows with wood, he had cut a small hole in the bottom panel of the bedroom doors for ventilation. He had also cut a hole in the ceiling of the tiny bedroom Michelle and Gina shared, so a fan up in the attic would pump air down.

The assistant prosecutor then showed the court a photograph of Castro's basement, asking about a large support pole in the center.

"That's a pole . . . that the women were restrained to at various points," Burke explained. "[It] was used to restrain the women in the early stages of captivity."

He also pointed out an old washing machine at the far end of the basement, where investigators had discovered more than $22,000 in cash.

"Did Mr. Castro use his cash . . . to run an internal barter system, if you will, with his victims?" asked Martin.

"On occasion," replied the agent.

"And would he," Martin continued, "after sexually abusing them, throw money at them, saying, 'Here, you're being paid for the sex?'"

"There were reports of that."

The assistant prosecutor then asked about a handwritten letter, dated April 4, 2004, that had been found near the kitchen counter.

"I know that to be a letter written by Ariel Castro," said Burke.

"Does he describe himself," asked Martin, "through his own choice of words as, 'I am a sexual predator'?"

"Yes," he replied.

"Does he describe his victimization of the women in this case?"

"Yes."

In his cross-examination, Craig Weintraub asked if his client's letter had expressed remorse.

"He wrote something to the effect that he was sorry for his conduct," said Burke.

"Hopefully you will agree with me too," continued Weintraub, "that . . . he was unsure of, but certainly believed and expressed in his letter, that he was sick and mentally ill. And other than that he had no explanation for why he could possibly do something like this?"

"Yes," replied Burke, as Ariel Castro looked on dispassionately.

Then Weintraub asked if he agreed it had been a "suicide letter," although he had never actually tried to kill himself?

"I don't know that I would concur that it was written as a suicide note," replied Special Agent Burke. "It did not give me that immediate impression."

"Thank you," said Weintraub. "Nothing further."

The State's next witness was Deputy David Jacobs of the Cuyahoga County Sheriff's Office, who had interrogated Ariel Castro. He testified that the defendant answered every question posed to him succinctly, even if they were incriminating. During the ten hours of questioning, spread over two days, Castro freely admitted taking the three women and imprisoning them.

"He used the word 'abduct,'" said Jacobs. "He referenced himself in the interview as a 'sexual predator.' I asked him at that point, 'What do you consider a sexual predator is?' And he said, 'Somebody that continually repeats offenses.'"

"Did he tell you why he was abducting young women off the streets of Cleveland?' asked Martin.

"We got into why he did it," replied Jacobs, "and his response was, 'to purely satisfy [my] sexual needs . . . and I know what I did was wrong.'"

The deputy also described how Castro had admitted to using his gun to control the girls.

"And are you aware that he used the gun . . . to play Russian roulette?" asked the assistant prosecutor.

"I'd asked him if this incident actually took place," said Jacobs. "His response was that he didn't recall. But if the girls said it, then it probably happened."

"And that he played a trust game," continued Martin. "He handed an empty revolver to a young woman and said, 'Here, put it to my head. Pull the trigger. If it's God's will that I die, I die. I'll say my prayers.' Did he play that game?"

"Yes, he did," said Jacobs.

Then Jaye Schlachet stood up to cross-examine Jacobs.

"Just one question," he said. "You went to see him and he completely cooperated with you, didn't he?"

"I don't think that's accurate," replied Jacobs. "I felt that some of the elements of the crime were minimized, but he was very cooperative through the interview."

"He talked himself right to the convictions, didn't he?" said the defender. "And he wasn't hesitant at all to tell you exactly what happened from his perspective. Right?"

"No, he wasn't," said Jacobs.

The next witness was forensic psychiatrist Dr. Gregory Saathoff, who consults with the FBI's Behavioral Analysis Unit. Dr. Saathoff said he had reviewed the video transcripts of all the victims' interviews, as well as interviewing Lillian Roldan.

Assistant Prosecutor Blaise Thomas asked why he had written in his report, "the scope and magnitude of Ariel Castro's crime is unprecedented."

"In terms of unrelated victims, the length of captivity and the location," said Dr. Saathoff, "as well as the fact that most cases of abduction are impulsive in nature and the victim is kept for a matter of minutes or hours. In this case, rather than a short abduction . . . there appeared to be a strategy here that extended over a period of many years. And this is in fact quite unusual and in fact unprecedented, according to the FBI's National Center for Analysis of Violent Crime."

"So he's in a class of one by himself?" asked Thomas.

"Well, certainly there are cases where there have been longer-term abductions in length," said the doctor, "but the specific nature of this—to abduct and keep this number of unrelated victims for this length of time within a neighborhood setting is completely unprecedented."

Then Thomas asked why he had described Castro "as a hoarder of humans."

Dr. Saathoff explained there was a definite pattern to his choice of victims.

"It was always on the same street," he said. "These victims were similar in terms of their stature, their age. They were female and they were also very trusting. And his use of ruses in order to get them into his vehicle and . . . into his house.

"Over the years he exposed them to significant degradation and violence. He enforced control over the most intimately private functions of their lives, which included food, bathing and toileting. So it was really a very complete and comprehensive captivity."

Thomas then asked about Ariel Castro's ongoing

duplicity with family, neighbors, friends and coworkers, to maintain his control over the situation.

"This is really the most significant part of the case," explained Dr. Saathoff, "that someone would be able to month after month, year after year devise ways to conceal the situation from family, friends, neighbors. For a time he maintained a relationship with a girlfriend, who was completely unaware that he had these women in the house."

Dr. Saathoff said he had read Ariel Castro's April 2004 letter and found two significant quotes in it.

"He stated, 'I live a normal life. I function around others like a normal person,'" said Dr. Saathoff. "In fact he appeared to have done that and was able to live this life around family and friends without them suspecting.

"[I] was also struck with . . . his statement, 'I had no idea Gina was so young. She looks a lot older.' But we certainly know that he was aware that Gina was a classmate of his daughter. He knew his daughter's age, and therefore to make that statement . . . caused some skepticism . . . as to whether or not he was actually being truthful in writing the document and making the statements that he made."

In cross-examination, Jaye Schlachet pointed out that Castro had also written that he believed he suffered from mental illness.

"Is that right?" asked the defense attorney.

"That's what the letter states," replied Dr. Saathoff.

"He talked about mental illness back in '04 in a letter he wrote. Didn't he?"

"He wrote, 'I'm a sexual predator who needs help but I don't want to get it,'" said Dr. Saathoff.

"Okay, and he talked about being sexually abused himself when he was a child?"

"Yes."

"And he talked about an addiction to masturbation and pornography and things like that. Didn't he?"

"Correct."

"Thank you," said Schlachet.

"Does any of that excuse his conduct in this case?" asked Blaise Thomas angrily.

"No," replied Dr. Saathoff.

At 11:28 A.M., the prosecution called its final witness, Dr. Frank Ochberg, who advises the FBI and the Secret Service on Stockholm syndrome and post-traumatic stress disorder. He had been hired by the Cuyahoga County Prosecutor's Office to consult on the case, and had reviewed the extensive FBI database. Although he had not interviewed the victims, he had read their journals and seen photographs and videos that had been taken during their captivity. He had also reviewed Ariel Castro's interrogation, and had a face-to-face interview with one of his daughters.

"I did what I felt was necessary," said the Michigan-based forensic psychiatrist, "to develop a sense of what these survivors went through and what they faced in the future."

"What were your findings?" asked Assistant Prosecutor Anna Faraglia. "How were these women hurt?"

"These women were hurt in many ways," he replied, "and I boiled it down to three. First is repeated episodes that were terrifying. And they were the kind of trauma that we meant when we define the post-traumatic stress disorder. The kind of trauma that you don't escape for years and sometimes a lifetime, after the images, smells, touches. They come back to you when you're asleep, when you're awake, when you're in the twilight zone between sleep and wakefulness."

Dr. Ochberg explained that Ariel Castro had actually changed the hard-wiring in their brains.

"Sometimes you feel you're going crazy," he told the judge, "because your mind isn't working the way it should. This is not normal memory. This is the brain in a different type of circuitry. It isn't simply an extreme of anxiety. They had that. That was a terror-induced state of mind."

The white-bearded psychiatrist said Castro inflicted a whole new dimension of psychological torture, by using "degradation, defilement and dehumanization."

"Being systematically and relentlessly deprived of your sense of self, your sense of dignity, your connection to others. And that has to do with not having access to sanitary facilities, the way you're fed, the way you're chained—all of that for a long, long time."

He said Castro had also robbed his victims of their family, home and school during those crucial ten years of their transitioning into womanhood.

"And that kind of deprivation," he explained, "isn't the same as being shot and degraded. It plays with your ability to know who to trust. This is the stage in which a human being is developing the capacity for real intimacy. This was not real intimacy. This was a perversion of intimacy."

Dr. Ochberg noted how Castro would portray his daughter with Amanda Berry as a love child, despite repeatedly forcing Michelle Knight to miscarry her babies.

"Whether he believed it in his own mind or whether he feigned believing it," said the doctor, "he tried to produce the belief that this daughter was a love child, not the product of forced sex in captivity. And when that happens, there is something that goes on in our minds and for a period of time we lack a real appreciation of what is real and what isn't. We become bonded to the person who aggresses against us. And that's the Stockholm syndrome."

"Doctor, how did these women cope?" asked Faraglia, "for 13,226 days before their escape?"

"First of all," he said, "among them are marvelous, compelling examples of resilience, of imagination, of humanity. I would start with Michelle. What an extraordinary human being. She served as doctor, nurse pediatrician, midwife. She did the delivery . . . and she did it under primitive circumstances. And when the baby wasn't breathing, she breathed into that baby. She brought life to that child."

Dr. Ochberg said he had also been moved by Amanda, who had raised Jocelyn under the most difficult circumstances.

"Amanda managed . . . to teach that child values and faith and school her," he said. "And there were times when there was interaction among them, and by and large that interaction showed the milk of human kindness, love, faith, optimism. So they coped and part of it was the Stockholm syndrome, but part of it are the gifts and personality and character that they had."

Finally, the assistant prosecutor asked about their prognosis for the future.

"I want to be on the side of optimism and encouragement and hope for them," he said. "But the damage that was done does not go away. They have life sentences. This was not trivial. I think they will, with the love and support of this whole community, and what they bring to the table, have a good chance to have a good life. But that doesn't mean that they will ever be free of the damage that was done."

"And would you agree with me, Doctor," said Faraglia, "that their injuries are that of a permanent nature?"

"Yes," he replied.

Then Judge Russo called a ten-minute recess to prepare for the victim-impact statements.

34

"I AM NOT A MONSTER"

At 11:49 A.M., Michelle Knight walked into the courtroom, escorted by a victim's advocate. Wearing a simple gray floral dress, Ariel Castro's first victim looked confident and assured as she hugged one of her attorneys, and took her place in the first row of the public gallery.

A few seconds later, a jaunty-looking Ariel Castro was brought back into court and smirked at his former captive, before sitting down at the defense table. He appeared animated and excited, and his attorneys tried to calm him down, as he would soon be addressing the court.

At 12:05, Assistant Prosecutor Anna Faraglia introduced Gina DeJesus's cousin Sylvia Colon, who would be delivering a statement on her behalf. Standing in front of Judge Russo, with the DeJesus family attorney Henry Hilow, Sylvia said that today closed a chapter in her family's lives.

"Today is the last day we want to think or talk about this," she said. "These events will not own a place in our thoughts or our hearts."

Sylvia told the judge that Gina was doing well.

"She laughs. She swims. She dances," said Sylvia. "And more importantly she loves and she's loved. She will finish school, go to college, fall in love. And if she chooses, she will get married and have children."

She said Gina no longer lives as a victim but as a survivor, and appealed to the media to give her family the privacy it needed to heal.

Then, she turned to the defendant, fixed him in the eye, and said: "To Ariel Castro. *Que dios se apiade de su alma!*" ("God have mercy on your soul!")

Beth Serrano then addressed Judge Russo, reading from a prepared statement.

"I am Amanda Berry's sister," she began. "The impact of these crimes on our family is something that we do not want to discuss with people we don't know."

Beth said it was impossible to put into words what she and her family had been through over the last ten years.

"For me, I lost a sister for all those years and I thought it was forever," she sobbed. "And you lost my mother forever. She died not knowing. My mother and sister, the two most loving people in the world."

Beth said although Amanda was not in court, she's "strong, beautiful and silent" and improving every day. Her biggest fear, though, was the way Jocelyn would discover the truth.

"Amanda's concern," she said, "is that her daughter will hear about things, or read about things said by the wrong people, the wrong way at the wrong time. Before Amanda thinks the time is right to tell her daughter."

Then Beth asked that Amanda be able to control how and when Jocelyn finds out about her father.

"Amanda did not control anything for a long time," she said. "Please . . . let her protect her daughter. She will do anything to protect her daughter."

Finally, Michelle Knight stood up and, after hugging Sylvia Colon and Beth Serrano, walked straight past Ariel Castro without giving him a look. Her attorney had advised against attending the sentencing and seeing Castro again, but Michelle was determined to "face my demon." She had spent the last few days writing her statement, which would finally free her from the tyranny of Ariel Castro.

"Good afternoon," she began, speaking clearly. "My name is Michelle Knight and I would like to tell you what this was like for me."

She told the judge that she had missed her son, Joey, every single day of her eleven-year captivity, crying herself to sleep thinking about him.

"I was so alone," she said. "Days turned into nights. Nights turned into days. The years turned into eternity."

Michelle said she knew no one cared about her, especially as Castro constantly reminded her of it. Christmas was the "most traumatic" day of the year for her, knowing there was no one out there looking for her.

"Nobody should ever have to go through what I went through," she said, "or anybody else, not even my worst enemy."

She called Gina DeJesus her "teammate," saying she nursed her back to health when she was dying from Castro's abuse. Their friendship had been the only good thing to come out of it.

"We said we will someday make it out alive," she said, "and we did."

Then Michelle took a deep breath and addressed her jailer directly.

"Ariel Castro," she began, as he stared at her, without a hint of emotion. "You took eleven years of my life away and I have got it back. I spent eleven years in hell, and now your hell is just beginning. I will overcome all this that happened, but you will face hell for eternity.

"From this moment on, I will not let you define me or affect who I am. I will live on. You will die a little every day."

Then Michelle asked what God would think of him going to church every Sunday, and then coming home to torture her, Amanda and Gina.

"The death penalty would be so much easier," she told him. "You don't deserve that. You deserve to spend life in prison. I can forgive you, but I will never forget."

Michelle told the judge that with the "guidance of God," she now wanted to help others that had suffered as she had.

"Writing this statement gave me the strength to be a stronger woman," she said, "and know . . . there is more good than evil. After eleven years, I am finally being heard and it's liberating. Thank you all. I love you. God bless you."

Assistant Prosecutor Faraglia then addressed Judge Russo about sentencing criteria.

"This case speaks volumes with regards to the defendant's actions," she told him. "If we look at the harm that has been caused to these victims, the only thing I need tell you is that 13,226 days of captivity."

She said that Castro had lured two of his innocent victims when they were just fourteen and sixteen, using his own daughters as bait.

"He locked the doors. He kept them chained. He used dirty socks when they screamed for help. There was duct tape and motorcycle helmets. That's what you need to consider, Your Honor."

She said that as well as dictating their most intimate

bodily functions, Castro "tormented" them by allowing them to watch their own vigils on television.

"And he even had the audacity to attend them and to talk to the family members," she said, "knowing full well that these women were in his captivity. They were right under his roof. Again, what kind of impact on these victims."

She asked the judge to punish Ariel Castro's "brazen behavior," and not show him any mercy.

"His actions have spoken so loud in this community," she said. "I think Michelle said it best to you, 'It was an eternity,' and that's why he deserves a new sentence. The minimum is a thousand years but this court can go higher, and the reason for our hearing today was to give you a picture of what happened at 2207 Seymour. It was by no means a way to disparage, to humiliate or to embarrass, or tell the story to a child. It was information that's being given to a court of law to impose a sentence. And that's what we did. Thank you."

Then Judge Russo asked Ariel Castro's lawyers if they had anything to say before their client addressed the court. Craig Weintraub said he had already expressed how the defense felt about the State's presentation today.

"We feel it was inappropriate," he said. "These are really private matters . . . but the sentence was agreed upon and Mr. Castro waived his appellant rights to challenge any of the facts in the sentencing of the case."

The judge then asked Tim McGinty if he had finished his presentation. The prosecutor said he wanted to give a rebuttal after the defendant had finished speaking.

"If you want to make a statement, make it now," said Judge Russo, losing patience. "Because if Mr. Castro wants to make a statement that will be the end of it. Okay."

"Your Honor," said McGinty, "as you noted these are

unprecedented crimes that call for an unprecedented sentence."

He told the judge that the defendant had taken advantage of "young vulnerable children," in "prior and calculated criminal acts." The three abductions had been a "disaster to the community," and today the State had attempted to help the court get a feel for the "extraordinary depravation" all the victims had suffered.

Calling Ariel Castro a "master manipulator," the prosecutor said there was no basis for his "sudden claim" that he suffered from mental illness.

"He has no psychiatric excuses," said McGinty. "He is responsible."

Comparing Castro to serial killers John Wayne Gacy and Ted Bundy, the prosecutor said the defendant was a sexual predator and should have sought help.

"He has no excuse," he said. "He takes no responsibility when questioned."

McGinty observed he even blamed the victims for getting in his car in the first place, and not doing what they were taught in school.

"He has no sincere remorse," said the prosecutor. "The only reason he pled guilty to this crime and this sentence was to avoid the death penalty. It's for himself. For no one else."

The prosecutor then spoke about Louwana Miller, who died without ever knowing Amanda was alive. And he revealed that Amanda wrote daily letters to her mother in her journal.

"Then she had to write to her deceased mother," he told the judge. "She had to sit there and tell her loving mother what she would have told her. She then had to learn of her own mother's funeral, and . . . that this man, the guy who goes to church on Sunday and comes home and beats and rapes her . . . had the audacity to go to their vigil."

Castro had also interacted with Gina's mother on Facebook, said the prosecutor, and brought missing posters into the house and put them up on the wall.

"He knows her mother is looking for her," he told the judge, "waiting for her, begging for her, praying for her. And he has her in his own home and he's torturing her."

McGinty said that even now Ariel Castro did not believe he had done anything wrong, and had absolutely no remorse.

"This man deserves as many years and as much punishment as this court can possibly give him," said the prosecutor. "We thank the courage of the victims. They've inspired law enforcement. They've inspired the prosecutors, and they've inspired the families, and they've inspired the other victims of the future."

At 12:38 P.M., Judge Michael Russo asked Ariel Castro if he wished to speak before being sentenced. And for the next seventeen minutes, he delivered a rambling, self-pitying and often defiant speech from the defense table, as his two attorneys looked on helplessly.

"First of all," Castro began, "I am a very emotional person. So I'm going to try and get it out."

He began by telling the judge how he had been a victim of sexual molestation as a child, leading to his lifelong obsession with pornography and "sexual problems."

"People are trying to paint me as a monster," he told the court, "and I'm not a monster. I'm sick."

Castro maintained he had always lived a "normal life," holding down a steady job with a wife and four children.

"And I still practiced the art of touching myself and viewing pornography," he said. "I believe I am addicted to porn to the point that it really makes me impulsive, and I just don't realize what I am doing is wrong. I'm not trying to make excuses here, 'cause I know . . . that I will be put away forever."

He then attacked his son, Anthony, for calling him an abusive father and husband in a recent television interview.

"I was never abusive until I met [Nilda]," he said. "She [was] saying I was a wife-beater. That is wrong."

Castro blamed Nilda Figueroa for all the violence during their relationship, saying she had provoked him to it.

"I couldn't get her to quiet down," he told the judge. "She would keep going and the situation would escalate until the point where she would put her hands on me, and that's how I reacted. I put my hands on her. I know that's [wrong]."

Castro said when they separated after twelve years, he found himself single again.

"I continued to practice the art of masturbation and pornography," he continued, "and it got so bad that I used to do it . . . two or three hours a day, nonstop. And when I was finished, I would just collapse, right there."

He then segued into how he had "picked up the first victim," saying it was completely unplanned.

"When I got up that day," he told the court, "I did not say, 'Oh, I'm gonna . . . try and find some women,' because it just wasn't my character. But I know it's wrong and I'm not trying to make excuses here."

Suddenly, he became emotional, complaining that everybody said he was violent when the opposite was true.

"I drove a school bus," he told the judge. "I'm a musician. I had a family. I do have value for human life."

He said his life had changed after Jocelyn had been born.

"As crazy as it may sound," he said, "my daughter just made every day for me. She never saw anything that was going on in the house, Your Honor. If anyone could ask her . . . she'll probably say, 'Yeah, my dad is the best dad in the world.' Because that's how I try and raise her in those six years, so she won't be traumatized."

Castro claimed that Jocelyn had always lived a "normal life," and he would take her out in public to experience life outside 2207 Seymour Avenue.

"And I will take her to church," he said, "and I will come home and just be a normal family. These accusations that I would come home and beat them are totally wrong. Your Honor, like I said before, I am not a violent person. I simply kept them there without being able to leave."

Then Castro explained that he had been "driven by sex" when he had abducted Gina DeJesus.

"I saw her walking with my daughter [Arlene]," he said, "but I did not know she was related to the DeJesus family. I know her dad, we went to school together."

Then he appeared to blame Amanda for getting into his car without even knowing who he was.

"I'm trying to make a point that I am not a violent predator," he said. "You are trying to make me look like a monster. I'm not a monster. I am a normal person. I am just sick. I have an addiction just like an alcoholic has an addiction. Alcoholics cannot control their addiction. That's why I can't control my addiction, Your Honor."

He then told the judge that most of the sex had been "consensual," and there had been a "lot of harmony" at 2207 Seymour Avenue.

"Practically all of it was consensual," he told Judge Russo. "These allegations about being forceful on them [are] totally wrong. Because there were times that they would even ask me for sex. Many times. And I learned that these girls are not virgins from their testimony to me. And they had multiple partners before me. All three of them."

Then, cradling his head in his hands, Ariel Castro apologized to his three victims, saying he was "truly sorry" for what had happened.

"I don't know why," he sobbed. "A man that had everything going for himself. I had a job. I had a home. I had vehicles. My musical talent. I had everything going for me, Your Honor."

Then he mentioned the *YouTube* video of Amanda onstage with Nelly, claiming it proved he had not hurt her.

"That girl did not go through torture," he told the judge, "because if that was true, do you think she would be out there partying already and having fun? I don't think so.

"I see Gina in the media. She looks normal. She acts normal. A person that's been tortured just does not act normal. They would act withdrawn and everything. On the contrary, they're the opposite. The victims are happy.

"I haven't seen much of Michelle. Because Michelle since day one, no one missed her. I never saw any fliers about her."

Then he blamed the FBI for incompetence, saying that if they had done a thorough investigation he would have been caught long ago.

"I feel that the FBI let these girls down when they questioned my daughter [Arlene]," he declared, "but they failed to question me. I'm her father. If they would have questioned me . . . it's possible that it would have ended right there."

He then turned around and looked at Michelle, Beth Serrano and the various members of the DeJesus family, all sitting in the public gallery.

"I am truly sorry," he told them, "to the DeJesus family, Michelle and Amanda. You guys know all the harmony that went on in that house. I ask God to forgive me and I apologize to my family also for putting them through all this. And I want to apologize to the State of Ohio and the City of Cleveland, for putting a dark cloud over this.

"I do also want to let you know that there was harmony in that home. There was harmony at home. I was a good person being brought up. I never had a record. I just hope they find it in their hearts to forgive me and maybe do some research on people [whose] addictions take over their lives."

He then tearfully apologized to his daughter, Jocelyn, for neglecting her health, by not taking her mother to a doctor during her difficult birth, when she almost died.

"God bless her, she's a miracle child," he said. "When she was born I know I could have taken her to the ER. And I chose not to. Thank God that nothing bad happened to her."

Finally, Castro apologized to Judge Russo for bringing the case into his courtroom, saying his true judgment day would come when he faced God.

"I believe in the Bible," he said. "I'll be praying and asking for forgiveness. And due to the fact that I do have a sexual addiction, I don't know how he's going to judge me. I only know the comment that the lady made for the DeJesus family at the end was uncalled for.

"So again, thank you, everyone. Thank you, victims. Please find it in your hearts to forgive me. Thank you."

After thanking Michelle Knight for her "remarkable restraint," Judge Russo asked Castro how he could possibly say he was not a violent person, after admitting to hundreds of sexually violent offenses. And although he might find the term "sexual predator" unpleasant, it fitted.

"It's confusing," argued Castro. "It makes it sound like I forced myself onto them. It never happened, you know, physically."

"By virtue of your plea that's what you did," said the judge. "You raped someone. That's what it means."

Judge Russo told the defendant that this was by far the

worst case that had ever come before him, and was unparalleled in its scope of kidnapping, torture and depravation.

"All this was organized," he said. "You used deception. You used chains and other means to hold captive three young women and ultimately a young child."

Judge Russo said there had been a definite strategy, as all the victims had been friends with his children.

"And that was your entrée," he said, "and that's how this evolved."

The judge noted that although Castro claimed to suffer from sexual addiction when he abducted Michelle Knight, he already had a steady girlfriend whom he neither harmed or abused.

"You had apparently, or outwardly, a normal relationship with Miss Roldan," said the judge. "Do you recall her?"

"Yes," replied Castro.

"Okay," Judge Russo continued, "so you are able to choose who you wish to victimize."

He said the defendant had caused Michelle serious physical and psychological harm.

"I think even without the testimony of the expert from Michigan, any person in America would understand that [someone] who is held captive for between nine and eleven years, sexually assaulted and such, will . . . have serious psychological harm as well as the physical harm."

The judge observed how Jocelyn Berry had been born into captivity, growing up in conditions that would never be tolerated in any Ohio prison.

"She grew up in a household where doors were locked," said Russo, "people were chained up, windows were covered. People were not allowed to come over and visit."

"Excuse me, Your Honor," interrupted Castro, "my daughter has never seen anyone with chains on."

Ignoring him, Judge Russo said the age of the victims

was very important, and as an adult Castro had taken advantage of them.

"They were young women, teenagers," he told Castro, "and they could not have imagined that an adult would trick them, and imprison them, and enslave them, and abuse them. You took advantage of their naïveté, and the fact that they were pleasant individuals that could not fathom this type of behavior."

Even more disturbing, said the judge, was "the relationship issue" and how he had exposed a young child to such "unbelievable conditions."

"In your mind there was harmony in a happy household," he told Castro. "I'm not sure there is anybody else in America that would agree with you. And there were many crimes committed in the vicinity of your young daughter. The women were still being raped and deprived of food, and living in difficult physical conditions."

Judge Russo said even if Castro was a victim of childhood sexual abuse, it was still no excuse for his crimes, as many people in similar situations move on and lead healthy lives, without abusing others.

The judge also questioned Castro's claim of suffering from mental illness, saying from what he had seen in the courtroom, he knew exactly what was going on and always answered questions.

"You just made a calculated decision . . . to do wrong," said Judge Russo, "and if anything, to me you exhibit antisocial personality disorder. I'm not a psychological expert, I certainly don't have the credentials of those who spoke here today, but you have extreme narcissism and it seems rather persuasive."

Judge Russo also spoke about his assertion that Nilda Figueroa was to blame for all the violence in their relationship.

"Now, you said your wife would irritate you," said the

judge, "she wouldn't stop talking and then you would respond. Well, my understanding from the records is that she suffered a broken nose twice, she had broken teeth and she otherwise was abused."

Russo called it "unfortunate" that Nilda had dropped her criminal complaint against him, as things might have been very different if she had gone ahead.

"I wish she had prosecuted for her sake," he told Castro, "and I know now that she has passed, but victims need to stand up for themselves so that the abuse stops. And so that those who are abusers, when possible, will receive proper treatment and redirection, and that's what the court is for."

Up to now, Ariel Castro had sat quietly without a word. But when Judge Russo challenged his claims of being a good school bus driver, he took issue.

"According to the Cleveland Metropolitan School District, your performance was not always acceptable," said the judge. "You left a child on the bus. You'd go shopping . . . and leave your school bus at Marc's. And you ended up eventually leaving that job. Is that right?"

"Your Honor, that's not right," replied Castro angrily. "That's not right. When I checked my bus, that's when I noticed the child was there on the bus."

"You were disciplined for that," the judge reminded him.

"And as for that case, the child never stayed alone."

"But you were disciplined for it," stated the judge.

"Yes, I was," he admitted.

"And ultimately, your work as a school bus driver ended. Correct?"

"Yes," replied Castro, gesticulating with his handcuffed hands, "but it wasn't my regular route. I did that to help them out when a driver missed work."

"All right," said Judge Russo, changing the subject.

"We're going to keep in mind the principles of sentencing for incapacitation, deterrents, rehabilitation and restitution. I'm certainly not sure in this instance that rehabilitation will be possible, but there certainly is a need here for incapacitation and deterrence."

Then the judge turned to sentencing Ariel Castro for the 937 counts, beginning with the two charges of aggravated murder, relating to Michelle Knight's forced miscarriages.

"May I say something?" asked the defendant.

"No," said Judge Russo, looking impatient. "Well, what do you want to say? You pled guilty to it."

"I know that," replied Castro testily. "But there was never any evidence in that. But I don't want to put these women through any more . . . so that's why I pled guilty to it. But there was never any incident of the murder of a fetus. That never happened."

"Mr. Castro," said the judge, "you talked to your attorneys and you made a decision to plead to count one as indicted. Is that correct?"

"Yes, I understand that," replied Castro, "I just want to tell the record, I never killed anyone and I am not a murderer."

Then Judge Russo read out each and every one of the 937 charges against him, sentencing him to serve the maximum time for each one, totaling life without parole plus a thousand years. He was also fined $100,000 and would have to forfeit everything he owned.

"The court imposed the maximum," he told the defendant, "because these are the worst form of the offenses there. Although Mr. Castro does not have a prior criminal conviction, the breadth and the scope of these crimes, and the merciless manner in which they were inflicted, requires that a maximum sentence on each of those counts be imposed. A person can only die in prison once.

"Your uncle is Julio [Castro] and his wife, Norma, correct?" asked the judge.

"Right," replied the defendant.

"They've been in this courtroom before. They are very wonderful people [and] have a great reputation in the community. They've operated a neighborhood store for over forty years. They were victims of a crime and the perpetrator of that crime had excuses also. In his case he blamed drug addiction and such. To the victim, excuses don't take away the harm that's involved."

"I understand," Castro replied.

The judge then ordered the defendant not to have any contact with his victims, by phone, letter or having a third party reach out to them.

"Do you understand that requirement?" asked the judge.

"Are you referring to my daughter also?" Castro asked.

"Yes," said Russo, "she's a victim. She's subject to three counts of endangering a child, so by law she's a victim."

"I know," said Castro, "but I heard . . . that I can file for parental rights for the future."

"Well," said the judge, "as in many other instances a person can file, whether they are going to be successful is a different matter, and it would take place in a different court. I'm imposing a no contact order. You should not try and contact them from the institution. Okay?"

Then Craig Weintraub leaned over and whispered in his client's ear, to stop him saying anything further on the subject.

At the end of the four-and-a-half-hour sentencing, Judge Russo ordered Ariel Castro to rise.

"Sir," he told him, "there's no place in this city, there's no place in this country, indeed there's no place in this world, for those who enslave others, those who sexually assault others and those who brutalize others. For more than ten years you have preyed upon three young women.

You have subjected them to harsh and violent conduct. You felt you were dominating them, but you were incorrect. You could not take away their dignity. Although they suffered terribly, Miss Knight, Miss DeJesus and Miss Berry did not give up hope. They have persevered. In fact they prevailed.

"These remarkable women again have their freedom, which is the most precious aspect of being an American. Mr. Castro, you forfeited that right. You now become a number with the Department of Rehabilitation and Correction. You will be confined for the remainder of your days. You are hereby remanded for transport to Lorain Correctional Institution."

Then Ariel Castro turned around and glared at Michelle Knight, who looked back at him defiantly.

"And now for Miss Knight, Miss DeJesus and Miss Berry, as well as your young daughter, we celebrate your futures. We acknowledge the faithfulness of your families, your friends and all others in this community who so fervently believed that you were alive. On behalf of the judges and the staff of this court, we wish each of you success and a sense of peace. Court adjourned."

A few minutes later in a holding cell downstairs, Ariel Castro broke down in tears, as he signed over the deed to 2207 Seymour Avenue to the Cleveland Land Bank, which would soon demolish it.

"I don't know why you have to tear my house down," he sobbed to prosecutors. "I have so many happy memories there with Gina, Amanda and Michelle."

35

YELLOW BALLOONS

On Friday morning, Ariel Castro's sentencing made headlines around the world. DAMN YOU FOREVER! screamed the *New York Post*, while the *Los Angeles Times* carried the headline, CLEVELAND KIDNAPPER ARIEL CASTRO: I'M NOT A MONSTER. I'M SICK.

Early that morning, a limousine pulled up outside the Cuyahoga County Jail in downtown Cleveland, with *Today* show anchor Matt Lauer and a TV crew. Then Lauer strolled up to the entrance, announcing that he was there to interview Ariel Castro. But to his embarrassment, Cuyahoga County Sheriff Frank Bova came out and informed the celebrity host that the interview was not going to happen.

"I won't allow it," Bova told him. "An Ariel Castro interview from jail isn't going to happen in Cleveland."

Then Lauer and his crew got back in the limousine and returned to the airport to fly back to New York.

A couple of hours later, Michelle Knight arrived at 2207 Seymour Avenue with a couple of friends. Although she did not go inside the house, she thanked the neighbors opposite who had helped in the escape.

Then she posed for pictures with Altagracia Tejeda on her porch, where Amanda Berry had first been spotted screaming for help. Michelle told Altagracia that she had seen her several times on her porch during her captivity.

"Did you see me?" Michelle asked her.

"Yes," said Altagracia.

At 6:00 P.M., after meeting his attorneys in his cell, a heavily shackled Ariel Castro was escorted past a line of reporters and TV camera crews in the garage below. Then he was put in a jail van and driven twenty-four miles to the Lorain Correctional Institution in Grafton, Ohio, where it would be determined in which state prison he should serve the rest of his life sentence.

Prior to his designated "high-priority transfer," a Cuyahoga County Jail nurse had filled out an Inmate Transfer Medical Information Sheet. It stated that Inmate Castro 643-371 had several medical issues, as well as a mental health diagnosis of Adjustment Disorder with Depressed Mood. It also noted a history of attempted suicides, although Castro had been taken off suicide watch some weeks earlier.

On his arrival at the Lorain Correctional Institution at 6:25 P.M., Castro appeared "blunted" and "subdued." As part of his processing, Castro filled out the state prison's suicide questionnaire and medical notification forms, as well as undergoing a mental health screening.

"The results of each screening process were unremarkable," an official prison report stated later, "with the inmate denying any history of mental illness and suicidal behavior, as well as any current suicidal ideation."

Castro told a nursing supervisor he had been depressed

since his arrest, and for the first week he had been put on suicide watch.

"[Castro] denies he actually was suicidal," read the report, "but just scared of the [general population] and wanted to ensure he would be alone."

Later that evening, Castro was examined by a prison psychiatrist. He denied any history of mental illness, repeating that he had only feigned being suicidal, to be kept away from the general population.

"The inmate seems fairly stable at the present time," the psychiatrist wrote. "He does not seem to be actively suicidal or self-injury behavior inclined."

Castro said he had many reasons to live, including his religious beliefs, family and children.

"He appears quite narcissistic," wrote the psychiatrist, "but does not show evidence of mood, anxiety or thought disorder."

But nevertheless he ordered Inmate Castro be placed on suicide watch and constant observation.

"Due to his life sentence and a high-profile nature of his crimes," wrote the psychiatrist, "he may pose some risk to his own safety and welfare, especially as the gravity of the situation begins to sink in."

On Sunday afternoon, Gina DeJesus was the star of the annual Cleveland Latino parade. She rode on top of a car with the sunroof open, waving a Puerto Rican flag, as part of Janet Garcia's campaign for city council.

With the elections just three months away, Garcia had enlisted the support of the DeJesus family in her campaign for Ward 14 against the incumbent Brian Cummins. And on Friday, a photograph of Gina and several family members wearing campaign shirts had suddenly appeared on Garcia's official Web site.

Later, Councilman Cummins would accuse his rival of exploiting Gina's newfound fame and popularity for votes. But the DeJesus family strongly refuted that Gina's appearance had anything to do with politics.

"People need to stop saying these negative things," said Felix DeJesus. "It's hurting my daughter Gina."

Nancy Ruiz said it had been Gina's idea to be in the parade, to thank the community.

"The only thing that I could think of," she said, "is seeing my daughter smiling and enjoying herself for the first time in nine years on top of that car."

At 8:43 A.M., on Monday, August 5, Ariel Castro was examined again by a Lorain Correctional Institution psychiatrist, who took him off suicide watch, finding there was no clinical reason to believe he was a threat to himself. Since his arrival the previous Friday, Castro had been psychologically evaluated on a daily basis, continuing to show "emotional stability" with no "problematic or self-harm behavior."

On Monday morning, Ariel Castro was transferred 135 miles south to the Correctional Reception Center in Orient, Ohio. On arrival he was given the same standard suicide questionnaire and medical notification forms that he filled out three days earlier.

During his psychiatric evaluation, Castro appeared "upset," complaining of being "verbally harassed" by the other inmates since his arrival.

"As the interview progressed," wrote his examiner, "he became more spontaneous, expressive, and reactive, smiling occasionally, in describing himself as 'always a happy person.'"

Castro's mood had alternated between being "irritated" and "happy," but his demeanor did not reflect dysphoria, overall distress or anxiety. Then the clinical psychiatrist asked Castro about his crimes, finding his insight into them "markedly impaired."

"His explanation for his criminal behavior," the psychiatrist later wrote, "focused on his 'sickness.' Referring to his long-standing addiction to pornography, and the mutual culpability of his victims."

Castro also appeared "oblivious" to the realities of his life sentence, and why he should be regarded as a monster.

"[He] is incredulous that the media and other inmates should treat him so poorly," the doctor wrote. "His goals involve going to 'a quiet place and do my time in peace.'"

In his report, the unnamed clinician found that Castro, who said he was not suicidal, was a low suicide risk at present. But he had a warning.

"However, as situational factors change for him," he wrote, "particularly if they should challenge his sense of entitlement and fragile grandiosity, the level of risk may increase, suggesting the need for periodic assessment of his mental status."

The psychiatrist diagnosed Ariel Castro as suffering from "Narcissistic Personality Disorder with Antisocial Features." He recommended that he be periodically examined for any changes in his "mental status or lethality risk, given his lengthy sentence, somewhat fragile self-esteem, and the notoriety of his crimes."

After his examination, Inmate Castro was housed in a far corner cell on the segregation section's second floor, well out of view of the other inmates.

Due to his notoriety, a special "operations order" was put into effect, limiting his movements in the segregation unit to ensure he never came into contact with any other inmates. He would spend twenty-three hours a day in his cell, being checked by guards every thirty minutes, and allowed out an hour for exercise.

* * *

Back in Cleveland, minutes after the Cuyahoga Land Bank announced that 2207 Seymour Avenue would be demolished early Wednesday morning, Anthony Castro and his sister Angie arrived to salvage family photographs and other memorabilia of their childhood growing up there. Under police supervision, the two Castro siblings went inside for what they termed a "demolition party."

When they came out carrying plastic bags of stuff, WOIO-TV news reporter Scott Taylor handed Anthony a copy of his father's 2004 confession note, asking why they had come.

"I went because we have photos," replied Anthony. "We have family mementos in there. I fully agree with the demolition of the house, but I don't want to see those things demolished with it."

Describing his father as a "hoarder," Anthony said the house was a "mess" after all the police activity.

"It's stressful to do this," he said, "but this is one of the last steps for our family to put this all behind us."

Soon after they drove off, the Cleveland Public Power company cut off electricity to the house, and Google Maps erased it from its "Street View."

The following day, Seymour Avenue was shut down to traffic, as workers went in the house and stripped it right down to the bare walls. With the current popularity of so-called "murderabillia," officials wanted to make sure that nothing could be removed from the "horror house," and auctioned off on eBay.

"We are taking a lot of precautions," said Cuyahoga Land Bank President Gus Frangos, "to keep scavengers from getting any material for that purpose."

At seven on Wednesday morning, Gina DeJesus's aunt Peggy Arida was at the controls of a giant excavator as it began razing 2207 Seymour Avenue to the ground. The demolition was watched by more than one hundred people, including Michelle Knight, who arrived clutching a bunch of yellow balloons. She was the only survivor to witness its destruction, being broadcast live on all local TV stations, as well as several national cable channels.

As the jaws of the excavator tore through the roof and the walls of the house, Prosecutor Tim McGinty addressed the media.

"This was one evil guy," he declared. "For ten years this house was the secret prison of a psychopath named Castro, but right now is a testament to the courage and relentless determination to live by the survivors, Michelle, Amanda and Gina. It will be gone."

McGinty said Councilmen Brian Cummins and Matt Zone would now work with the community to decide what the site should be used for.

Then, holding a bunch of yellow balloons and surrounded by neighbors, Michelle said a prayer for all the missing people still out there, asking God to give them the strength to know that they were loved.

"It was important for me to be here today," she explained to reporters, "because nobody was there for me when I was missing."

"Michelle," asked a female TV reporter, "what do these yellow balloons represent?"

"It represents all the millions of children that were never found," she said, "and the ones that passed away that were never heard."

"People have seen you over these few weeks," asked the same reporter, "and the incredible strength that you have and the source of inspiration that you truly have given everyone. When . . . people call you an incredible role model, how do you respond?"

"I feel very liberated," Michelle replied, "that people

think of me as a hero and a role model, and I would love to continue being that."

Then, as Pastor Horst Hoyer rang the bells of the Immanuel Evangelical Lutheran Church, Michelle and the neighbors released the yellow balloons into the sky, as 2207 Seymour Avenue was reduced to rubble.

36

RETRIBUTION

On Saturday, August 10, five days after he arrived in the Correctional Reception Center, Ariel Castro began writing a journal. For the next three weeks he would write occasional entries in what he called "A Day in the Life of a Prisoner," chronicling his life in captivity.

"I eat, brush and go back to bed," he wrote in his first entry, "get up, lay down, get up, lay down. This goes on all day. I pace in my cell, meditate, stare at the walls as I daydream a lot."

He complained about "warm" food and the way he had been treated by one of his prison guards.

"[He] mistreats me," wrote Castro, "for no apparent reason."

Castro had already received visits from his mother and sister, and had officially requested a guitar to play in his cell.

On Wednesday, August 14, he wrote that he believed that someone had "tampered" with his food, giving him chest pains and making him throw up. That day the prison medical staff was called to his cell twice, after he complained of chest pains, dizziness and nausea.

Over the next few days, Castro became so paranoid that his food was being poisoned that he started flushing it down the toilet. He also lazed around his cell totally naked, having to be told to dress several times, when female guards were on duty. Later, a corrections officer described his behavior as "demanding and pompous."

On Thursday, August 22, Castro complained in his journal about his treatment from prison guards. He wrote that his cell and its toilet were "filthy," and he had asked an officer for a mop so he could clean. He had also requested clean underwear and bed linen, which had not arrived.

"Still nothing gets done," he wrote in frustration. "I don't know if I can take this neglect anymore, and the way I'm treated!"

He also wrote about finding "hair and plastic" in his food, which was always served in "a pool of water."

On Monday, August 26, the Cuyahoga Land Bank demolished the two houses to the left of Ariel Castro's house. The next day workers moved in to seed the empty lots and plant wildflowers, making it look presentable. But neighbors were divided about what should be done with it.

"It was touchy," explained Councilman Brian Cummins. "Someone wanted to put a white picket fence across the whole frontage to keep people out. Others said they're 'going to hang things on it and use it as a memorial.' So we had this back-and-forth."

Daniel Javier, who lives across Seymour Avenue, said he wanted to keep it simple.

"Leave the place like it is," he said. "No statues, no angels, nothing. Put a few little chairs and tables where older people can come and play dominoes—nothing for the kids because . . . we don't want no drugs."

As the days passed, Ariel Castro became increasingly anxious about his situation, venting his despair in his diary.

"I will never see light at the end of the tunnel," he wrote, "but that's all right, it's what I chose. I've lots of time on my hands now to think and read, write, exercise. I want to make a bigger effort to try to commit to god."

Ironically, he also worried about how warm his cell would be in the winter, after so many years of punishing his prisoners with lack of heat.

"I'm very sensitive to cold draft," he wrote, "it literally drives me to get under the covers . . . I also get depressed and don't want to do anything but just lay here, I guess we'll just have to wait and see when I get to that bridge."

He also fretted about being insulted by guards.

"Most of the guards here are okay," he noted, "but the younger ones don't take the job seriously or they are rude to me for no apparent reason. Sometimes I drift into a negative thought, I check myself and try harder not to go there."

On Wednesday, August 28, he wrote that he was "really getting frustrated." Three days later he said he was near breaking point.

"I will not take this kind of treatment much longer," he wrote. "I feel as though I'm being pushed over the edge, one day at a time."

The next day, he complained when a supervisor brought him his meal, saying his "brown rice looks like dog shit," before the supervisor took his dirty underwear to be washed and didn't bring it back.

"It's nearly 9:00 P.M., he wrote, "still no underclothing to wear."

*   *   *

At 1:29 P.M. on Tuesday, September 3, 2013, Inmate Ariel Castro met with two members of the Correctional Reception Center's Protective Control Committee, to discuss where he would serve out the rest of his life. He told the committee that he favored a prison facility nearer his family, asking about mail and visitation privileges.

"I believe I need protective control," he said, "[based upon] the high-profile nature of my charges."

Castro was then told about the Allen Correctional Institution in Lima, Ohio, less than a three-hour drive from Cleveland, which seemed to please him.

"He appeared happy that the placement would be closer for his family," said a report of the meeting. "He asked questions about other potential placements and CRC staff explained that those placements would not be safe for him. He also asked questions about getting mail."

The meeting finished at 1:52 and Castro was returned to his cell after the committee agreed to recommend he be moved to Lima soon.

For the rest of the afternoon, Ariel Castro remained in his cell. He was supposed to be checked every thirty minutes by guards, but they missed eight scheduled rounds that day.

At 5:29, a prison supervisor brought Castro his evening meal, but he refused to eat it, believing it had been tampered with. Half an hour later he returned it untouched to the supervisor.

At 8:54, a prison guard checked in on Castro's cell and he appeared to be fine.

Then, as soon as he left, Ariel Castro started his preparations to die. He first created a shrine, carefully laying out photographs of his children and all his family members on a poster board on his desk. The he wrote out their names on sheets of paper, placing each by their photographs.

After laying out several personal items around his cell, he opened his Bible to the Gospel of Saint John, chapters one and two, leaving it on the floor. He also wrote out a passage from chapter three on a sheet of paper: "No one can see the Kingdom of God unless they are born again."

Castro then took off his bedsheet and tied it in knots to form a ligature. After securing several inches of it around the window frame, seven feet off the ground, he wound a foot-long section around his neck and undid his shorts until they fell to his ankles. Then, facing his cell door, he dropped to his knees, as the ligature tightened, pulling the last breath out of him.

At nine-fifteen, Officer Caleb Ackley began his regular evening cell count. Three minutes later, he reached Ariel Castro's cell, 2103, and saw his lifeless body dangling from the window frame.

"[He had] a sheet tied around his neck and attached to the window seal [sic]," Officer Ackley later wrote, "his knees were slightly bent and his shorts were around his ankles."

Ackley raised the alarm and within seconds Officer Ryan Murphy arrived. Then they lifted up Castro's body to release the pressure off his neck, pulling the sheet out of the window and ripping it.

"We then lowered the inmate to the floor," wrote Ackley. "I instructed Officer Murphy to bring me [a knife] to remove the remainder of the sheet from the inmate's neck."

After cutting off the sheet, Ackley started CPR chest compressions to try to revive Castro. For the next few minutes he and two other officers took turns applying CPR in cycles of thirty chest compressions each. But there was no response. At 9:22, a nurse arrived and continued the CPR.

At 9:25, an ambulance was called and for the next forty-five minutes, until paramedics arrived, a rotation of prison guards and nurses took turns applying CPR to Castro. Two correction officers entered with video cameras and started filming the resuscitation attempts.

Finally, at 10:05, the paramedics arrived after getting lost on the way. They placed Castro's body on a backboard and onto a gurney, wheeling it out of the cell, which was then secured with yellow tape. Ariel Castro's body was then carried down the stairs into the waiting ambulance.

At 10:24, the ambulance driver turned on the flashing lights and siren, and drove to the Ohio State University Wexner Medical Center in Columbus. Attempts to resuscitate Castro continued, as a correctional officer filmed. Midway, the ambulance stopped to pick up more medics, who came on board to join in the attempts to revive Castro.

When they arrived at the hospital, a doctor pronounced Ariel Castro dead at 10:52, and he was taken to the morgue. Four minutes later, the video camera was turned off.

At 12:03 Wednesday morning, after getting a tip-off, WOIO-TV broke into regular programming to report Ariel Castro had hung himself in his cell. For the next two and a half hours they broadcast live, from the studio and the former site of the Castro house on Seymour Avenue.

Just after midnight, Ariel Castro's cousin Maria Montes received a text informing her of the news. Then she turned on the television to find every station reporting her uncle's suicide.

"I cried a little bit," she said. "It wasn't for him. I cried for those girls . . . and just wondering if they knew, what they thought, how they felt."

Montes said she was also concerned for Castro's elderly

mother, Lillian Rodriguez, who had already been through so much.

"I just hope this doesn't kill her," said Montes.

In the wake of Castro's suicide, the Ohio Department of Corrections issued a statement:

> *Inmate Ariel Castro was found hanging in his cell at 9:20 P.M. at the Correctional Reception Center in Orient. He was housed in protective custody which means he was in a cell by himself and rounds are required every 30 minutes at staggered intervals. Upon finding inmate Castro, prison medical staff began performing lifesaving measures. Shortly after, he was transported to OSUMC where he was pronounced dead at 10:52 P.M. A thorough review of this incident is underway and more information can be provided as it becomes available pending the state of the investigation.*

On Wednesday morning, the Ohio Department of Rehabilitation announced it would conduct a "thorough review" of the incident, to determine exactly what happened. Many questions were being asked about how Ariel Castro was able to commit suicide while under maximum security. There were even reports that guards had turned a blind eye and let him kill himself.

Even more embarrassing was that, only three weeks earlier, convicted killer Billy Slagle had hung himself in his cell at the Chillicothe Correctional Institution, just forty miles south of Orient. Three days away from his execution by lethal injection, Slagle had left a suicide note, asking how Ariel Castro had avoided the death penalty and he had not.

On the *Today* show, defense attorney Craig Weintraub claimed that he had warned the Ohio prison authorities several times that Ariel Castro was a suicide risk, but no one had taken any notice.

"There is no doubt that he had psychological problems . . . and was deeply disturbed," he told reporter Willie Geist. "I understand the public in general is probably going to say, 'Well, good riddance.' But this is a human being, we are in a civilized society, and we expect that the person will be protected when they're institutionalized. I would doubt the prison officials would dispute that they have an obligation to ensure that there won't be a suicide or anything else. And we pray that there wasn't anything else."

Prosecutor Tim McGinty told reporters that Ariel Castro had taken the coward's way out.

"This man couldn't take, even for a month, a small portion of what he had dished out for more than a decade," said McGinty.

Michelle Knight agreed, saying that she understood why he had hung himself.

"He couldn't face what he did with his head held up high," she said. "He had to face it like a coward because he was ashamed and embarrassed of what he had done. And he didn't want what he did to us to happen to him."

EPILOGUE

In the wake of Ariel Castro's suicide, the Ohio branch of the American Civil Liberties Union called for a full investigation into his death. And the Ohio authorities announced two separate investigations: one to examine the circumstances of his death, and the other to determine if he had received adequate medical and psychological care prior to his death.

Franklin County Coroner Jan Gorniak said that an autopsy on Ariel Castro's body had determined his death was a "hanging suicide." She noted depressions on his wrists, injuries to his neck and chin, and that he had bitten his tongue as he died. It also revealed that the five-foot-seven-inch Castro weighed 168 pounds, ten pounds less than when he had arrived at Lima, almost a month earlier.

On Friday morning, as Castro's body was released to his family, *Today* aired part of his interrogation video, which had been leaked. Castro spoke about an early close call soon after he had snatched Michelle, when Lillian

Roldan had asked him why a television upstairs was turned on. After watching the *Today* piece, Roldan said she could not even remember the incident.

Over the next few weeks, Anthony Castro devoted himself to finding a cemetery that would take his father's remains, but was turned down again and again.

"Anthony is trying to work the body," said Cesi Castro, "but I don't know how he's doing it."

By October 1, the Cleveland Courage Fund stood at $1.4 million and still growing daily. A week later, the Ohio Department for Rehabilitation and Correction published its findings. It made lurid headlines by speculating whether Ariel Castro might have died of autoerotic asphyxiation, as he was found naked from the waist down.

Coroner Jan Gorniak scoffed at the idea of Castro accidentally killing himself, trying to get a sexual thrill by depriving the brain of oxygen during masturbation.

"I did the autopsy myself," she told CNN. "I saw the ligature. I saw the pictures of the cell. It was a suicide."

The report also criticized prison guards for failing to check his cell at least eight times on the day he died, and then falsifying logbooks to cover it up.

In mid-October, Dr. Phil McGraw arrived in Cleveland to interview Michelle Knight for a two-part special. She was seen filming with Dr. Phil at the Family Dollar store from where she was abducted, later posing for photographs with Commander Keith Sulzer and other Cleveland police officers.

"Michelle Knight's story of horror and courageous survival almost defied description," read a press release from Dr. Phil, "and has changed me like no other in twelve years of doing the show. Her dark journey from victim to victor is beyond compelling."

At the end of October, Amanda Berry and Gina

DeJesus signed a book deal to tell their story. The deal, for an undisclosed sum, was brokered by the Jones Day law firm. Michelle was invited to participate but declined, as she now had her own attorney handling her affairs.

In early November, soon after the Dr. Phil special was aired to huge ratings, Michelle Knight signed her own book deal, to write a memoir with a ghostwriter to be published on the first anniversary of her escape.

That Thanksgiving, Michelle moved out of the halfway house and into her own apartment in a fashionable part of Cleveland. Since her escape she had started getting tattooed and pierced as a therapeutic symbol of her new-found freedom.

She had also started boxing and regularly practiced on a red punching bag, with Ariel Castro's face drawn on it in Magic Marker.

"I just wanted to put his face right here," she told *The Guardian,* "and hit it."

She also announced plans to change her name to Lily, her favorite flower, and was writing her own songs and recording them in a Cleveland studio. But her real passion was cooking, and Michelle told *People* magazine she wanted to open her own "multicultural" restaurant, serving different dishes from around the world.

Michelle had also been in touch with her son Joey's adoptive parents, and had been sent photographs of him as a teenager. But for the moment she had agreed not to contact him until his adoptive parents were ready, as it would be too unsettling.

Fernando Colon hired a lawyer to handle his appeal against his conviction for molesting Emily and Arlene Castro, and is still awaiting a date for it to be heard.

* * *

On May 6, 2014—the first anniversary of the escape—Michelle Knight, now thirty-three, officially forgave Ariel Castro. In an interview with Savannah Guthrie of the *Today* show to promote her new book, *Finding Me: A Decade of Darkness, a Life Reclaimed,* Michelle said she no longer bore him any grudges.

"If I did something wrong," she explained, "even if it was a small thing, I would want somebody to forgive me. So I can forgive him for what he's done wrong because that's the way of life."

That afternoon, Amanda Berry and Gina DeJesus and their families went to the White House, where they met President Barack Obama and Vice President Joe Biden. After a VIP tour of the White House followed by lunch, they posed for photographs in the Oval Office with the president and the vice president, who congratulated them on their bravery and fortitude.

That night, Amanda and Gina were guests of honor at the National Center for Missing and Exploited Children's annual Hope Awards dinner. During the glittering evening, Amanda, who looked glamorous in a fashionable evening gown, delivered a speech to the guests.

"If I could only say one thing," she said, fighting back tears, "it would be this: Never give up hope, because miracles do happen."

Then the crowd rose to their feet for a standing ovation.